Microsoft

MICROSOFT
VISUAL C# .NET
LANGUAGE REFERENCE

Microsoft
.net

PUBLISHED BY
Microsoft Press
A Division of Microsoft Corporation
One Microsoft Way
Redmond, Washington 98052-6399

Library of Congress Cataloging-in-Publication Data
Microsoft Visual C# .NET : Language Reference / Microsoft Corporation.
     p. cm.
   Includes index.
   ISBN 0-7356-1554-3
   1. C# (Computer program language) I. Microsoft Corporation.

  QA76.73.C154 M53   2002
  005.26'8-dc21   2001056824

Printed and bound in the United States of America.

1 2 3 4 5 6 7 8 9   QWT   7 6 5 4 3 2

Distributed in Canada by Penguin Books Canada Limited.

A CIP catalogue record for this book is available from the British Library.

Microsoft Press books are available through booksellers and distributors worldwide. For further information about international editions, contact your local Microsoft Corporation office or contact Microsoft Press International directly at fax (425) 936-7329. Visit our Web site at www.microsoft.com/mspress. Send comments to *mspinput@microsoft.com*.

Acquisitions Editor: Juliana Aldous
Project Editor: Denise Bankaitis

Body Part No. X08-64087

Contents

PART 2   C# Keywords *(continued)*

PART 3   C# Features 169

PART 3   C# Features *(continued)*

PART 1

Introduction to C#

Programming in C#

Visual C#® is a programming language introduced in Visual Studio® .NET. This book provides reference information on programming in Visual C#. It focuses on programming topics rather than on the C# language specification.

This book is divided into the following sections:

1. **Introduction**   Establishes the general approach of the book and the general look of a C# program.

2. **C# Keywords**   Describes for each keyword its use, possible contexts, sample code and outputs, and recommendations of best programming practices.

3. **C# Features**   Discusses various elements of C# programming, including the use of operators, attributes, preprocessor directives, arrays, constructors and destructors, indexers, properties, passing parameters, the main method, conditional methods, delegates, events, and XML. This section presents definitions, sample code designed to meet specific needs, code behavior and output, and recommendations of best programming practices.

Note   Much of the longer sample code contained in this book is available for download in the Visual Studio .NET online documentation.

The following table shows the typographic conventions used in this documentation.

Convention	Description	Example
Monospace	Indicates source code, code examples, input to the command line, application output, code lines embedded in text, and variables and code elements.	`using System;`
Bold	Indicates most predefined programming elements, including namespaces, classes, delegates, objects, interfaces, methods, functions, macros, structures, constructors, properties, events, enumerations, fields, operators, statements, directives, data types, keywords, exceptions, non-HTML attributes, and configuration tags, as well as registry keys, subkeys, and values. Also indicates the following HTML elements: attributes, directives, keywords, values, and headers.	the **base** keyword

(continued)

(continued)

Convention	Description	Example
Bold *(continued)*	In addition, indicates required user input, including command-line options, that must be entered exactly as shown.	
Italic	Indicates placeholders, most often method or function parameters and HTML placeholders; these placeholders represent information that must be supplied by the implementation or the user. For command-line input, indicates parameter values.	*identifier*, the interface name

General Structure of a C# Program

C# programs can consist of one or more files. Each file can contain one or more namespaces. A namespace can contain types such as classes, structs, interfaces, enumerations, and delegates, in addition to other namespaces. The following is the skeleton of a C# program that contains all of these elements.

```
// A skeleton of a C# program
using System;
namespace MyNamespace1
{
    class MyClass1
    {
    }
    struct MyStruct
    {
    }
    interface IMyInterface
    {
    }
    delegate int MyDelegate();
    enum MyEnum
    {
    }
    namespace MyNamespace2
    {
    }
    class MyClass2
    {
        public static void Main(string[] args)
        {
        }
    }
}
```

C# Keywords

The Keywords

Keywords are predefined reserved identifiers that have special meanings to the compiler. They cannot be used as identifiers in your program unless they include @ as a prefix. For example, @if is a legal identifier but if is not because it is a keyword.

The following lists each keyword used in C# and the section within this part of the book that discusses that keyword.

abstract	Access Modifiers		enum	Type Keywords
as	Operator Keywords		event	Access Modifiers
base	Access Keywords		explicit	Conversion Keywords
bool	Type Keywords		extern	Access Modifiers
break	Statement Keywords		false	Literal Keywords; Operator Keywords
byte	Type Keywords			
case	Statement Keywords		finally	Statement Keywords
catch	Statement Keywords		fixed	Statement Keywords
char	Type Keywords		float	Type Keywords
checked	Statement Keywords		for	Statement Keywords
class	Reference Types		foreach	Statement Keywords
const	Access Modifiers		goto	Statement Keywords
continue	Statement Keywords		if	Statement Keywords
decimal	Type Keywords		implicit	Conversion Keywords
default	Statement Keywords		in	Statement Keywords
delegate	Reference Types		int	Type Keywords
do	Statement Keywords		interface	Reference Types
double	Type Keywords		internal	Modifiers
else	Statement Keywords		is	Operator Keywords
			lock	Statement Keywords

long	Type Keywords	static	Access Modifiers
namespace	Namespace Keywords	string	Reference Types
new	Operator Keywords	struct	Type Keywords
null	Literal Keywords	switch	Statement Keywords
object	Reference Types	this	Access Keywords
operator	Conversion Keywords	throw	Statement Keywords
out	Method Parameter	true	Literal Keywords; Operator Keywords
override	Access Modifiers		
params	Method Parameter	try	Statement Keywords
private	Modifiers	typeof	Operator Keywords
protected	Modifiers	uint	Type Keywords
public	Modifiers	ulong	Type Keywords
readonly	Access Modifiers	unchecked	Statement Keywords
ref	Method Parameter	unsafe	Access Modifiers
return	Statement Keywords	ushort	Type Keywords
sbyte	Type Keywords	using	Namespace Keywords
sealed	Access Modifiers	virtual	Access Modifiers
short	Type Keywords	void	Reference Types
sizeof	Operator Keywords	volatile	Access Modifiers
stackalloc	Operator Keywords	while	Statement Keywords

Access Keywords

This section introduces the following access keywords:

- **base** Access the members of the base class.
- **this** Refer to the current object for which a method is called.

base

The **base** keyword is used to access members of the base class from within a derived class:

- Call a method on the base class that has been overridden by another method.
- Specify which base-class constructor should be called when creating instances of the derived class.

A base class access is permitted only in a constructor, an instance method, or an instance property accessor.

It is an error to use the **base** keyword from within a static method.

Example

In this example, both the base class, Person, and the derived class, Employee, have a method named Getinfo. By using the **base** keyword, it is possible to call the Getinfo method on the base class, from within the derived class.

```
// keywords_base.cs
// Accessing base class members
using System;
    public class Person
    {
        protected string ssn = "444-55-6666";
        protected string name = "John L. Malgraine";

        public virtual void GetInfo()
        {
            Console.WriteLine("Name: {0}", name);
            Console.WriteLine("SSN: {0}", ssn);
        }
    }
    class Employee: Person
    {
        public string id = "ABC567EFG";

        public override void GetInfo()
        {
            // Calling the base class GetInfo method:
            base.GetInfo();
            Console.WriteLine("Employee ID: {0}", id);
        }
    }

class TestClass {
    public static void Main()
    {
        Employee E = new Employee();
        E.GetInfo();
    }
}
```

Output

```
Name: John L. Malgraine
SSN: 444-55-6666
Employee ID: ABC567EFG
```

For additional examples, see the sections "new" on page 65, "virtual" on page 51, and "override" on page 44.

Example

This example shows how you can specify the base-class constructor called when creating instances of a derived class.

```
// keywords_base2.cs
using System;
public class MyBase
{
    int num;
    public MyBase() {
        Console.WriteLine("in MyBase()");
    }
    public MyBase(int i )
    {
        num = i;
        Console.WriteLine("in MyBase(int i)");
    }

    public int GetNum()
    {
        return num;
    }
}

public class MyDerived : MyBase
{
    static int i = 32;

    // This constructor will call MyBase.MyBase()
    public MyDerived(int ii)  : base()
    {
    }

    // This constructor will call MyBase.MyBase(int i)
    public MyDerived()  : base(i)
    {
    }

    public static void Main()
    {
        MyDerived md = new MyDerived();
        MyDerived md1 = new MyDerived(1);
    }
}
```

Output

```
in MyBase(int i)
in MyBase()
```

this

The **this** keyword refers to the current instance for which a method is called. Static member functions do not have a **this** pointer. The **this** keyword can be used to access members from within constructors, instance methods, and instance accessors.

The following are common uses of **this**:

- To qualify members hidden by similar names, for example:

```
public Employee(string name, string alias)
{
    this.name = name;
    this.alias = alias;
}
```

- To pass an object as a parameter to other methods, for example:

```
CalcTax(this);
```

- To declare indexers, for example:

```
public int this [int param]
{
    get
    {
        return array[param];
    }
    set
    {
        array[param] = value;
    }
}
```

It is an error to refer to **this** in a static method, static property accessor, or variable initializer of a field declaration.

Example

In this example, **this** is used to qualify the Employee class members, name and alias, which are hidden by similar names. It is also used to pass an object to the method CalcTax, which belongs to another class.

```csharp
// keywords_this.cs
// this example
using System;
public class Employee
{
    public string name;
    public string alias;
    public decimal salary = 3000.00m;

    // Constructor:
    public Employee(string name, string alias)
    {
        // Use this to qualify the fields, name and alias:
        this.name = name;
        this.alias = alias;
    }

    // Printing method:
    public void printEmployee()
    {
        Console.WriteLine("Name: {0}\nAlias: {1}", name, alias);
        // Passing the object to the CalcTax method by using this:
        Console.WriteLine("Taxes: {0:C}", Tax.CalcTax(this));
    }
}
public class Tax
{
    public static decimal CalcTax(Employee E)
    {
        return (0.08m*(E.salary));
    }
}

public class MainClass
{
    public static void Main()
    {
        // Create objects:
        Employee E1 = new Employee ("John M. Trainer", "jtrainer");

        // Display results:
        E1.printEmployee();
    }
}
```

Output

```
Name: John M. Trainer
Alias: jtrainer
Taxes: $240.00
```

For additional examples, see the sections "class" on page 149 and "struct" on page 138.

Conversion Keywords

This section describes keywords used in type conversions:

- explicit

- implicit

- operator

A conversion enables an expression of one type to be treated as another type. Conversions can be implicit or explicit, and this determines whether an explicit cast is required. For instance, in the conversion from type int to type long is implicit, so expressions of type int can implicitly be treated as type long. The opposite conversion, from type long to type int, is explicit and so an explicit cast is required.

```
int a = 123;
long b = a;        // implicit conversion from int to long
int c = (int) b;   // explicit conversion from long to int
```

Some conversions are defined by the language. Programs may also define their own conversions.

explicit

The **explicit** keyword is used to declare an explicit user-defined type conversion operator. For example:

```
class MyType
{
    public static explicit operator MyType(int i)
    {
        // code to convert from int to MyType
    }
}
```

Unlike implicit conversion, explicit conversion operators must be invoked via a cast.

```
int i;
MyType x = (MyType)i;   // int-to-MyType requires cast
```

Omitting the cast results in a compile-time error.

If a conversion operation can cause exceptions or lose information, you should mark it **explicit**. This prevents the compiler from silently invoking the conversion operation with possibly unforeseen consequences.

Example

The following example defines a struct, Digit, that represents a single decimal digit. An operator is defined for conversions from byte to Digit, but because not all bytes can be converted to a Digit, the conversion is explicit.

```
// cs_keyword_explicit.cs
using System;
struct Digit
{
    byte value;
    public Digit(byte value)
    {
        if (value<0 || value>9) throw new ArgumentException();
        this.value = value;
    }

    // define explicit byte-to-Digit conversion operator:
    public static explicit operator Digit(byte b)
    {
        Console.WriteLine("conversion occurred");
        return new Digit(b);
    }
}

class Test
{
    public static void Main()
    {
        byte b = 3;
        Digit d = (Digit)b; // explicit conversion
    }
}
```

Output

```
conversion occurred
```

implicit

The **implicit** keyword is used to declare an implicit user-defined type conversion operator. For example:

```
class MyType
{
    public static implicit operator int(MyType m)
    {
        // code to convert from MyType to int
    }
}
```

Implicit conversion operators can be called implicitly, without being specified by explicit casts in the source code.

```
MyType x;
int i = x; // implicitly call MyType's MyType-to-int conversion operator
```

By eliminating unnecessary casts, implicit conversions can improve source code readability. However, because implicit conversions can occur without the programmer's specifying them, care must be taken to prevent unpleasant surprises. In general, implicit conversion operators should never throw exceptions and never lose information so that they can be used safely without the programmer's awareness. If a conversion operator cannot meet those criteria, it should be marked **explicit**.

Example

The following example defines a struct, `Digit`, that represents a single decimal digit. An operator is defined for conversions from `Digit` to `byte`, and because any `Digit` can be converted to a `byte`, the conversion is implicit.

```
// cs_keyword_implicit.cs
using System;
struct Digit
{
    byte value;

    public Digit(byte value)
    {
        if (value < 0 || value > 9) throw new ArgumentException();
        this.value = value;
    }
```

(continued)

(continued)

```
    // define implicit Digit-to-byte conversion operator:
    public static implicit operator byte(Digit d)
    {
        Console.WriteLine( "conversion occurred" );
        return d.value;
    }
}

class Test
{
    public static void Main()
    {
        Digit d = new Digit(3);

        // implicit (no cast) conversion from Digit to byte
        byte b = d;
    }
}
```

Output

```
conversion occurred
```

operator

The **operator** keyword is used to declare an operator in a class or struct declaration. An operator declaration can take one of the following four forms:

```
public static result-type operator unary-operator ( op-type operand )
public static result-type operator binary-operator (
    op-type operand,
    op-type2 operand2
)
public static implicit operator conv-type-out ( conv-type-in operand )
public static explicit operator conv-type-out ( conv-type-in operand )
```

where:

result-type
> The type of the operator's result.

unary-operator
> One of: + - ! ~ ++ -- true false

op-type
> The type of the first (or only) parameter.

operand
> The name of the first (or only) parameter.

binary-operator
> One of: + - * / % & | ^ << >> == != > < >= <=

op-type2
> The type of the second parameter.

operand2
> The name of the second parameter.

conv-type-out
> The target type of a type conversion operator.

conv-type-in
> The type of the input to a type conversion operator.

Remarks

The first two forms declare user-defined operators that overload built-in operators. Note that not all the built-in operators can be overloaded (see "Overloadable Operators" on page 170). At least one of op-type and op-type2 must be the enclosing type (that is, the type of which the operator is a member). This prevents redefining the integer addition operator, for instance.

The last two forms declare conversion operators. Exactly one of *conv-type-in* and *conv-type-out* must be the enclosing type (that is, a conversion operator can only convert from its enclosing type to some other type, or from some other type to its enclosing type).

Operators can only take value parameters, not ref or out parameters.

Any operator declaration can be preceded by an optional attribute list.

Example

The following is an extremely simplified class for rational numbers. It overloads the + and * operators to perform fractional addition and multiplication, and also provides an operator that converts fractions to doubles.

```
// cs_keyword_operator.cs
using System;
class Fraction
{
    int num, den;
    public Fraction(int num, int den)
    {
        this.num = num;
        this.den = den;
    }

    // overload operator +
    public static Fraction operator +(Fraction a, Fraction b)
    {
        return new Fraction(a.num * b.den + b.num * a.den,
            a.den * b.den);
    }
```

(continued)

(continued)

```
// overload operator *
public static Fraction operator *(Fraction a, Fraction b)
{
    return new Fraction(a.num * b.num, a.den * b.den);
}

// define operator double
public static implicit operator double(Fraction f)
{
    return (double)f.num / f.den;
}
}

class Test
{
    public static void Main()
    {
        Fraction a = new Fraction(1, 2);
        Fraction b = new Fraction(3, 7);
        Fraction c = new Fraction(2, 3);
        Console.WriteLine((double)(a * b + c));
    }
}
```

Output

```
0.880952380952381
```

Literal Keywords

C# has the following literal keywords:

- null

- true

- false

null

The **null** keyword is a literal that represents a null reference, one that does not refer to any object. **null** is the default value of reference-type variables.

See Also

Default Values Table (pg. 164)

true

In C#, the **true** keyword can be used as an overloaded operator or as a literal:

- true Operator
- true Literal

true Operator

User-defined types can define a **true** operator that returns the bool value true to indicate true and returns false otherwise. This is useful for types that represent true, false, and null (neither true nor false), as used in databases.

Such types can be used for the controlling expression in if, do, while, and for statements and in conditional expressions.

If a type defines operator **true**, it must also define operator false.

A type cannot directly overload the conditional logical operators (&& and ||), but an equivalent effect can be achieved by overloading the regular logical operators and operators **true** and **false**.

true Literal

The **true** keyword is a literal of type bool representing the boolean value true.

Example
```
// cs_keyword_true.cs
using System;
class test
{
   public static void Main()
   {
      bool a = true;
      Console.WriteLine( a ? "yes" : "no" );
   }
}
```

Output
Yes

See Also
Operators (pg. 169), false (pg. 16, 74)

false

In C#, the **false** keyword can be used as an overloaded operator or as a literal:

- false Operator
- false Literal

false Operator

User-defined types can define a **false** operator that returns the bool value true to indicate false and returns false otherwise. This is useful for types that represent true, false, and null (neither true nor false), as used in databases.

Such types can be used for the controlling expression in if, do, while, and for statements and in conditional expressions.

If a type defines operator **false**, it must also define operator true.

A type cannot directly overload the conditional logical operators (&& and ||), but an equivalent effect can be achieved by overloading the regular logical operators and operators **true** and **false**.

false Literal

The **false** keyword is a literal of type bool representing the boolean value false.

Example

```
// cs_keyword_false.cs
using System;
class test
{
    public static void Main()
    {
        bool a = false;
        Console.WriteLine( a ? "yes" : "no" );
    }
}
```

Output

```
No
```

See Also

Operators (pg. 169), true (pg. 15, 73)

Method Parameter Keywords

If a parameter is declared for a method without **ref** or **out**, the parameter can have a value associated with it. That value can be changed in the method, but the changed value will not be retained when control passes back to the calling procedure. By using a method parameter keyword, you can change this behavior.

This section describes the keywords you can use when declaring method parameters:

- params

- ref

- out

params

The **params** keyword lets you specify a method parameter that takes an argument where the number of arguments is variable.

No additional parameters are permitted after the **params** keyword in a method declaration, and only one **params** keyword is permitted in a method declaration.

Example

```
// cs_params.cs
using System;
public class MyClass
{

    public static void UseParams(params int[] list)
    {
        for ( int i = 0 ; i < list.Length ; i++ )
            Console.WriteLine(list[i]);
        Console.WriteLine();
    }

    public static void UseParams2(params object[] list)
    {
        for ( int i = 0 ; i < list.Length ; i++ )
            Console.WriteLine((object)list[i]);
        Console.WriteLine();
    }
```

(continued)

(continued)

```
public static void Main()
{
    UseParams(1, 2, 3);
    UseParams2(1, 'a', "test");

    int[] myarray = new int[3] {10,11,12};
    UseParams(myarray);
}
}
```

Output

```
1
2
3

1
a
test

10
11
12
```

ref

The **ref** method parameter keyword on a method parameter causes a method to refer to the same variable that was passed into the method. Any changes made to the parameter in the method will be reflected in that variable when control passes back to the calling method.

To use a **ref** parameter, the argument must explicitly be passed to the method as a **ref** argument. The value of a **ref** argument will be passed to the **ref** parameter.

An argument passed to a **ref** parameter must first be initialized. Compare this to an out parameter, whose argument does not have to be explicitly initialized before being passed to an **out** parameter.

An overload will occur if declarations of two methods differ only in their use of **ref**.

A property is not a variable and cannot be passed as a **ref** parameter.

For information on passing an array, see "Passing Arrays Using ref and out" on page 254.

Example

```
// cs_ref.cs
using System;
public class MyClass
{
    public static void TestRef(ref char i)
    {
        // The value of i will be changed in the calling method
        i = 'b';
    }

    public static void TestNoRef(char i)
    {
        // The value of i will be unchanged in the calling method
        i = 'c';
    }

    // This method passes a variable as a ref parameter; the value of the
    // variable is changed after control passes back to this method.
    // The same variable is passed as a value parameter; the value of the
    // variable is unchanged after control is passed back to this method.
    public static void Main()
    {

        char i = 'a';    // variable must be initialized
        TestRef(ref i);  // the arg must be passed as ref
        Console.WriteLine(i);
        TestNoRef(i);
        Console.WriteLine(i);
    }
}
```

Output

```
b
b
```

out

The **out** method parameter keyword on a method parameter causes a method to refer to the same variable that was passed into the method. Any changes made to the parameter in the method will be reflected in that variable when control passes back to the calling method.

Declaring an **out** method is useful when you want a method to return multiple values. A method that uses an **out** parameter can still return a value. A method can have more than one **out** parameter.

To use an **out** parameter, the argument must explicitly be passed to the method as an **out** argument. The value of an **out** argument will not be passed to the **out** parameter.

A variable passed as an **out** argument need not be initialized. However, the **out** parameter must be assigned a value before the method returns.

An overload will occur if declarations of two methods differ only in their use of **out**.

A property is not a variable and cannot be passed as an **out** parameter.

For information on passing an array, see "Passing Arrays Using ref and out" on page 254.

Example

```
// cs_out.cs
using System;
public class MyClass
{
    public static int TestOut(out char i)
    {
        i = 'b';
        return -1;
    }

    public static void Main()
    {
        char i;    // variable need not be initialized
        Console.WriteLine(TestOut(out i));
        Console.WriteLine(i);
    }
}
```

Output

```
-1
b
```

Modifiers

Modifiers are used to modify declarations of types and type members. This section introduces the C# modifiers:

Modifier	Purpose
Access Modifiers • public • private • internal • protected	Specify the declared accessibility of types and type members.

Modifier	Purpose
abstract	Indicate that a class is intended only to be a base class of other classes.
const	Specify that the value of the field or the local variable cannot be modified.
event	Declare an event.
extern	Indicate that the method is implemented externally.
override	Provide a new implementation of a virtual member inherited from a base class.
readonly	Declare a field that can only be assigned values as part of the declaration or in a constructor in the same class.
sealed	Specify that a class cannot be inherited.
static	Declare a member that belongs to the type itself rather than to a specific object.
unsafe	Declare an unsafe context.
virtual	Declare a method or an accessor whose implementation can be changed by an overriding member in a derived class.
volatile	Indicate that a field can be modified in the program by something such as the operating system, the hardware, or a concurrently executing thread.

Access Modifiers

Access modifiers are keywords used to specify the declared accessibility of a member or a type. This section introduces the four access modifiers:

- public
- protected
- internal
- private

The following five accessibility levels can be specified using the access modifiers:

public   protected   internal   internal protected   private

This section also introduces the following topics:

- Accessibility Levels
- Accessibility Domain
- Restrictions on Using Accessibility Levels

Accessibility Levels

When access is allowed to a member, it said to be accessible. Otherwise, it is inaccessible. Use the access modifiers, public, protected, internal, or private, to specify one of the following declared accessibilities for members.

Declared accessibility	Meaning
public	Access is not restricted.
protected	Access is limited to the containing class or types derived from the containing class.
internal	Access is limited to the current project.
protected internal	Access is limited to the current project or types derived from the containing class.
private	Access is limited to the containing type.

Only one access modifier is allowed for a member or type, except for the **protected internal** combination.

Access modifiers are not allowed on namespaces. Namespaces have no access restrictions.

Depending on the context in which a member declaration takes place, only certain declared accessibilities are permitted. If no access modifier is specified in a member declaration, a default accessibility is used.

Top-level types, which are not nested into other types, can only have **internal** or **public** accessibility. The default accessibility for these types is **internal**.

Nested types, which are members of other types, can have declared accessibilities as indicated in the following table.

Members of	Default member accessibility	Allowed declared accessibility of the member
enum	**public**	None
class	**private**	**public** **protected** **internal** **private** **protected internal**
interface	**public**	None
struct	**private**	**public** **internal** **private**

The accessibility of a nested type depends on its accessibility domain, which is determined by both the declared accessibility of the member and the accessibility domain of the immediately containing type. However, the accessibility domain of a nested type cannot exceed that of the containing type.

See Also

Accessibility Domain (pg. 23), Restrictions on Using Accessibility Levels (pg. 24)

Accessibility Domain

The accessibility domain of a member specifies where, in the program sections, a member can be referenced. If the member is nested within another type, its accessibility domain is determined by both the accessibility level of the member and the accessibility domain of the immediately containing type.

The accessibility domain of a top-level type is at least the program text of the project in which it is declared. That is, the entire source files of this project. The accessibility domain of a nested type is at least the program text of the type in which it is declared. That is, the type body, including any nested types. The accessibility domain of a nested type never exceeds that of the containing type. These concepts are demonstrated in the following example.

Example

This example contains a top-level type, T1, and two nested classes, M1 and M2. The classes contain fields with different declared accessibilities. In the Main method, a comment follows each statement to indicate the accessibility domain of each member. Notice that the statements that attempt to reference the inaccessible members are commented out. If you want to see the compiler errors caused by referencing an inaccessible member, remove the comments one at a time.

```
// cs_Accessibility_Domain.cs
using System;
namespace MyNameSpace
{
    public class T1
    {
        public static int myPublicInt;
        internal static int myInternalInt;
        private static int myPrivateInt = 0;

        public class M1
        {
            public static int myPublicInt;
            internal static int myInternalInt;
            private static int myPrivateInt = 0;
        }
```

(continued)

(continued)

```
    private class M2
    {
        public static int myPublicInt = 0;
        internal static int myInternalInt = 0;
        private static int myPrivateInt = 0;
    }
}

public class MainClass
{
    public static int Main()
    {
        // Access to T1 fields:
        T1.myPublicInt = 1;        // Access is unlimited
        T1.myInternalInt = 2;      // Accessible only in current project
        // T1.myPrivateInt = 3;    // Error: inaccessible outside T1

        // Access to the M1 fields:
        T1.M1.myPublicInt = 1;        // Access is unlimited
        T1.M1.myInternalInt = 2;      // Accessible only in current project
        // T1.M1.myPrivateInt = 3;    // Error: inaccessible outside M1

        // Access to the M2 fields:
        // T1.M2.myPublicInt = 1;     // Error: inaccessible outside T1
        // T1.M2.myInternalInt = 2;   // Error: inaccessible outside T1
        // T1.M2.myPrivateInt = 3;    // Error: inaccessible outside M2

        return 0;
    }
}
}
```

See Also
Accessibility Levels (pg. 22), Restrictions on Using Accessibility Levels (pg. 24)

Restrictions on Using Accessibility Levels

When you declare a type, it is essential to see if that type has to be *at least as accessible as* another member or type. For example, the direct base class must be at least as accessible as the derived class. The following declarations will result in a compiler error, because the base class BaseClass is less accessible than MyClass:

```
class BaseClass {...}
public class MyClass: BaseClass {...} // Error
```

The following table summarizes the restrictions on using declared accessibility levels.

Context	Remarks
Classes	The direct base class of a class type must be at least as accessible as the class type itself.
Interfaces	The explicit base interfaces of an interface type must be at least as accessible as the interface type itself.
Delegates	The return type and parameter types of a delegate type must be at least as accessible as the delegate type itself.
Constants	The type of a constant must be at least as accessible as the constant itself.
Fields	The type of a field must be at least as accessible as the field itself.
Methods	The return type and parameter types of a method must be at least as accessible as the method itself.
Properties	The type of a property must be at least as accessible as the property itself.
Events	The type of an event must be at least as accessible as the event itself.
Indexers	The type and parameter types of an indexer must be at least as accessible as the indexer itself.
Operators	The return type and parameter types of an operator must be at least as accessible as the operator itself.
Constructors	The parameter types of a constructor must be at least as accessible as the constructor itself.

Example

The following example contains erroneous declarations of different types. The comment following each declaration indicates the expected compiler error.

```
// Restrictions_on_Using_Accessibility_Levels.cs
// CS0052 expected as well as CS0053, CS0056, and CS0057
// To make the program work, change access level of both class B
// and MyPrivateMethod() to public.

using System;

// A delegate:
delegate int MyDelegate();

class B
{
    // A private method:
    static int MyPrivateMethod()
    {
        return 0;
    }
}
```

(continued)

(continued)

```
public class A
{
    // Fields:
    public B myField = new B();    // Error: The type B is less accessible
                                   // than the field A.myField.
    // Constants:
    public readonly B myConst = new B();    // Error: The type B is less accessible
                                            // than the constant A.myConst.

    // Methods:
    public B MyMethod()
    {
        return new B();    // Error: The type B is less accessible
    }                      // than the method A.MyMethod.

    // Properties:
    public  B MyProp
    {
        set
        {
        }
    }   // Error: The type B is less accessible than the property A.MyProp

    // Delegates:
    MyDelegate d = new MyDelegate(B.MyPrivateMethod);
    // Even when B is declared public, you still get the error:
    // "The parameter B.MyPrivateMethod is not accessible due to
    // protection level."

    // Operators:
    public static B operator + (A m1, B m2)
    {
        return new B();    // Error: The type B is less accessible
                           // than the operator A.operator +(A,B)
    }
    static void Main()
    {
        Console.Write("Compiled successfully");
    }
}
```

See Also

Accessibility Domain (pg. 23), Accessibility Levels (pg. 22)

internal

The **internal** keyword is an access modifier for types and type members. Internal members are accessible only within files in the same assembly.

A common use of internal access is in component-based development because it enables a group of components to cooperate in a private manner without being exposed to the rest of the application code. For example, a framework for building graphical user interfaces could provide Control and Form classes that cooperate using members with internal access. Since these members are internal, they are not exposed to code that is using the framework.

It is an error to reference a member with internal access outside the assembly within which it was defined.

> **Caution**   An **internal virtual** method can be overridden in some languages (such as textual IL using Ilasm.exe) even though it cannot be overridden using C#.

For a comparison of **internal** with the other access modifiers, see "Accessibility Levels" on page 22.

Example

This example contains two files, Assembly1.cs and Assembly2.cs. The first file contains an internal base class, BaseClass. In the second file, an attempt to access the member of the base class will produce an error.

File Assembly1.cs

```
// Assembly1.cs
// compile with: /target:library
internal class BaseClass
{
   public static int IntM = 0;
}
```

File Assembly2.cs

```
// Assembly2.cs
// compile with: /reference:Assembly1.dll
// CS0122 expected
class TestAccess
{
   public static void Main()
   {
      BaseClass myBase = new BaseClass();    // error, BaseClass not visible outside assembly
   }
}
```

See Also

Accessibility Levels (pg. 22)

private

The **private** keyword is a member access modifier. Private access is the least permissive access level. Private members are accessible only within the body of the class or the struct in which they are declared.

Nested types in the same body can also access those private members.

It is a compile-time error to reference a private member outside the class or the struct in which it is declared.

For a comparison of private with the other access modifiers, see "Accessibility Levels" on page 22.

Example

In this example, the Employee class contains a public member, Name, and a private member, Salary. The public member can be accessed directly, while the private member must be accessed through the public method AccessSalary().

```
// private_keyword.cs
using System;
class Employee
{
   public string name = "xx";
   double salary = 100.00;   // private access by default
   public double AccessSalary() {
      return salary;
   }
}
class MainClass
{
   public static void Main()
   {
      Employee e = new Employee();

      // Accessing the public field:
      string n = e.name;

      // Accessing the private field:
      double s = e.AccessSalary();
   }
}
```

In the preceding example, if you attempt to access the private members directly by using a statement like this:

```
double s = e.salary;
```

you will get the error message:

```
'Employee.Salary' is inaccessible due to its protection level.
```

See Also

Accessibility Levels (pg. 22)

protected

The **protected** keyword is a member access modifier. A protected member is accessible from within the class in which it is declared, and from within any class derived from the class that declared this member.

A protected member of a base class is accessible in a derived class only if the access takes place through the derived class type. For example, consider the following code segment:

```
class A
{
    protected int x = 123;
}

class B : A
{
    void F()
    {
        A a = new A();
        B b = new B();
        a.x = 10;    // Error
        b.x = 10;    // OK
    }
}
```

The statement `a.x =10` generates an error because A is not derived from B.

Struct members cannot be protected because the struct cannot be inherited.

It is an error to reference a protected member from a class, which is not derived from the protected member's class.

For a comparison of protected with the other access modifiers, see "Accessibility Levels" on page 22.

Example

In this example, the class `MyDerivedC` is derived from `MyClass`; therefore, you can access the protected members of the base class directly from the derived class.

```
// protected_keyword.cs
using System;
class MyClass
{
    protected int x;
    protected int y;
}
```

(continued)

(continued)

```
class MyDerivedC: MyClass
{
    public static void Main()
    {
        MyDerivedC mC = new MyDerivedC();

        // Direct access to protected members:
        mC.x = 10;
        mC.y = 15;
        Console.WriteLine("x = {0}, y = {1}", mC.x, mC.y);
    }
}
```

Output

```
x = 10, y = 15
```

If you change the access levels of x and y to **private**, the compiler will issue the error messages:

```
'MyClass.y' is inaccessible due to its protection level.
'MyClass.x' is inaccessible due to its protection level.
```

See Also

Accessibility Levels (pg. 22)

public

The **public** keyword is an access modifier for types and type members. Public access is the most permissive access level. There are no restrictions on accessing public members.

For a comparison of **public** with the other access modifiers, see "Accessibility Levels" on page 22.

Example

In the following example, two classes are declared, MyClass1 and MyClass2. The public members x and y of the MyClass1 are accessed directly from MyClass2.

```
// protected_public.cs
// Public access
using System;
class MyClass1
{
    public int x;
    public int y;
}
```

```
class MyClass2
{
    public static void Main()
    {
        MyClass1 mC = new MyClass1();

        // Direct access to public members:
        mC.x = 10;
        mC.y = 15;
        Console.WriteLine("x = {0}, y = {1}", mC.x, mC.y);
    }
}
```

Output

```
x = 10, y = 15
```

If you change the **public** access level to **private** or **protected**, you will get the error message:

```
'MyClass1.y' is inaccessible due to its protection level.
```

See Also

Accessibility Levels (pg. 22)

abstract

The **abstract** modifier can be used with classes, methods, and properties.

Use the **abstract** modifier in a class declaration to indicate that a class is intended only to be a base class of other classes.

Abstract classes have the following features:

- An abstract class cannot be instantiated.

- An abstract class may contain abstract methods and accessors.

- It is not possible to modify an abstract class with the sealed modifier, which means that the class cannot be inherited.

- A non-abstract class derived from an abstract class must include actual implementations of all inherited abstract methods and accessors.

Use the **abstract** modifier in a method or property declaration to indicate that the method or property does not contain implementation.

Abstract methods have the following features:

- An abstract method is implicitly a virtual method.

- Abstract method declarations are only permitted in abstract classes.

- Because an abstract method declaration provides no actual implementation, there is no method body; the method declaration simply ends with a semicolon and there are no braces ({ }) following the signature. For example:

```
public abstract void MyMethod();
```

- The implementation is provided by an overriding method, which is a member of a non-abstract class.

- It is an error to use the **static**, **virtual**, or **override** modifiers in an abstract method declaration.

Abstract properties behave like abstract methods, except for the differences in declaration and invocation syntax.

- It is an error to use the **abstract** modifier on a static property.

- An abstract inherited property can be overridden in a derived class by including a property declaration that uses the **override** modifier.

An abstract class must provide implementation for all interface members.

An abstract class that implements an interface might map the interface methods onto abstract methods. For example:

```
interface I
{
   void M();
}
abstract class C: I
{
   public abstract void M();
}
```

Example

In this example, the class MyDerivedC is derived from an abstract class MyBaseC. The abstract class contains an abstract method, MyMethod(), and two abstract properties, GetX() and GetY().

```
// abstract_keyword.cs
// Abstract Classes
using System;
abstract class MyBaseC    // Abstract class
{
   protected int x = 100;
   protected int y = 150;
   public abstract void MyMethod();    // Abstract method

   public abstract int GetX    // Abstract property
   {
      get;
   }
```

```
    public abstract int GetY    // Abstract property
    {
        get;
    }
}

class MyDerivedC: MyBaseC
{
    public override void MyMethod()
    {
        x++;
        y++;
    }

    public override int GetX    // overriding property
    {
        get
        {
            return x+10;
        }
    }

    public override int GetY    // overriding property
    {
        get
        {
            return y+10;
        }
    }

    public static void Main()
    {
        MyDerivedC mC = new MyDerivedC();
        mC.MyMethod();
        Console.WriteLine("x = {0}, y = {1}", mC.GetX, mC.GetY);
    }
}
```

Output

```
x = 111, y = 161
```

In the preceding example, if you attempt to instantiate the abstract class by using a statement like this:

```
MyBaseC mC1 = new MyBaseC();    // Error
```

you will get the following error message:

```
Cannot create an instance of the abstract class 'MyBaseC'.
```

See Also

virtual (pg. 51), override (pg. 44)

const

The keyword **const** is used to modify a declaration of a field or local variable. It specifies that the value of the field or the local variable cannot be modified. A constant declaration introduces one or more constants of a given type. The declaration takes the form:

```
[attributes] [modifiers] const type declarators;
```

where:

attributes (optional)
> Optional declarative information. For more information on attributes and attribute classes, see "Attributes" on page 211.

modifiers (optional)
> Optional modifiers that include the **new** modifier and one of the four access modifiers.

type
> One of the types: **byte**, **char**, **short**, **int**, **long**, **float**, **double**, **decimal**, **bool**, **string**, an enum type, or a reference type.

declarators
> A comma-separated list of declarators. A declarator takes the form:
>
> *identifier = constant-expression*

The *attributes* and *modifiers* apply to all of the members declared by the constant declaration.

The *type* of a constant declaration specifies the type of the members introduced by the declaration. A constant expression must yield a value of the target type, or of a type that can be implicitly converted to the target type.

A constant expression is an expression that can be fully evaluated at compile time. Therefore, the only possible values for constants of reference types are **string** and **null**.

Remarks

The constant declaration can declare multiple constants, for example:

```
public const double x = 1.0, y = 2.0, z = 3.0;
```

The **static** modifier is not allowed in a constant declaration.

A constant can participate in a constant expression, for example:

```
public const int c1 = 5.0;
public const int c2 = c1 + 100;
```

Example

```
// const_keyword.cs
// Constants
using System;
public class ConstTest
{
   class MyClass
   {
      public int x;
      public int y;
      public const int c1 = 5;
      public const int c2 = c1 + 5;

      public MyClass(int p1, int p2)
      {
         x = p1;
         y = p2;
      }
   }

   public static void Main()
   {
      MyClass mC = new MyClass(11, 22);
      Console.WriteLine("x = {0}, y = {1}", mC.x, mC.y);
      Console.WriteLine("c1 = {0}, c2 = {1}", MyClass.c1, MyClass.c2 );
   }
}
```

Output

```
x = 11, y = 22
c1 = 5, c2 = 10
```

Example

This example demonstrates using constants as local variables.

```
// const_keyword2.cs
using System;
public class TestClass
{
   public static void Main()
   {
      const int c = 707;
      Console.WriteLine("My local constant = {0}", c);
   }
}
```

Output

```
My local constant = 707
```

event

Specifies an event.

```
[attributes] [modifiers] event type declarator;
[attributes] [modifiers] event type member-name {accessor-declarations};
```

where:

attributes (optional)

Optional declarative information. For more information on attributes and attribute classes, see "Attributes" on page 211.

modifiers (optional)

Optional modifiers that include:

- abstract

- new

- override

- static

- virtual

- one of the four access modifiers

type

The delegate to which you want to associate this event.

declarator

The name of the event.

member-name

The name of the event.

accessor-declarations (optional)

Declaration of the accessors, which are used to add and remove event handlers in client code. The accessor functions are add and remove. It is an error to define one but not the other.

Remarks

The **event** keyword lets you specify a delegate that will be called upon the occurrence of some "event" in your code. The delegate can have one or more associated methods that will be called when your code indicates that the event has occurred. An event in one program can be made available to other programs that target the .NET Framework Common Language Runtime.

* The following steps must be taken in order to create and use C# events:

1. Create or identify a delegate. If you are defining your own event, you must also ensure that there is a delegate to use with the event keyword. If the event is predefined, in the .NET Framework for example, then consumers of the event need only know the name of the delegate.

2. Create a class that contains:

   a. An event created from the delegate.

   b. (optional) A method that verifies that an instance of the delegate declared with the **event** keyword exists. Otherwise, this logic must be placed in the code that fires the event.

   c. Methods that call the event. These methods can be overrides of some base class functionality.

   This class defines the event.

3. Define one or more classes that connect methods to the event. Each of these classes will include:

   * Associate one or more methods, using the += and -= operators, with the event in the base class.

   * The definition of the method(s) that will be associated with the event.

4. Use the event:

   * Create an object of the class that contains the event declaration.

   * Create an object of the class that contains the event definition, using the constructor that you defined.

For more information on events, see "Events Tutorial" on page 328.

Examples

A basic example of defining and using events can be found in the Events Tutorial. The following examples in this topic also demonstrate events.

Example	Comment
Example 1	Declaring an event in an interface and implementing it in a class.
Example 2	Using a hash table to store event instances.
Example 3	Implementing, via event properties, two interfaces that have an event with the same name.

Example 1

This example shows that it is possible to declare an event in an interface and implement it in a class:

```
// event_keyword.cs
using System;
public delegate void MyDelegate();   // delegate declaration

public interface I
{
   event MyDelegate MyEvent;
   void FireAway();
}

public class MyClass: I
{
   public event MyDelegate MyEvent;
   public void FireAway()
   {
      if (MyEvent != null)
         MyEvent();
   }
}

public class MainClass
{
   static private void f()
   {
      Console.WriteLine("This is called when the event fires.");
   }

   static public void Main ()
   {
      I i = new MyClass();

      i.MyEvent += new MyDelegate(f);
      i.FireAway();
   }
}
```

Example 2

One use for *accessor-declarations* is to expose a large number of events without allocating a field for each event, but instead using a hash table to store the event instances. This is only useful if you have a very large number of events, but you expect most of the events will not be implemented.

```
// event_keyword2.cs
using System;
using System.Collections;

public delegate void MyDelegate1(int i);
public delegate void MyDelegate2(string s);
public delegate void MyDelegate3(int i, object o);
public delegate void MyDelegate4();

public class PropertyEventsSample
{
    private Hashtable eventTable = new Hashtable();

    public event MyDelegate1 Event1
    {
        add
        {
            eventTable["Event1"] = (MyDelegate1)eventTable["Event1"] + value;
        }
        remove
        {
            eventTable["Event1"] = (MyDelegate1)eventTable["Event1"] - value;
        }
    }

    public event MyDelegate1 Event2
    {
        add
        {
            eventTable["Event2"] = (MyDelegate1)eventTable["Event2"] + value;
        }
        remove
        {
            eventTable["Event2"] = (MyDelegate1)eventTable["Event2"] - value;
        }
    }

    public event MyDelegate2 Event3
    {
        add
        {
            eventTable["Event3"] = (MyDelegate2)eventTable["Event3"] + value;
        }
        remove
        {
            eventTable["Event3"] = (MyDelegate2)eventTable["Event3"] - value;
        }
    }
```

(continued)

(continued)

```csharp
    public event MyDelegate3 Event4
    {
        add
        {
            eventTable["Event4"] = (MyDelegate3)eventTable["Event4"] + value;
        }
        remove
        {
            eventTable["Event4"] = (MyDelegate3)eventTable["Event4"] - value;
        }
    }

    public event MyDelegate3 Event5
    {
        add
        {
            eventTable["Event5"] = (MyDelegate3)eventTable["Event5"] + value;
        }
        remove
        {
            eventTable["Event5"] = (MyDelegate3)eventTable["Event5"] - value;
        }
    }

    public event MyDelegate4 Event6
    {
        add
        {
            eventTable["Event6"] = (MyDelegate4)eventTable["Event6"] + value;
        }
        remove
        {
            eventTable["Event6"] = (MyDelegate4)eventTable["Event6"] - value;
        }
    }
}

public class MyClass
{
    public static void Main()
    {
    }
}
```

Example 3

Another use for event properties covers the situation where you are implementing two interfaces, each with an event of the same name. In such a case, you must use an explicit implementation event property:

```
// event_keyword3.cs
using System;

public delegate void MyDelegate1();

public interface I1
{
   event MyDelegate1 MyEvent;
}

public delegate int MyDelegate2(string s);

public interface I2
{
   event MyDelegate2 MyEvent;
}

public class ExplicitEventsSample: I1, I2
{
   public event MyDelegate1 MyEvent;  // normal implementation of I1.MyEvent.

   event MyDelegate2 I2.MyEvent    // explicit implementation of I2.MyEvent
   {
      add
      {
         MyEvent2Storage += value;
      }
      remove
      {
         MyEvent2Storage -= value;
      }
   }

   private MyDelegate2 MyEvent2Storage;  // underlying storage for I2.MyEvent.

   private void FireEvents()
   {
      if (MyEvent != null)
         MyEvent();
      if (MyEvent2Storage != null)
         MyEvent2Storage("hello");
   }
}

public class MyClass
{
   public static void Main()
   {
   }
}
```

See Also

Events Tutorial (pg. 328)

extern

Use the **extern** modifier in a method declaration to indicate that the method is implemented externally. A common use of the extern modifier is with the **DllImport** attribute.

It is an error to use the abstract and **extern** modifiers together to modify the same member. Using the **extern** modifier means that the method is implemented outside the C# code, while using the **abstract** modifier means that the method implementation is not provided in the class.

Because an external method declaration provides no actual implementation, there is no method body; the method declaration simply ends with a semicolon and there are no braces ({ }) following the signature. For example:

```
public static extern int MyMethod(int x);
```

Note The **extern** keyword is more limited in use than in C++.

For more information on attributes, see "Attributes" on page 211.

Example

In this example, the program receives a string from the user and displays it inside a message box. The program uses the MessageBox method imported from the User32.dll library.

```
using System;
using System.Runtime.InteropServices;
class MyClass
{
    [DllImport("User32.dll")]
    public static extern int MessageBox(int h, string m, string c, int type);

    public static int Main()
    {
        string myString;
        Console.Write("Enter your message: ");
        myString = Console.ReadLine();
        return MessageBox(0, myString, "My Message Box", 0);
    }
}
```

Sample Run

```
Enter your message: Where do you want to go today?
```

When the previous text is entered, a message box that contains the text will pop up on the screen.

Example

This example uses two files, CM.cs and Cmdll.c, to demonstrate **extern**. The C file is an external DLL that is invoked from within the C# program.

File: Cmdll.c

```
// cmdll.c
// compile with: /LD /MD
int __declspec(dllexport) MyMethod(int i)
{
    return i*10;
}
```

File: CM.cs

```
// cm.cs
using System;
using System.Runtime.InteropServices;
public class MyClass
{
    [DllImport("Cmdll.dll")]
    public static extern int MyMethod(int x);
    public static void Main()
    {
        Console.WriteLine("MyMethod() returns {0}.", MyMethod(5));
    }
}
```

Output

```
MyMethod() returns 50.
```

Compilation

To build the project, use the following steps:

- Compile Cmdll.c to a DLL using the Visual C++® command line:

    ```
    cl /LD /MD Cmdll.c
    ```

- Compile CM.cs using the command line:

    ```
    csc CM.cs
    ```

This will create the executable file CM.exe. When you run this program, MyMethod will pass the value 5 to the DLL file, which returns the value multiplied by 10.

override

Use the **override** modifier to modify a method or a property. An override method provides a new implementation of a member inherited from a base class. The method overridden by an override declaration is known as the overridden base method. The overridden base method must have the same signature as the override method.

You cannot override a non-virtual or static method. The overridden base method must be virtual, abstract, or override.

An override declaration cannot change the accessibility of the virtual method. Both the override method and the virtual method must have the same access level modifier.

You cannot use the following modifiers to modify an override method:

new   static   virtual   abstract

An overriding property declaration must specify the exact same access modifier, type, and name as the inherited property, and the overridden property must be virtual, abstract, or override.

Example

See the example for the virtual keyword.

From within the derived class that has an override method, you still can access the overridden base method that has the same name by using the **base** keyword. For example, if you have a virtual method MyMethod(), and an override method on a derived class, you can access the virtual method from the derived class by using the call:

```
base.MyMethod()
```

Compare this to the C++ way, where you use the scope resolution operator (::) and the base class name, for example:

```
My_Base_Class_Name::MyMethod()
```

Example

In this example, there is a base class, Square, and a derived class, Cube. Because the area of a cube is the sum of the areas of six squares, it is possible to calculate it by calling the Area() method on the base class.

```
// cs_override_keyword.cs
// Calling overriden methods from the base class
using System;
class TestClass
{
    public class Square
    {
        public double x;
```

```
   // Constructor:
   public Square(double x)
   {
      this.x = x;
   }

   public virtual double Area()
   {
      return x*x;
   }
}

class Cube: Square
{
   // Constructor:
   public Cube(double x): base(x)
   {
   }

   // Calling the Area base method:
   public override double Area()
   {
      return (6*(base.Area()));
   }
}

public static void Main()
{
   double x = 5.2;
   Square s = new Square(x);
   Square c = new Cube(x);
   Console.WriteLine("Area of Square = {0:F2}", s.Area());
   Console.WriteLine("Area of Cube = {0:F2}", c.Area());
}
}
```

Output

```
Area of Square = 27.04
Area of Cube = 162.24
```

See Also

abstract (pg. 31), virtual (pg. 51)

readonly

The **readonly** keyword is a modifier that you can use on fields. When a field declaration includes a **readonly** modifier, assignments to the fields introduced by the declaration can only occur as part of the declaration or in a constructor in the same class.

You can assign a value to a readonly field only in the following contexts:

- When the variable is initialized in the declaration, for example:

  ```
  public readonly int y = 5;
  ```

- For an instance field, in the instance constructors of the class that contains the field declaration, or for a static field, in the static constructor of the class that contains the field declaration. These are also the only contexts in which it is valid to pass a readonly field as an **out** or **ref** parameter.

Example

```
// cs_readonly_keyword.cs
// Readonly fields
using System;
public class ReadOnlyTest
{
   class MyClass
   {
      public int x;
      public readonly int y = 25; // Initialize a readonly field
      public readonly int z;

      public MyClass()
      {
         z = 24;    // Initialize a readonly instance field
      }

      public MyClass(int p1, int p2, int p3)
      {
         x = p1;
         y = p2;
         z = p3;
      }
   }

   public static void Main()
   {
      MyClass p1= new MyClass(11, 21, 32);   // OK
      Console.WriteLine("p1: x={0}, y={1}, z={2}" , p1.x, p1.y, p1.z);
      MyClass p2 = new MyClass();
      p2.x = 55;   // OK
      Console.WriteLine("p2: x={0}, y={1}, z={2}" , p2.x, p2.y, p2.z);
   }
}
```

Output

```
p1: x=11, y=21, z=32
p2: x=55, y=25, z=24
```

In the preceding example, if you use a statement like this:

```
p2.y = 66;          // Error
```

you will get the compiler error message:

```
The left-hand side of an assignment must be an l-value
```

which is the same error you get when you attempt to assign a value to a constant.

sealed

A sealed class cannot be inherited. It is an error to use a sealed class as a base class. Use the **sealed** modifier in a class declaration to prevent accidental inheritance of the class.

It is not permitted to use the abstract modifier with a sealed class.

Structs are implicitly sealed; therefore, they cannot be inherited.

Example

```
// cs_sealed_keyword.cs
// Sealed classes
using System;
sealed class MyClass
{
    public int x;
    public int y;
}

class MainClass
{
    public static void Main()
    {
        MyClass mC = new MyClass();
        mC.x = 110;
        mC.y = 150;
        Console.WriteLine("x = {0}, y = {1}", mC.x, mC.y);
    }
}
```

Output

```
x = 110, y = 150
```

In the preceding example, if you attempt to inherit from the sealed class by using a statement like this:

```
class MyDerivedC: MyClass {}    // Error
```

you will get the error message:

```
'MyDerivedC' cannot inherit from sealed class 'MyBaseC'.
```

static

Use the **static** modifier to declare a static member, which belongs to the type itself rather than to a specific object. The **static** modifier can be used with fields, methods, properties, operators, and constructors, but cannot be used with indexers, destructors, or types.

Remarks

- A constant or type declaration is implicitly a static member.

- A static member cannot be referenced through an instance. Instead, it is referenced through the type name. For example, consider the following class:

```
public class MyBaseC
{
   public struct MyStruct {
      public static int x = 100;
   }
}
```

To refer to the static member x, use the fully qualified name (unless it is accessible from the same scope):

```
MyBaseC.MyStruct.x
```

- While an instance of a class contains a separate copy of all instance fields of the class, there is only one copy of each static field.

- It is not possible to use **this** to reference static methods or property accessors.

> **Note** The **static** keyword is more limited in use than in C++.

To demonstrate instance members, consider a class that represents a company employee. Assume that the class contains a method to count employees and a field to store the number of employees. Both the method and the field do not belong to any instance employee. Instead they belong to the company class. Therefore, they should be declared as static members of the class.

For more information on constructors, see "Instance Constructors" on page 261.

Example

This example reads the name and ID of a new employee, increments the employee counter by one, and displays the information for the new employee as well as the new number of employees. For simplicity, this program reads the current number of employees from the keyboard. In a real application, this information should be read from a file.

```
// cs_static_keyword.cs
// Static members
using System;
public class Employee
{
    public string id;
    public string name;

    public Employee ()
    {
    }

    public Employee (string name, string id)
    {
        this.name = name;
        this.id = id;
    }

    public static int employeeCounter;

    public static int AddEmployee()
    {
        return ++employeeCounter;
    }
}

class MainClass: Employee
{
    public static void Main()
    {
        Console.Write("Enter the employee's name: ");
        string name = Console.ReadLine();
        Console.Write("Enter the employee's ID: ");
        string id = Console.ReadLine();
        // Create the employee object:
        Employee e = new Employee (name, id);
        Console.Write("Enter the current number of employees: ");
        string n = Console.ReadLine();
        Employee.employeeCounter = Int32.Parse(n);
        Employee.AddEmployee();
```

(continued)

(continued)

```
        // Display the new information:
        Console.WriteLine("Name: {0}", e.name);
        Console.WriteLine("ID:   {0}", e.id);
        Console.WriteLine("New Number of Employees: {0}",
                          Employee.employeeCounter);
    }
}
```

Input

```
Tara Strahan
AF643G
15
```

Sample Output

```
Enter the employee's name: Tara Strahan
Enter the employee's ID: AF643G
Enter the current number of employees: 15
Name: Tara Strahan
ID:   AF643G
New Number of Employees: 16
```

unsafe

The **unsafe** keyword denotes an unsafe context. Unsafe context is required for any operation involving pointers.

unsafe is applied as a modifier in the declaration of callable members such as methods, properties, constructors, and extenders (but not static constructors).

```
static unsafe void FastCopy ( byte[] src, byte[] dst, int count )
{
    // unsafe context: can use pointers here
}
```

The scope of the unsafe context extends from the parameter list to the end of the function, so pointers can also be used in the parameter list:

```
static unsafe void FastCopy ( byte* ps, byte* pd, int count ) {...}
```

To compile unmanaged code you must specify the /unsafe compiler option. Unmanaged code is not verifiable by the Common Language Runtime.

Example

```
// cs_unsafe_keyword.cs
// compile with: /unsafe
using System;
class UnsafeTest
{
    unsafe static void SquarePtrParam (int* p)
    // unsafe method: takes pointer to int
    {
        *p *= *p;
    }

    unsafe public static void Main()
    // unsafe method: uses address-of operator (&)
    {
        int i = 5;
        SquarePtrParam (&i);
        Console.WriteLine (i);
    }
}
```

Output

25

See Also

fixed Statement (pg. 116)

virtual

The **virtual** keyword is used to modify a method or property declaration, in which case the method or the property is called a virtual member. The implementation of a virtual member can be changed by an overriding member in a derived class.

When a virtual method is invoked, the run-time type of the object is checked for an overriding member. The overriding member in the most derived class is called, which might be the original member, if no derived class has overridden the member.

By default, methods are non-virtual. You cannot override a non-virtual method.

You cannot use the **virtual** modifier with the following modifiers:

static   abstract   override

Virtual properties behave like abstract methods, except for the differences in declaration and invocation syntax.

- It is an error to use the **virtual** modifier on a static property.

- A virtual inherited property can be overridden in a derived class by including a property declaration that uses the **override** modifier.

Example

In this example, the class Dimensions contains the two coordinates x, y, and the Area() virtual method. Different shape classes such as Circle, Cylinder, and Sphere inherit the Dimensions class, and the surface area is calculated for each figure. Each derived class has it own override implementation of Area(). The program calculates and displays the proper area for each figure by invoking the proper implementation of Area() according to the object associated with the method.

```
// cs_virtual_keyword.cs
// Virtual and override
using System;
class TestClass
{
   public class Dimensions
   {
      public const double pi = Math.PI;
      protected double x, y;
      public Dimensions()
      {
      }
      public Dimensions (double x, double y)
      {
         this.x = x;
         this.y = y;
      }

      public virtual double Area()
      {
         return x*y;
      }
   }

   public class Circle: Dimensions
   {
      public Circle(double r): base(r, 0)
      {
      }

      public override double Area()
      {
         return pi * x * x;
      }
   }
```

```
class Sphere: Dimensions
{
    public Sphere(double r): base(r, 0)
    {
    }

      public override double Area()
    {
        return 4 * pi * x * x;
    }
}

class Cylinder: Dimensions
{
    public Cylinder(double r, double h): base(r, h)
    {
    }

    public override double Area()
    {
        return 2*pi*x*x + 2*pi*x*y;
    }
}

public static void Main()
{
    double r = 3.0, h = 5.0;
    Dimensions c = new Circle(r);
    Dimensions s = new Sphere(r);
    Dimensions l = new Cylinder(r, h);
    // Display results:
    Console.WriteLine("Area of Circle   = {0:F2}", c.Area());
    Console.WriteLine("Area of Sphere   = {0:F2}", s.Area());
    Console.WriteLine("Area of Cylinder = {0:F2}", l.Area());
}
}
```

Output

```
Area of Circle   = 28.27
Area of Sphere   = 113.10
Area of Cylinder = 150.80
```

In the preceding example, notice that the inherited classes Circle, Sphere, and Cylinder are all using constructors that initialize the base class, for example:

```
public Cylinder(double r, double h): base(r, h) {}
```

This is analogous to the C++ initialization list.

See Also

abstract (pg. 31), override (pg. 44)

volatile

The **volatile** keyword indicates that a field can be modified in the program by something such as the operating system, the hardware, or a concurrently executing thread.

```
volatile declaration
```

where:

declaration
>   The declaration of a field.

Remarks

The system always reads the current value of a volatile object at the point it is requested, even if the previous instruction asked for a value from the same object. Also, the value of the object is written immediately on assignment.

The **volatile** modifier is usually used for a field that is accessed by multiple threads without using the lock statement to serialize access. Using the **volatile** modifier ensures that one thread retrieves the most up-to-date value written by another thread.

The type of a field marked as volatile is restricted to the following types:

- Any reference type.

- Any pointer type (in an unsafe context).

- The types sbyte, byte, short, ushort, int, uint, char, float, bool.

- An enum type with an enum base type of byte, sbyte, short, ushort, int, or uint.

Example

The following sample shows how to declare a public field variable as volatile.

```
// csharp_volatile.cs
class Test
{
    public volatile int i;

    Test(int _i)
    {
        i = _i;
    }
    public static void Main()
    {

    }
}
```

Namespace Keywords

This section describes the keywords that are associated with using namespaces:

- namespace

- using

namespace

The **namespace** keyword is used to declare a scope. This namespace scope lets you organize code and gives you a way to create globally-unique types.

```
namespace name[.name1] ...] {
    type-declarations
}
```

where:

name, name1
    A namespace name can be any legal identifier. A namespace name can contain periods.

type-declarations
    Within a namespace, you can declare one or more of the following types:

- another namespace

- class

- interface

- struct

- enum

- delegate

Remarks

Even if you do not explicitly declare one, a default namespace is created. This unnamed namespace, sometimes called the global namespace, is present in every file. Any identifier in the global namespace is available for use in a named namespace.

Namespaces implicitly have public access and this is not modifiable.

"Namespace Keywords" discusses namespaces in more detail.

For a discussion of the access modifiers you can assign to elements within a namespace, see "Access Modifiers" on page 21.

It is possible to define a namespace in two or more declarations. For example, the following sample defines both classes as part of namespace `MyCompany`:

```
namespace MyCompany.Proj1
{
   class MyClass
   {
   }
}

namespace MyCompany.Proj1
{
   class MyClass1
   {
   }
}
```

Example

The following example shows how to call a static method in a nested namespace.

```
// cs_namespace_keyword.cs
using System;
namespace SomeNameSpace
{
   public class MyClass
   {
      public static void Main()
      {
         Nested.NestedNameSpaceClass.SayHello();
      }
   }

   namespace Nested    // a nested namespace
   {
      public class NestedNameSpaceClass
      {
         public static void SayHello()
         {
            Console.WriteLine("Hello");
         }
      }
   }
}
```

Output

```
Hello
```

See Also

using (pg. 57)

using

The **using** keyword has two major uses:

- using Directive   Creates an alias for a namespace.

- using Statement   Defines a scope at the end of which an object will be disposed.

See Also

namespace (pg. 55)

using Directive

The **using** directive has two uses:

- Create an alias for a namespace (a **using** alias).

- Permit the use of types in a namespace, such that, you do not have to qualify the use of a type in that namespace (a **using** directive).

```
using [alias = ]class_or_namespace;
```

where:

alias (optional)
    A user-defined symbol that you want to represent a namespace. You will then be able to use *alias* to represent the namespace name.

class_or_namespace
    The namespace name that you want to either use or alias, or the class name that you want to alias.

Remarks

Create a **using** alias to make it easier to qualify an identifier to a namespace or class.

Create a **using** directive to use the types in a namespace without having to specify the namespace. A **using** directive does not give you access to any namespaces that may be nested in the namespace you specify.

Namespace come in two categories: user-defined and system-defined. User-defined namespaces are namespaces defined in your code. See the documentation for the .NET Framework for a list of the system-defined namespaces.

Example

The following sample shows how to define and use a **using** alias for a namespace:

```
// cs_using_directive.cs
using MyAlias = MyCompany.Proj.Nested;  // define an alias to represent a namespace

namespace MyCompany.Proj
{
   public class MyClass
   {
      public static void DoNothing()
      {
      }
   }

   namespace Nested   // a nested namespace
   {
      public class ClassInNestedNameSpace
      {
         public static void SayHello()
         {
            System.Console.WriteLine("Hello");
         }
      }
   }

}

public class UnNestedClass
{
   public static void Main()
   {
      MyAlias.ClassInNestedNameSpace.SayHello();   // using alias
   }
}
```

Output

```
Hello
```

Example

The following sample shows how to define a **using** directive and a **using** alias for a class:

```
// cs_using_directive2.cs
using System;    // using directive
using AliasToMyClass = NameSpace1.MyClass;    // using alias for a class

namespace NameSpace1
{
   public class MyClass
   {
      public override string ToString()
      {
         return "You are in NameSpace1.MyClass";
      }
   }
}

namespace NameSpace2
{
   class MyClass
   {
   }
}

namespace NameSpace3
{
   using NameSpace1;    // using directive
   using NameSpace2;    // using directive

   class Test
   {
      public static void Main()
      {
         AliasToMyClass somevar = new AliasToMyClass();
         Console.WriteLine(somevar);
      }
   }
}
```

Output

```
You are in NameSpace1.MyClass
```

See Also

namespace (pg. 55), using Statement (pg. 60)

using Statement

The **using** statement defines a scope at the end of which an object will be disposed.

```
using (expression | type identifier = initializer)
{
}
```

where:

expression
> An expression you want to call **Dispose** on upon exiting the **using** statement.

type
> The type of *identifier*.

identifier
> The name, or identifer, of the type *type*. It is possible to define more than one *identifier* of type *type*. Precede each *identifier* = *initializer* with a comma.

initializer
> An expression that creates an object.

Remarks

You create an instance in a **using** statement to ensure that **Dispose** is called on the object when the **using** statement is exited. A **using** statement can be exited either when the end of the **using** statement is reached or if, for example, an exception is thrown and control leaves the statement block before the end of the statement.

The object you instantiate must implement the **System.IDisposable** interface.

Example

```
// cs_using_statement.cs
// compile with /reference:System.Drawing.dll
using System.Drawing;
class a
{
   public static void Main()
   {
      using (Font MyFont = new Font("Arial", 10.0f), MyFont2 = new Font("Arial", 10.0f))
      {
         // use MyFont and MyFont2
      }   // compiler will call Dispose on MyFont and MyFont2
```

```
    Font MyFont3 = new Font("Arial", 10.0f);
    using (MyFont3)
    {
        // use MyFont3
    }   // compiler will call Dispose on MyFont3

    }
}
```

See Also

using Directive (pg. 57)

Operator Keywords

This section introduces the following keywords:

- as   Convert an object to a compatible type.

- is   Check the run-time type of an object.

- new

  - new operator   Create objects.

  - new modifier   Hide an inherited member.

- sizeof   Obtain the size of a type.

- typeof   Obtain the **System.Type** object for a type.

- true   Return the boolean value true.

- false   Return the boolean value false.

- stackalloc   Allocate a block of memory on the stack.

The following keywords, which can be used as operators and as statements, are covered in the Statements section:

- checked   Specify checked context.

- unchecked   Specify unchecked context.

See Also

Operators (pg. 169)

as

The **as** operator is used to perform conversions between compatible types. The **as** operator is used in an expression of the form:

```
expression as type
```

where:

expression
> An expression of a reference type.

type
> A reference type.

Remarks

The **as** operator is like a cast except that it yields null on conversion failure instead of raising an exception. More formally, an expression of the form:

```
expression as type
```

is equivalent to:

```
expression is type ? (type)expression : (type)null
```

except that `expression` is evaluated only once.

Example

```
// cs_keyword_as.cs
// The as operator
using System;
class MyClass1
{
}

class MyClass2
{
}

public class IsTest
{
    public static void Main()
    {
        object [] myObjects = new object[6];
        myObjects[0] = new MyClass1();
        myObjects[1] = new MyClass2();
        myObjects[2] = "hello";
        myObjects[3] = 123;
        myObjects[4] = 123.4;
        myObjects[5] = null;
```

```
        for (int i=0; i<myObjects.Length; ++i)
        {
            string s = myObjects[i] as string;
            Console.Write ("{0}:", i);
            if (s != null)
                Console.WriteLine ( "'" + s + "'" );
            else
                Console.WriteLine ( "not a string" );
        }
    }
}
```

Output

```
0:not a string
1:not a string
2:'hello'
3:not a string
4:not a string
5:not a string
```

See Also

is (pg. 63), ?: Operator (pg. 187)

is

The **is** operator is used to check whether the run-time type of an object is compatible with a given type. The **is** operator is used in an expression of the form:

```
expression is type
```

Where:

expression
    An expression of a reference type.

type
    A type.

Remarks

An **is** expression evaluates to true if both of the following conditions are met:

- *expression* is not **null**.

- *expression* can be cast to *type*. That is, a cast expression of the form (type)(expression) will complete without throwing an exception.

A compile-time warning will be issued if the expression expression is type is known to always be true or always be false.

The **is** operator cannot be overloaded.

Example

```csharp
// cs_keyword_is.cs
// The is operator
using System;
class Class1
{
}

class Class2
{
}

public class IsTest
{
   public static void Test (object o)
   {
      Class1 a;
      Class2 b;

      if (o is Class1)
      {
         Console.WriteLine ("o is Class1");
         a = (Class1)o;
         // do something with a
      }

      else if (o is Class2)
      {
         Console.WriteLine ("o is Class2");
         b = (Class2)o;
         // do something with b
      }

      else
      {
         Console.WriteLine ("o is neither Class1 nor Class2.");
      }
   }
   public static void Main()
   {
      Class1 c1 = new Class1();
      Class2 c2 = new Class2();
      Test (c1);
      Test (c2);
      Test ("a string");
   }
}
```

Output

```
o is Class1
o is Class2
o is neither Class1 nor Class2.
```

See Also

typeof (pg. 71), as (pg. 62)

new

In C#, the **new** keyword can be used as an operator or as a modifier.

* new operator   Used to create objects on the heap and invoke constructors.

* new modifier   Used to hide an inherited member from a base class member.

new Operator

The **new** operator is used to create objects and invoke constructors, for example:

```
Class1 MyClass  = new Class1();
```

It is also used to invoke the default constructor for value types, for example:

```
int myInt = new int();
```

In the preceding statement, myInt is initialized to 0, which is the default value for the type **int**. The statement has the same effect as:

```
int myInt = 0;
```

For a complete list of default values, see "Default Values Table" on page 164.

Remember that it is an error to declare a default constructor for a struct, because every value type implicitly has a public default constructor. It is possible though to declare parameterized constructors on a struct type.

Value-type objects such as structs are created on the stack, while reference-type objects such as classes are created on the heap.

The **new** operator cannot be overloaded.

Example

In the following example, a struct object and a class object are created and initialized by using the
new operator and then assigned values. The default and the assigned values are displayed

```csharp
// cs_operator_new.cs
// The new operator
using System;
class NewTest
{
    struct MyStruct
    {
        public int x;
        public int y;
        public MyStruct (int x, int y)
        {
            this.x = x;
            this.y = y;
        }
    }

    class MyClass
    {
        public string name;
        public int id;

        public MyClass ()
        {
        }

        public MyClass (int id, string name)
        {
            this.id = id;
            this.name = name;
        }
    }

    public static void Main()
    {
        // Create objects using default constructors:
        MyStruct Location1 = new MyStruct();
        MyClass Employee1 = new MyClass();

        // Display values:
        Console.WriteLine("Default values:");
        Console.WriteLine("    Struct members: {0}, {1}",
            Location1.x, Location1.y);
        Console.WriteLine("    Class members: {0}, {1}",
            Employee1.name, Employee1.id);
```

```
      // Create objects using parameterized constructors::
      MyStruct Location2 = new MyStruct(10, 20);
      MyClass Employee2 = new MyClass(1234, "John Martin Smith");

      // Display values:
      Console.WriteLine("Assigned values:");
      Console.WriteLine("    Struct members: {0}, {1}",
          Location2.x, Location2.y);
      Console.WriteLine("    Class members: {0}, {1}",
          Employee2.name, Employee2.id);
   }
}
```

Output

```
Default values:
    Struct members: 0, 0
    Class members: , 0
Assigned values:
    Struct members: 10, 20
    Class members: John Martin Smith, 1234
```

Notice in the example that the default value of a string is **null**. Therefore, it was not displayed.

new Modifier

Use the **new** modifier to explicitly hide a member inherited from a base class. To hide an inherited member, declare it in the derived class using the same name, and modify it with the **new** modifier.

Consider the following class:

```
public class MyBaseC
{
    public int x;
    public void Invoke();
}
```

Declaring a member with the name Invoke in a derived class will hide the method Invoke in the base class, that is:

```
public class MyDerivedC : MyBaseC
{
    new public void Invoke();
}
```

However, the field x will not be affected because it is not hidden by a similar name.

Name hiding through inheritance takes one of the following forms:

- A constant, field, property, or type introduced in a class or struct hides all base class members with the same name.
- A method introduced in a class or struct hides properties, fields, and types, with the same name, in the base class. It also hides all base class methods with the same signature.
- An indexer introduced in a class or struct hides all base class indexers with the same signature.

It is an error to use both **new** and override on the same member.

Using **new** and **virtual** together guarantees a new point of specialization.

Using the **new** modifier in a declaration that does not hide an inherited member generates a warning.

Example

In this example, a base class, MyBaseC, and a derived class, MyDerivedC, use the same field name x, thus hiding the value of the inherited field. The example demonstrates the use of the **new** modifier. It also demonstrates how to access the hidden members of the base class by using the fully qualified names.

```
// cs_modifier_new.cs
// The new modifier
using System;
public class MyBaseC
{
    public static int x = 55;
    public static int y = 22;
}

public class MyDerivedC : MyBaseC
{
    new public static int x = 100;    // Name hiding
    public static void Main()
    {
        // Display the overlapping value of x:
        Console.WriteLine(x);

        // Access the hidden value of x:
        Console.WriteLine(MyBaseC.x);

        // Display the unhidden member y:
        Console.WriteLine(y);
    }
}
```

Output

```
100
55
22
```

If you remove the **new** modifier, the program will still compile and run, but you will get the warning:

```
The keyword new is required on 'MyDerivedC.x' because it hides inherited member 'MyBaseC.x'.
```

You can also use the **new** modifier to modify a nested type if the nested type is hiding another type, as demonstrated in the following example.

Example

In this example, a nested class, MyClass, hides a class with the same name in the base class. The example demonstrates using the **new** modifier to eliminate the warning message, as well as accessing the hidden class members by using the fully qualified names.

```
// cs_modifer_new_nested.cs
// Using the new modifier with nested types
using System;
public class MyBaseC
{
   public class MyClass
   {
      public int x = 200;
      public int y;
   }
}

public class MyDerivedC : MyBaseC
{
   new public class MyClass    // nested type hiding the base type members
   {
      public int x = 100;
      public int y;
      public int z;
   }

   public static void Main()
   {
      // Creating object from the overlapping class:
      MyClass S1  = new MyClass();

      // Creating object from the hidden class:
      MyBaseC.MyClass S2 = new MyBaseC.MyClass();

      Console.WriteLine(S1.x);
      Console.WriteLine(S2.x);
   }
}
```

Output

```
100
200
```

See Also

Modifiers (pg. 20)

sizeof

The **sizeof** operator is used to obtain the size in bytes for a value type. A **sizeof** expression takes the form:

```
sizeof(type)
```

where:

type
    The value type for which the size is obtained.

Remarks

The **sizeof** operator can be applied only to value types, not reference types.

The **sizeof** operator can only be used in the unsafe mode.

The **sizeof** operator cannot be overloaded.

Example

```
// cs_operator_sizeof.cs
// compile with: /unsafe

// Using the sizeof operator
using System;
class SizeClass
{
    // Notice the unsafe declaration of the method:
    unsafe public static void SizesOf()
    {
        Console.WriteLine("The size of short is {0}.", sizeof(short));
        Console.WriteLine("The size of int is {0}.", sizeof(int));
        Console.WriteLine("The size of long is {0}.", sizeof(long));
    }
}

class MainClass
{
    public static void Main()
    {
        SizeClass.SizesOf();
    }
}
```

```
The size of short is 2.
The size of int is 4.
The size of long is 8.
```

typeof

The **typeof** operator is used to obtain the **System.Type** object for a type. A **typeof** expression takes the form:

```
typeof(type)
```

where:

type
> The type for which the **System.Type** object is obtained.

Remarks

The **typeof** operator cannot be overloaded.

To obtain the run-time type of an expression, you can use the .NET Framework method **GetType**.

Example

```
// cs_operator_typeof.cs
// Using typeof operator
using System;
using System.Reflection;

public class MyClass
{
    public int intI;
    public void MyMeth()
    {
    }

    public static void Main()
    {
        Type t = typeof(MyClass);

        // alternatively, you could use
        // MyClass t1 = new MyClass();
        // Type t = t1.GetType();

        MethodInfo[] x = t.GetMethods();
        foreach (MethodInfo xtemp in x)
        {
            Console.WriteLine(xtemp.ToString());
        }
```

(continued)

(continued)

```
        Console.WriteLine();

        MemberInfo[] x2 = t.GetMembers();
        foreach (MemberInfo xtemp2 in x2)
        {
            Console.WriteLine(xtemp2.ToString());
        }
    }
}
```

Output

```
Int32 GetHashCode()
Boolean Equals(System.Object)
System.String ToString()
Void MyMeth()
Void Main()
System.Type GetType()

Int32 intI
Int32 GetHashCode()
Boolean Equals(System.Object)
System.String ToString()
Void MyMeth()
Void Main()
System.Type GetType()
Void .ctor()
```

Example

```
// cs_operator_typeof2.cs
// Using GetType method
using System;
class GetTypeTest
{
    public static void Main()
    {
        int radius = 3;
        Console.WriteLine("Area = {0}", radius*radius*Math.PI);
        Console.WriteLine("The type is {0}",
                (radius*radius*Math.PI).GetType());
    }
}
```

Output

```
Area = 28.2743338823081
The type is System.Double
```

See Also

is (pg. 63)

true

In C#, the **true** keyword can be used as an overloaded operator or as a literal:

- true Operator
- true Literal

true Operator

User-defined types can define a **true** operator that returns the bool value true to indicate true and returns false otherwise. This is useful for types that represent true, false, and null (neither true nor false), as used in databases.

Such types can be used for the controlling expression in if, do, while, and for statements and in conditional expressions.

If a type defines operator **true**, it must also define operator false.

A type cannot directly overload the conditional logical operators (&& and ||), but an equivalent effect can be achieved by overloading the regular logical operators and operators **true** and **false**.

true Literal

The **true** keyword is a literal of type bool representing the boolean value true.

Example

```
// cs_keyword_true.cs
using System;
class test
{
   public static void Main()
   {
      bool a = true;
      Console.WriteLine( a ? "yes" : "no" );
   }
}
```

Output

```
yes
```

See Also

Operators (pg. 169), false (pg. 16, 74)

false

In C#, the **false** keyword can be used as an overloaded operator or as a literal:

- false Operator
- false Literal

false Operator

User-defined types can define a **false** operator that returns the bool value true to indicate false and returns false otherwise. This is useful for types that represent true, false, and null (neither true nor false), as used in databases.

Such types can be used for the controlling expression in if, do, while, and for statements and in conditional expressions.

If a type defines operator **false**, it must also define operator true.

A type cannot directly overload the conditional logical operators (&& and ||), but an equivalent effect can be achieved by overloading the regular logical operators and operators **true** and **false**.

false Literal

The **false** keyword is a literal of type bool representing the boolean value false.

Example

```
// cs_keyword_false.cs
using System;
class test
{
   public static void Main()
   {
      bool a = false;
      Console.WriteLine( a ? "yes" : "no" );
   }
}
```

Output

```
no
```

See Also

Operators (pg. 169), true (pg. 15, 73)

stackalloc

Allocates a block of memory on the stack.

```
type * ptr = stackalloc type [ expr ];
```

where:

type
> An unmanaged type.

ptr
> A pointer name.

expr
> An integral expression.

Remarks

A block of memory of sufficient size to contain *expr* elements of type *type* is allocated on the stack, not the heap; the address of the block is stored in pointer *ptr*. This memory is not subject to garbage collection and therefore does not have to be pinned (via fixed). The lifetime of the memory block is limited to the lifetime of the method in which it is defined.

stackalloc is only valid in local variable initializers.

Because A.2 Pointer types are involved, **stackalloc** requires unsafe context.

stackalloc is similar to _alloca in the C run-time library.

Example

```
// cs_keyword_stackallow.cs
// compile with: /unsafe
using System; class Test
{
    public static unsafe void Main()
    {
        int* fib = stackalloc int[100];
        int* p = fib;
        *p++ = *p++ = 1;
        for (int i=2; i<100; ++i, ++p)
            *p = p[-1] + p[-2];
        for (int i=0; i<10; ++i)
            Console.WriteLine (fib[i]);
    }
}
```

Output

```
1
1
2
3
5
8
13
21
34
55
```

Statement Keywords

Statements are program instructions. Except as described, statements are executed in sequence. C# has the following categories of statements.

Category	C# keywords
Selection statements	if, else, switch, case
Iteration statements	do, for, foreach, in, while
Jump statements	break, continue, default, goto, return
Exception handling statements	throw, try-catch, try-finally
Checked and unchecked	checked, unchecked
fixed Statement	fixed
lock Statement	lock

Selection Statements

A selection statement causes the program control to be transferred to a specific flow based upon whether a certain condition is true or not.

The following keywords are used in selection statements:

- if
- else
- switch
- case

See Also

Selection Statements (pg. 76)

if-else

The **if** statement is a control statement that executes a block of code if an expression evaluates to **true**. It takes the form:

```
if (expression)
    statement1
[else
    statement2]
```

where:

expression
> An expression that can be implicitly converted to **bool** or a type that contains overloading of the true and false operators.

statement1
> The embedded statement(s) to be executed if *expression* is **true**.

statement2
> The embedded statement(s) to be executed if *expression* is **false**.

Remarks

If *expression* is **true**, *statement1* is executed. If the optional **else** clause exists and *expression* evaluates to **false**, *statement2* is executed. After executing the **if** statement, control is transferred to the next statement.

If any of the two results of the **if** statement (**true** or **false**) results in executing more than one statement, multiple statements can be conditionally executed by including them into blocks.

The statement(s) to be executed upon testing the condition can be of any kind, including another **if** statement nested into the original **if** statement. In nested **if** statements, the **else** clause belongs to the last **if** that does not have a corresponding **else**. For example:

```
if (x > 10)
    if (y > 20)
        Console.Write("Statement_1");
    else
        Console.Write("Statement_2");
```

In this example, Statement_2 will be displayed if the condition (y > 20) evaluates to **false**. However, if you want to associate Statement_2 with the condition (x >10), use braces:

```
if (x > 10)
{
    if (y > 20)
        Console.Write("Statement_1");
}
else
    Console.Write("Statement_2");
```

In this case, Statement_2 will be displayed if the condition (x > 10) evaluates to **false**.

Example

In this example, you enter a character from the keyboard and the program checks if the input character is an alphabetic character. If so, it checks if it is lowercase or uppercase. In each case, the proper message is displayed.

```
// statements_if_else.cs
// if-else example
using System;
public class IfTest
{
   public static void Main()
   {
      Console.Write("Enter a character: ");
      char c = (char) Console.Read();
      if (Char.IsLetter(c))
         if (Char.IsLower(c))
            Console.WriteLine("The character is lowercase.");
         else
            Console.WriteLine("The character is uppercase.");
      else
         Console.WriteLine("The character is not an alphabetic character.");
   }
}
```

Input

2

Sample Output

```
Enter a character: 2
The character is not an alphabetic character.
```

Additional sample might look as follows:

Run #2:

```
Enter a character: A
The character is uppercase.
```

Run #3:

```
Enter a character: h
The character is lowercase.
```

It is also possible to extend the **if** statement to handle multiple conditions using the following else-if arrangement:

```
if (Condition_1)
    Statement_1;
else if (Condition_2)
    Statement_2;
else if (Condition_3)
    Statement_3;
...
else
    Statement_n;
```

Example

This example checks if the input character is lowercase, uppercase, or a number. Otherwise, it is not an alphanumeric character. The program makes use of the else-if ladder.

```
// statements_if_else2.cs
// else-if
using System;
public class IfTest
{
    public static void Main()
    {
        Console.Write("Enter a character: ");
        char c = (char) Console.Read();

        if (Char.IsUpper(c))
            Console.WriteLine("The character is uppercase.");
        else if (Char.IsLower(c))
            Console.WriteLine("The character is lowercase.");
        else if (Char.IsDigit(c))
            Console.WriteLine("The character is a number.");
        else
            Console.WriteLine("The character is not alphanumeric.");
    }
}
```

Input

```
E
```

Sample Output

```
Enter a character: E
The character is uppercase.
```

Additional sample runs might look as follows:

Run #2

```
Enter a character: e
The character is lowercase.
```

Run #3:

```
Enter a character: 4
The character is a number.
```

Run #4:

```
Enter a character: $
The character is not alphanumeric.
```

See Also

switch (pg. 80)

switch

The **switch** statement is a control statement that handles multiple selections by passing control to one of the **case** statements within its body. The **switch** statement takes the form:

```
switch (expression)
{
    case constant-expression:
        statement
        jump-statement
    [default:
        statement
        jump-statement]
}
```

Where:

expression
>   An integral or string type expression.

statement
>   The embedded statement(s) to be executed if control is transferred to the **case** or the **default**.

jump-statement
>   A jump statement that transfers control out of the **case** body.

constant-expression
>   Control is transferred to a specific **case** according to the value of this expression.

Remarks

Control is transferred to the **case** statement whose *constant-expression* matches *expression*. The **switch** statement can include any number of **case** instances, but no two case constants within the same **switch** statement can have the same value. Execution of the statement body begins at the selected statement and proceeds until the *jump-statement* transfers control out of the **case** body.

Notice that the *jump-statement* is required after each block, including the last block whether it is a **case** statement or a **default** statement. Unlike the C++ **switch** statement, C# does not support an explicit fall through from one case label to another. If you want, you can use **goto** a switch-case, or **goto default**.

If *expression* does not match any *constant-expression*, control is transferred to the *statement*(s) that follow the optional **default** label. If there is no **default** label, control is transferred outside the **switch**.

Example

```
// statements_switch.cs
using System;
class SwitchTest
{
    public static void Main()
    {
        Console.WriteLine("Coffee sizes: 1=Small 2=Medium 3=Large");
        Console.Write("Please enter your selection: ");
        string s = Console.ReadLine();
        int n = int.Parse(s);
        int cost = 0;
        switch(n)
        {
            case 0:
            case 1:
                cost += 25;
                break;
            case 2:
                cost += 25;
                goto case 1;
            case 3:
                cost += 50;
                goto case 1;
            default:
                Console.WriteLine("Invalid selection. Please select 1, 2, or 3.");
                break;
        }
        if (cost != 0)
            Console.WriteLine("Please insert {0} cents.", cost);
        Console.WriteLine("Thank you for your business.");
    }
}
```

Input

2

Sample Output

```
Coffee sizes: 1=Small 2=Medium 3=Large
Please enter your selection: 2
Please insert 50 cents.
Thank you for your business.
```

In the preceding example, an integral type variable, n, was used for the switch cases. Notice that you can also use the string variable, s, directly. In this case, you can use switch cases like these:

```
switch(s)
{
    case "1":
        ...
    case "2":
        ...
}
```

See Also

if (pg. 240)

Iteration Statements

You can create loops by using the iteration statements. Iteration statements cause embedded statements to be executed a number of times, subject to the loop-termination criteria. These statements are executed in order, except when a jump statement is encountered.

The following keywords are used in iteration statements:

- do
- for
- foreach
- in
- while

do

The **do** statement executes a statement or a block of statements repeatedly until a specified expression evaluates to **false**. It takes the following form:

```
do statement while (expression);
```

where:

expression
>   An expression that can be implicitly converted to **bool** or a type that contains overloading of the true and false operators. The expression is used to test the loop-termination criteria.

statement
>   The embedded statement(s) to be executed.

Remarks

Unlike the while statement, the body loop of the **do** statement is executed at least once regardless of the value of the *expression*.

Example

```csharp
// statements_do.cs
using System;
public class TestDoWhile
{
    public static void Main ()
    {
        int x;
        int y = 0;

        do
        {
            x = y++;
            Console.WriteLine(x);
        }

        while(y < 5);
    }
}
```

Output

```
0
1
2
3
4
```

Example

Notice in this example that although the condition evaluates to **false**, the loop will be executed once.

```
// statements_do2.cs
using System;
class DoTest {
   public static void Main()
   {
      int n = 10;
      do
      {
         Console.WriteLine("Current value of n is {0}", n);
         n++;
      } while (n < 6);
   }
}
```

Output

```
Current value of n is 10
```

for

The **for** loop executes a statement or a block of statements repeatedly until a specified expression evaluates to **false**. It takes the following form:

```
for ([initializers]; [expression]; [iterators]) statement
```

where:

initializers
    A comma separated list of expressions or assignment statements to initialize the loop counters.

expression
    An expression that can be implicitly converted to **bool** or a type that contains overloading of the true and false operators. The expression is used to test the loop-termination criteria.

iterators
    Expression statement(s) to increment or decrement the loop counters.

statement
    The embedded statement(s) to executed.

Remarks

The **for** statement executes the *statement* repeatedly as follows:

- First, the *initializers* are evaluated.

- Then, while the *expression* evaluates to **true**, the *statement*(s) are executed and the *iterators* are evaluated.

- When the *expression* becomes **false**, control is transferred outside the loop.

Because the test of *expression* takes place before the execution of the loop, a **for** statement executes zero or more times.

All of the expressions of the **for** statement are optional; for example, the following statement is used to write an infinite loop:

```
for (;;) {
    ...
}
```

Example

```
// statements_for.cs
// for loop
using System;
public class ForLoopTest
{
    public static void Main()
    {
        for (int i = 1; i <= 5; i++)
            Console.WriteLine(i);
    }
}
```

Output

```
1
2
3
4
5
```

foreach, in

The **foreach** statement repeats a group of embedded statements for each element in an array or an object collection. The **foreach** statement is used to iterate through the collection to get the desired information, but should not be used to change the contents of the collection to avoid unpredictable side effects. The statement takes the following form:

```
foreach (type identifier in expression) statement
```

where:

type
> The type of *identifier*.

identifier
> The iteration variable that represents the collection element.

expression
> Object collection or array expression. The type of the collection element must be convertible to the *identifier* type.

statement
> The embedded statement(s) to be executed.

Remarks

The embedded statements continue to execute for each element in the array or collection. After the iteration has been completed for all the elements in the collection, control is transferred to the next statement following the **foreach** block.

For more information on the **foreach** keyword, including code samples, see the following sections:

- Using foreach with Arrays

- Using foreach with Collections

Using foreach with Arrays

When used with an array, the foreach statement repeats the embedded statement(s) for each element in the array.

Example

In this example, an array of integers is searched for even and odd numbers. A counter for each type of number stores the number of occurrences.

```
// statements_foreach_arrays.cs
// Using foreach with arrays
using System;
class MainClass
{
   public static void Main()
   {
      int odd = 0, even = 0;
      int[] arr = new int [] {0,1,2,5,7,8,11};

      foreach (int i in arr)
      {
         if (i%2 == 0)
            even++;
         else
            odd++;
      }

      Console.WriteLine("Found {0} Odd Numbers, and {1} Even Numbers.",
                        odd, even) ;
   }
}
```

Output

```
Found 4 Odd Numbers, and 3 Even Numbers.
```

See Also

foreach, in (pg. 86); Arrays (pg. 248); Using foreach with Collections (pg. 87)

Using foreach with Collections

To iterate through a collection, the collection must meet specific requirements. For example, in the following foreach statement:

```
foreach (ItemType item in myCollection)
```

myCollection must meet the following requirements:

* The collection type:

  * Must be one of the types: **interface**, **class**, or **struct**.

  * Must include an instance method named **GetEnumerator** that returns a type, for example, Enumerator (explained below).

* The type Enumerator (a class or struct) must contain:

  * A property named **Current** that returns ItemType or a type that can be converted to it. The property accessor returns the current element of the collection.

  * A **bool** method, named **MoveNext**, that increments the item counter and returns **true** if there are more items in the collection.

There are three approaches to using collections:

1. Create a collection using the above instructions. This collection can only be used in a C# program.

2. Create a generic collection using the above instructions, in addition to implementing the **IEnumerable** interface. This collection can be used from other languages such as Visual Basic®.

3. Use one of the predefined collections in the collection classes.

The following examples demonstrate the three approaches.

Example	Demonstrates	Comment
Example 1	A C#-specific collection.	This example creates a collection by using the instructions above.
Example 2a	A generic collection.	This example creates a collection by using the instructions above and implements the **IEnumerable** and **IEnumerator** interfaces.
Example 2b	A generic collection with a Dispose method.	Same as Example 2a except that a user-defined enumerator inherits from **IDisposable** and implements a **Dispose** method.
Example 3	Using one of the predefined collection classes.	This example creates a **Hashtable** instance and uses the **Hashtable** class members to manipulate the collection. The **Hashtable** class represents a dictionary of associated keys and values, implemented as a hash table.

For more information on the interfaces **IEnumerator** and **IEnumerable**, and the **Hashtable** class, see the "System.Collections" section in the .NET Framework SDK.

Example 1

```
// statements_foreach_collections.cs
// Using foreach with C#-specific collections:
using System;

// Declare the collection:
public class MyCollection
{
   int[] items;

   public MyCollection()
   {
      items = new int[5] {12, 44, 33, 2, 50};
   }

   public MyEnumerator GetEnumerator()
   {
      return new MyEnumerator(this);
   }
}
```

```
    // Declare the enumerator class:
    public class MyEnumerator
    {
        int nIndex;
        MyCollection collection;
        public MyEnumerator(MyCollection coll)
        {
            collection = coll;
            nIndex = -1;
        }

        public bool MoveNext()
        {
            nIndex++;
            return(nIndex < collection.items.GetLength(0));
        }

        public int Current
        {
            get
            {
                return(collection.items[nIndex]);
            }
        }
    }
}

public class MainClass
{
    public static void Main()
    {
        MyCollection col = new MyCollection();
        Console.WriteLine("Values in the collection are:");

        // Display collection items:
        foreach (int i in col)
        {
            Console.WriteLine(i);
        }
    }
}
```

Output

```
Values in the collection are:
12
44
33
2
50
```

Example 2a

This example repeats the same algorithm of Example 1, but uses a generic collection that can be enumerated from other languages such as Visual Basic. This type of collection must implement the **IEnumerable** interface from the **System.Collections** namespace.

```
// statements_foreach_generic_collection.cs
// Using foreach with a generic collection
using System;
using System.Collections;

// Declare the collection and implement the IEnumerable interface:
public class MyCollection: IEnumerable
{
    int[] items;
    public MyCollection()
    {
        items = new int[5] {12, 44, 33, 2, 50};
    }

    public MyEnumerator GetEnumerator()
    {
        return new MyEnumerator(this);
    }

    // Implement the GetEnumerator() method:
    IEnumerator IEnumerable.GetEnumerator()
    {
        return GetEnumerator();
    }

    // Declare the enumerator and implement the IEnumerator interface:
    public class MyEnumerator: IEnumerator
    {
        int nIndex;
        MyCollection collection;
        public MyEnumerator(MyCollection coll)
        {
            collection = coll;
            nIndex = -1;
        }

        public void Reset()
        {
            nIndex = -1;
        }
```

```
      public bool MoveNext() {
         nIndex++;
         return(nIndex < collection.items.GetLength(0));
      }

      public int Current
      {
         get
         {
            return(collection.items[nIndex]);
         }
      }

      // The current property on the IEnumerator interface:
      object IEnumerator.Current
      {
         get
         {
            return(Current);
         }
      }
   }
}

public class MainClass
{
   public static void Main(string [] args)
   {
      MyCollection col = new MyCollection();
      Console.WriteLine("Values in the collection are:");

      // Display collection items:
      foreach (int i in col)
      {
         Console.WriteLine(i);
      }
   }
}
```

Output

```
Values in the collection are:
12
44
33
2
50
```

Example 2b

This example is the same as Example 2a except that it also implements a **Dispose** method. **Dispose** is implemented in a user-defined enumerator that inherits from **IDisposable**.

The **foreach** statement provides support for disposable enumerators. If an enumerator implements the **IDisposable** interface, the **foreach** statement guarantees that the **Dispose** method is called on the enumerator no matter how the enumeration loop is terminated.

```
// statements_foreach_generic_collection2.cs
// Using foreach with a generic collection
using System;
using System.Collections;

// Declare the collection and implement the IEnumerable interface:
public class MyCollection: IEnumerable
{
    int[] items;
    public MyCollection()
    {
        items = new int[5] {12, 44, 33, 2, 50};
    }

    public MyEnumerator GetEnumerator()
    {
        return new MyEnumerator(this);
    }

    // Implement the GetEnumerator() method:
    IEnumerator IEnumerable.GetEnumerator()
    {
        return GetEnumerator();
    }

    // Declare the enumerator and implement the IEnumerator
    // and IDisposable interfaces
    public class MyEnumerator: IEnumerator, IDisposable
    {
        int nIndex;
        MyCollection collection;
        public MyEnumerator(MyCollection coll)
        {
            collection = coll;
            nIndex = -1;
        }

        public void Reset()
        {
            nIndex = -1;
        }
```

```csharp
        public bool MoveNext()
        {
            nIndex++;
            return (nIndex < collection.items.GetLength(0));
        }

        public int Current
        {
            get
            {
                return (collection.items[nIndex]);
            }
        }

        // The current property on the IEnumerator interface:
        object IEnumerator.Current
        {
            get
            {
                return (Current);
            }
        }

        public void Dispose()
        {
            Console.WriteLine("In Dispose");
            collection = null;
        }
    }
}

public class MainClass
{
    public static void Main(string [] args)
    {
        MyCollection col = new MyCollection();
        Console.WriteLine("Values in the collection are:");

        // Display collection items:
        foreach (int i in col)
        {
            Console.WriteLine(i);
        }
    }
}
```

Output

```
Values in the collection are:
12
44
33
2
50
In Dispose
```

Example 3

In this example, the predefined **Hashtable** collection class is used. By using the **System.Collections** namespace in your program, you can have access to the **Hashtable** class and its members. To add entries to the **Hashtable** object, use the **Add** method.

```
// statements_foreach_hashtable.cs
// Using the Hashtable collection class
using System;
using System.Collections;
public class MainClass
{
    public static void Main(string [] args)
    {
        // Declare a Hashtable object:
        Hashtable ziphash = new Hashtable();

        // Add entries using the Add() method:
        ziphash.Add("98008", "Bellevue");
        ziphash.Add("98052", "Redmond");
        ziphash.Add("98201", "Everett");
        ziphash.Add("98101", "Seattle");
        ziphash.Add("98371", "Puyallup");

        // Display contents:
        Console.WriteLine("Zip code        City");
        foreach (string zip in ziphash.Keys)
        {
            Console.WriteLine(zip + "            " + ziphash[zip]);
        }
    }
}
```

Output

```
Zip code        City
98201           Everett
98052           Redmond
98101           Seattle
98008           Bellevue
98371           Puyallup
```

See Also

foreach, in (pg. 86); Using foreach with Arrays (pg. 86)

while

The **while** statement executes a statement or a block of statements until a specified expression evaluates to **false**. It takes the form:

```
while (expression) statement
```

where:

expression
> An expression that can be implicitly converted to **bool** or a type that contains overloading of the true and false operators. The expression is used to test the loop-termination criteria.

statement
> The embedded statement(s) to be executed.

Remarks

Because the test of *expression* takes place before each execution of the loop, a **while** loop executes zero or more times.

A **while** loop can be terminated when a **break**, **goto**, **return**, or **throw** statement transfers control outside the loop. To pass control to the next iteration without exiting the loop, use the **continue** statement.

Example

```
// statements_while.cs
using System;
class WhileTest
{
    public static void Main()
    {
        int n = 1;

        while (n < 6)
        {
            Console.WriteLine("Current value of n is {0}", n);
            n++;
        }
    }
}
```

Output

```
Current value of n is 1
Current value of n is 2
Current value of n is 3
Current value of n is 4
Current value of n is 5
```

Jump Statements

Branching is performed using jump statements, which cause an immediate transfer of the program control. The following keywords are used in jump statements:

- break

- continue

- default

- goto

- return

break

The **break** statement terminates the closest enclosing loop or conditional statement in which it appears. Control is passed to the statement that follows the terminated statement, if any. The **break** statement takes the form:

```
break;
```

Example

In this example, the conditional statement contains a counter that is supposed to count from 1 to 100; however, the **break** statement terminates the loop after 4 counts.

```
// statements_break.cs
using System;
class BreakTest
{
    public static void Main()
    {
        for (int i = 1; i <= 100; i++)
        {
            if (i == 5)
                break;
            Console.WriteLine(i);
        }
    }
}
```

Output

```
1
2
3
4
```

Example

This example demonstrates the use of **break** in a **switch** statement.

```csharp
// statements_break2.cs
// break and switch
using System;
class Switch
{
    public static void Main()
    {
        Console.Write("Enter your selection (1, 2, or 3): ");
        string s = Console.ReadLine();
        int n = Int32.Parse(s);

        switch(n)
        {
            case 1:
                Console.WriteLine("Current value is {0}", 1);
                break;
            case 2:
                Console.WriteLine("Current value is {0}", 2);
                break;
            case 3:
                Console.WriteLine("Current value is {0}", 3);
                break;
            default:
                Console.WriteLine("Sorry, invalid selection.");
                break;
        }
    }
}
```

Input

```
1
```

Sample Output

```
Enter your selection (1, 2, or 3): 1
Current value is 1
```

If you entered 4, the output would be:

```
Enter your selection (1, 2, or 3): 4
Sorry, invalid selection.
```

continue

The **continue** statement passes control to the next iteration of the enclosing iteration statement in which it appears. It takes the form:

```
continue;
```

Example

In this example, a counter is initialized to count from 1 to 10. By using the **continue** statement in conjunction with the expression (i < 9), the statements between **continue** and the end of the **for** body are skipped.

```
// statements_continue.cs
using System;
class ContinueTest
{
    public static void Main()
    {
        for (int i = 1; i <= 10; i++)
        {
            if (i < 9)
                continue;
            Console.WriteLine(i);
        }
    }
}
```

Output

```
9
10
```

goto

The **goto** statement transfers the program control directly to a labeled statement. It takes one of the following forms:

```
goto identifier;
goto case constant-expression;
goto default;
```

where:

identifier
    A label.

constant-expression
    A switch-case label.

Remarks

In the first form, the *identifier* indicates a label located in the current body, the same lexical scope, or an enclosing scope of the **goto** statement.

A common use of **goto** is to transfer control to a specific switch-case label or the default label in a **switch** statement.

The **goto** statement is also useful to get out of deeply nested loops.

A warning message may be issued if the label has never been referenced in the program.

Example

For an example of using **goto** to transfer control to a specific switch-case label, see the example for "switch" on page 80.

Example

The following example demonstrates using **goto** to break out from nested loops.

```
// statements_goto.cs
// Nested search loops
using System;
public class GotoTest1
{
    public static void Main()
    {
        int x = 200, y = 4;
        int[,] myArray = new int[x,y];

        // initialize the array:
        for (int i = 0; i < x; i++)
            for (int j = 0; j < y; j++)
                myArray[i,j] = ++i;

        // Read input:
        Console.Write("Enter the number to search for: ");

        // input a char
        string s = Console.ReadLine();
        int myNumber = Int32.Parse(s);

        // Search:
        for (int i = 0; i < x; i++)
            for (int j = 0; j < y; j++)
                if (myArray[i,j] == myNumber)
                    goto Found;

        Console.WriteLine("The number {0} was not found.", myNumber);
        goto Finish;
```

(continued)

(continued)

```
    Found:
        Console.WriteLine("The number {0} is found.", myNumber);

    Finish:
        Console.WriteLine("End of search.");
    }
}
```

Input

44

Sample Output

```
Enter the number to search for: 44
The number 44 is found.
End of search.
```

Example

```
// statements_goto2.cs
// CS0159 expected
// Labels outside the scope
using System;
class UnreachableCode
{
    public static void Main()
    {
        int x = 55;
        Console.WriteLine("x = {0}", x);

        if (x == 55)
        {
            x = 135;
            goto A;    // Error
        }

        x = x + 1;

        for (int i=1; i<=5; i++)
        {
            A: Console.WriteLine(i);
        }

        Console.WriteLine("x = {0}", x);
    }
}
```

In the preceding example, the **goto** statement is referencing a label A outside its scope. The compiler will issue the error message:

```
No such label 'A' within the scope of the goto statement
```

A warning message may also be issued because the label has never been referenced.

If you move the label A to the beginning of the **for** loop, the program would compile and run normally, that is:

```
A:      for (int i=1; i<=5; i++) {    // Now the program compiles.
```

return

The **return** statement terminates execution of the method in which it appears and returns control to the calling method. It can also return the value of the optional *expression*. If the method is of the type **void**, the **return** statement can be omitted. The **return** statement takes the form:

```
return [expression];
```

where:

expression
> The value returned by a method. The *expression* is not used with methods of the type **void**.

Example

In the following example, the method A( ) returns the variable Area as a **double** value.

```csharp
// statements_return.cs
using System;
class ReturnTest
{
    static double CalculateArea(int r)
    {
        double area;
        area = r*r*Math.PI;
        return area;
    }

    public static void Main()
    {
        int radius = 5;
        Console.WriteLine("The area is {0:0.00}", CalculateArea(radius));
    }
}
```

Output

```
The area is 78.54
```

Exception Handling Statements

C# provides built-in support for handling anomalous situations, known as exceptions, which may occur during the execution of your program. These exceptions are handled by code that is outside the normal flow of control. The **try**, **throw**, **catch**, and **finally** keywords implement exception handling.

The following exception handling topics are explained in this section:

- throw
- try-catch
- try-finally
- try-catch-finally

throw

The **throw** statement is used to signal the occurrence of an anomalous situation (exception) during the program execution. The **throw** statement takes the form:

```
throw [expression];
```

where:

expression
> The exception object. This is omitted when rethrowing the current exception object in a **catch** clause.

Remarks

The thrown exception is an object whose class is derived from **System.Exception**, for example:

```
class MyException : System.Exception {}
throw new MyException();
```

Usually the **throw** statement is used with try-catch or try-finally statements. When an exception is thrown, the program looks for the **catch** statement that handles this exception.

Example

This example demonstrates how to throw an exception using the **throw** statement.

```
// throw example
using System;
public class ThrowTest
{
    public static void Main()
    {
        string s = null;
```

```
        if (s == null)
        {
            throw(new ArgumentNullException());
        }

        Console.Write("The string s is null"); // not executed
    }
}
```

Output

The following exception occurs:

```
System.ArgumentNullException
```

Example

See the examples for "try-catch" on page 103, "try-finally" on page 107, and "try-catch-finally" on page 108.

try-catch

The try-catch statement consists of a **try** block followed by one or more **catch** clauses, which specify handlers for different exceptions. The try-catch statement takes one of the forms:

```
try try-block
catch (exception-declaration-1) catch-block-1
catch (exception-declaration-2) catch-block-2
...
try try-block catch catch-block
```

where:

try-block
    Contains the code segment expected to raise the exception.

exception-declaration, exception-declaration-1, exception-declaration-2
    The exception object declaration.

catch-block, catch-block-1, catch-block-2
    Contains the exception handler.

Remarks

The *try-block* contains the guarded code block that may cause the exception. The block is executed until an exception is thrown or it is completed successfully. For example, the following attempt to cast a **null** object raises the **NullReferenceException** exception:

```
object o2 = null;
try
{
    int i2 = (int) o2;   // Error
}
```

The **catch** clause can be used without arguments, in which case it catches any type of exception, and referred to as the general catch clause. It can also take an object argument derived from **System.Exception**, in which case it handles a specific exception. For example:

```
catch (InvalidCastException e)
{
}
```

It is possible to use more than one specific **catch** clause in the same try-catch statement. In this case, the order of the **catch** clauses is important because the **catch** clauses are examined in order. Catch the more specific exceptions before the less specific ones.

A throw statement can be used in the **catch** block to rethrow the exception, which has been caught by the **catch** statement. For example:

```
catch (InvalidCastException e)
{
    throw (e);    // Rethrowing exception e
}
```

If you want to rethrow the exception currently handled by a parameterless **catch** clause, use the **throw** statement without arguments. For example:

```
catch
{
    throw;
}
```

Do not initialize variables inside a **try** block because the **try** block is not guaranteed to be executed. An exception can occur before the block is completed. For example, in the following code segment, the variable x is initialized inside the **try** block. An attempt to use this variable outside the **try** block, such as the Write(x) statement, will generate the following compiler error: Use of unassigned local variable.

```
public static void Main()
{
    int x;
    try
    {
        x = 123;    //   Don't do that.
        // ...
    }
    catch
    {
        // ...
    }
    Console.Write(x);    // Error: Use of unassigned local variable 'x'.
}
```

For more information on **catch**, see the section "try-catch-finally" on page 108.

Example

In this example, the **try** block contains a call to the method MyFn() that may cause an exception. The **catch** clause contains the exception handler that simply displays a message on the screen. When the **throw** statement is called from inside MyFn(), the system looks for the **catch** statement and displays the message Exception caught.

```
// Rethrowing exceptions:
using System;
class MyClass
{
    public static void Main()
    {
        MyClass x = new MyClass();
        try
        {
            string s = null;
            x.MyFn(s);
        }

        catch (Exception e)
        {
            Console.WriteLine("{0} Exception caught.", e);
        }
    }

    public void MyFn(string s)
    {
        if (s == null)
            throw(new ArgumentNullException());
    }
}
```

Output

The following exception occurs:

```
System.ArgumentNullException
```

Example

In this example, two catch statements are used. The most specific exception, which comes first, is caught.

```csharp
// Ordering catch clauses
using System;
class MyClass
{
    public static void Main()
    {
        MyClass x = new MyClass();
        try
        {
            string s = null;
            x.MyFn(s);
        }

        // Most specific:
        catch (ArgumentNullException e)
        {
            Console.WriteLine("{0} First exception caught.", e);
        }

        // Least specific:
        catch (Exception e)
        {
            Console.WriteLine("{0} Second exception caught.", e);
        }

    }

    public void MyFn(string s)
    {
        if (s == null)
            throw new ArgumentNullException();
    }
}
```

Output

The following exception occurs:

```
System.ArgumentNullException
```

In the preceding example, if you start with the least specific catch clause, you will get the error message:

```
A previous catch clause already catches all exceptions of this or a super type
('System.Exception')
```

However, to catch the least specific exception, replace the throw statement by the following one:

```
throw new Exception();
```

See Also

throw (pg. 102), try-finally (pg. 107)

try-finally

The **finally** block is useful for cleaning up any resources allocated in the try block. Control is always passed to the finally block regardless of how the try block exits. The try-finally statement takes the form:

```
try try-block finally finally-block
```

where:

try-block
>   Contains the code segment expected to raise the exception.

finally-block
>   Contains the exception handler and the cleanup code.

Remarks

Whereas **catch** is used to handle exceptions that occur in a statement block, **finally** is used to guarantee a statement block of code executes regardless of how the preceding **try** block is exited.

Example

In this example, there is one illegal conversion statement that causes an exception. When you run the program, you get a run-time error message, but the **finally** clause will still be executed and display the output.

```
// try-finally
using System;
public class TestTryFinally
{
   public static void Main()
   {
      int i = 123;
      string s = "Some string";
      object o = s;

      try
      {
         // Illegal conversion; o contains a string not an int
         i = (int) o;
      }

      finally
      {
         Console.Write("i = {0}", i);
      }
   }
}
```

Output

The following exception occurs:

```
System.InvalidCastException
```

Although an exception was caught, the output statement included in the **finally** block will still be executed, that is:

```
i = 123
```

For more information on **finally**, see the section "try-catch-finally" on page 108.

See Also

throw (pg. 102), try-catch (pg. 103)

try-catch-finally

A common usage of **catch** and **finally** together is to obtain and use resources in a **try** block, deal with exceptional circumstances in a **catch** block, and release the resources in the **finally** block.

Example

```csharp
// try-catch-finally
using System;
public class EHClass
{
   public static void Main ()
   {
      try
      {
         Console.WriteLine("Executing the try statement.");
         throw new NullReferenceException();
      }

      catch(NullReferenceException e)
      {
         Console.WriteLine("{0} Caught exception #1.", e);
      }

      catch
      {
         Console.WriteLine("Caught exception #2.");
      }

      finally
      {
         Console.WriteLine("Executing finally block.");
      }
   }
}
```

Output

```
Executing the try statement.
System.NullReferenceException: Attempted to dereference a null object reference.
   at EHClass.Main() Caught exception #1.
Executing finally block.
```

See Also

throw (pg. 102)

Checked and Unchecked

C# statements can execute in either checked or unchecked context. In a checked context, arithmetic overflow raises an exception. In an unchecked context, arithmetic overflow is ignored and the result is truncated.

- checked   Specify checked context.

- unchecked   Specify unchecked context.

If neither **checked** nor **unchecked** is specified, the default context depends on external factors such as compiler options.

The following operations are affected by the overflow checking:

- Expressions using the following predefined operators on integral types:

  ++ -- - (unary) + - * /

- Explicit numeric conversions between integral types.

The /checked compiler option lets you specify checked or unchecked context for all integer arithmetic statements that are not explicitly in the scope of a **checked** or **unchecked** keyword.

checked

The **checked** keyword is used to control the overflow-checking context for integral-type arithmetic operations and conversions. It can be used as an operator or a statement according to the following forms.

The **checked** statement:

```
checked block
```

The **checked** operator:

```
checked (expression)
```

where:

block
>   The statement block that contains the expressions to be evaluated in a checked context.

expression
>   The expression to be evaluated in a checked context. Notice that the expression must be in parentheses ( ).

Remarks

In a checked context, if an expression produces a value that is outside the range of the destination type, the result depends on whether the expression is constant or non-constant. Constant expressions cause compile time errors, while non-constant expressions are evaluated at run time and raise exceptions.

If neither **checked** nor unchecked is used, a constant expression uses the default overflow checking at compile time, which is **checked**. Otherwise, if the expression is non-constant, the run-time overflow checking depends on other factors such as compiler options and environment configuration.

The following three examples demonstrate the **checked** and **unchecked** operators on non-constant expressions. All use the same algorithm, but different checking contexts. The overflow checking is evaluated at run time.

- Example 1: Using a **checked** expression.

- Example 2: Using an **unchecked** expression.

- Example 3: Using default overflow checking.

Only the first example throws an overflow exception at run time, in which case, you have the option to go to the debugging mode, or abort the program execution. The other two examples produce truncated values.

See also the unchecked examples on using the **checked** and **unchecked** statements.

Example 1

```
// statements_checked.cs
// The overflow of non-constant expressions is checked at run time
using System;

class OverFlowTest
{
    static short x = 32767;    // Max short value
    static short y = 32767;

    // Using a checked expression
    public static int myMethodCh()
    {
        int z = 0;

        try
        {
            z =  checked((short)(x + y));
        }
        catch (System.OverflowException e)
        {
            System.Console.WriteLine(e.ToString());
        }
        return z;    // Throws the exception OverflowException
    }

    public static void Main()
    {
        Console.WriteLine("Checked output value is: {0}", myMethodCh());
    }
}
```

Sample Output

When you run the program, it throws the exception OverflowException. You can debug the program or abort execution.

```
System.OverflowException: An exception of type System.OverflowException was thrown.
   at OverFlowTest.myMethodCh()
Checked output value is: 0
```

Example 2

```
// statements_checked2.cs
// Using unchecked expressions
// The overflow of non-constant expressions is checked at run time
using System;

class OverFlowTest
{
   static short x = 32767;    // Max short value
   static short y = 32767;

   public static int myMethodUnch()
   {
      int z =  unchecked((short)(x + y));
      return z;   // Returns -2
   }

   public static void Main()
   {
      Console.WriteLine("Unchecked value is: {0}", myMethodUnch());
   }
}
```

Output

```
Unchecked value is: -2
```

Example 3

```
// statements_checked3.cs
// Using default overflow checking
// The overflow of non-constant expressions is checked at run time
using System;

class OverFlowTest
{
   static short x = 32767;    // Max short value
   static short y = 32767;

   public static int myMethodUnch()
   {
      int z =  (short)(x + y);
      return z;   // Returns -2
   }

   public static void Main()
   {
      Console.WriteLine("Default checking ouput value is: {0}", myMethodUnch());
   }
}
```

```
Default checking ouput value is: -2
```

See Also

unchecked (pg. 113)

unchecked

The **unchecked** keyword is used to control the overflow-checking context for integral-type arithmetic operations and conversions. It can be used as an operator or a statement according to the following forms.

The **unchecked** statement:

```
unchecked block
```

The **unchecked** operator:

```
unchecked (expression)
```

where:

block
> The statement block that contains the expressions to be evaluated in an unchecked context.

expression
> The expression to be evaluated in an unchecked context. Notice that the expression must be in parentheses ( ).

Remarks

In an unchecked context, if an expression produces a value that is outside the range of the destination type, the result is truncated.

If neither checked nor **unchecked** is used, a constant expression uses the default overflow checking at compile time, which is **checked**. Otherwise, if the expression is non-constant, the run-time overflow checking depends on other factors such as compiler options and environment configuration.

The following are three examples demonstrating the checked and unchecked statements. All use the same algorithm, but different checking contexts. The three examples are using constant expressions, for which the overflow checking is evaluated at compile time.

- Example 1: Using the **unchecked** statement.
- Example 2: Using default overflow checking.
- Example 3: Using the **checked** statement.

Only the **unchecked** statement produces a truncated value. The other two statements produce compile-time errors.

See also the checked examples on using the **checked** and **unchecked** operators.

Example 1

```
// statements_unchecked.cs
// Using the unchecked statement with constant expressions
// Overflow is checked at compile time
using System;

class TestClass
{
    const int x = 2147483647;    // Max int
    const int y = 2;

    public int MethodUnCh()
    {
        // Unchecked statement:
        unchecked
        {
            int z = x * y;
            return z;    // Returns -2
        }
    }

    public static void Main()
    {
        TestClass myObject = new TestClass();
        Console.WriteLine("Unchecked output value: {0}",
            myObject.MethodUnCh());
    }
}
```

Output

```
Unchecked output value: -2
```

Example 2

```
// statements_unchecked2.cs
// CS0220 expected
// Using default overflow checking with constant expressions
// Overflow is checked at compile time
using System;

class TestClass
{
    const int x = 2147483647;    // Max int
    const int y = 2;
```

```
   public int MethodDef()
   {
      // Using default overflow checking:
      int z = x * y;
      return z;    // Compiler error
   }

   public static void Main()
   {
      TestClass myObject = new TestClass();
      Console.WriteLine("Default checking value: {0}",
         myObject.MethodDef());
   }
}
```

Output

The warning: `The operation overflows at compile time in checked mode.`

Example 3

```
// statements_unchecked3.cs
// CS0220 expected
// Using the checked statement with constant expressions
// Overflow is checked at compile time
using System;

class TestClass
{
   const int x = 2147483647;    // Max int
   const int y = 2;

   public int MethodCh()
   {
      // Checked statement:
      checked
      {
         int z = (x * y);
         return z;    // Compiler error
      }
   }

   public static void Main()
   {
      TestClass myObject = new TestClass();
      Console.WriteLine("Checked value: {0}", myObject.MethodCh());
   }
}
```

Output

The warning: `The operation overflows at compile time in checked mode.`

See Also

checked (pg. 110)

fixed Statement

Prevents relocation of a variable by the garbage collector.

```
fixed ( type* ptr = expr ) statement
```

where:

type
> An unmanaged type or void.

ptr
> A pointer name.

expr
> An expression that is implicitly convertible to *type**.

statement
> Executable statement or block.

Remarks

The **fixed** statement is only permitted in an unsafe context.

The **fixed** statement sets a pointer to a managed variable and "pins" that variable during the execution of *statement*. Without **fixed**, pointers to managed variables would be of little use since garbage collection could relocate the variables unpredictably. (In fact, the C# compiler will not allow you to set a pointer to a managed variable except in a **fixed** statement.)

```
// assume class Point { public int x, y; }
Point pt = new Point();    // pt is a managed variable, subject to g.c.
fixed ( int* p = &pt.x ){  // must use fixed to get address of pt.x and
    *p = 1;                //   pin pt in place while we use the pointer
}
```

You can initialize a pointer with the address of an array or a string:

```
fixed (int* p = arr) ...  // equivalent to p = &arr[0]
fixed (char* p = str) ... // equivalent to p = &str[0]
```

You can initialize multiple pointers, as long as they are all of the same type:

```
fixed (byte* ps = srcarray, pd = dstarray) {...}
```

To initialize pointers of different type, simply nest **fixed** statements:

```
fixed (int* p1 = &p.x)
   fixed (double* p2 = &array[5])
      // do something with p1 and p2
```

Pointers initialized in fixed statements cannot be modified.

After *statement* is executed, any pinned variables are unpinned and subject to garbage collection. Therefore, do not point to those variables outside the **fixed** statement.

In unsafe mode, you can allocate memory on the stack, where it is not subject to garbage collection and therefore does not need to be pinned. For more information, see the section "stackalloc" on page 75.

Example

```
// statements_fixed.cs
// compile with: /unsafe
using System;

class Point {
   public int x, y;
}

class FixedTest
{
   // unsafe method: takes pointer to int
   unsafe static void SquarePtrParam (int* p)
   {
      *p *= *p;
   }

   unsafe public static void Main()
   {
      Point pt = new Point();
      pt.x = 5;
      pt.y = 6;
      // pin pt in place:
      fixed (int* p = &pt.x)
      {
         SquarePtrParam (p);
      }
      // pt now unpinned
      Console.WriteLine ("{0} {1}", pt.x, pt.y);
   }
}
```

Output

25 6

See Also

unsafe (pg. 50)

lock Statement

The **lock** keyword marks a statement block as a critical section.

```
lock(expression) statement_block
```

where:

expression

Specifies the object that you want to lock on. *expression* must be a reference type.

Typically, *expression* will either be this, if you want to protect an instance variable, or typeof(*class*), if you want to protect a static variable (or if the critical section occurs in a static method in the given class).

statement_block

The statements of the critical section.

Remarks

lock ensures that one thread does not enter a critical section while another thread is in the critical section of code.

Example 1

The following sample shows a simple use of threads in C#.

```
// statements_lock.cs
using System;
using System.Threading;

class ThreadTest
{
    public void runme()
    {
        Console.WriteLine("runme called");
    }

    public static void Main()
    {
        ThreadTest b = new ThreadTest();
        Thread t = new Thread(new ThreadStart(b.runme));
        t.Start();
    }
}
```

Output

```
runme called
```

Example 2

The following sample uses threads and **lock**. As long as the **lock** statement is present, the statement block is a critical section and balance will never become a negative number.

```csharp
// statements_lock2.cs
using System;
using System.Threading;

internal class Account
{
    int balance;

    Random r = new Random();

    internal Account(int initial)
    {
        balance = initial;
    }

    internal int Withdraw(int amount)
    {

        if (balance < 0)
        {
            throw new Exception("Negative Balance");
        }

        // Comment out the next line to see the effect of leaving out the lock keyword
        lock (this)
        {
            if (balance >= amount)
            {
                Thread.Sleep(5);
                balance = balance - amount;
                return amount;
            }

            else
            {
                return 0; // transaction rejected
            }
        }
    }
}
```

(continued)

(continued)

```
    internal void DoTransactions()
    {
        for (int i = 0; i < 100; i++)
        {
            Withdraw(r.Next(-50, 100));
        }
    }
}

internal class Test
{
    static internal Thread[] threads = new Thread[10];

    public static void Main()
    {
        Account acc = new Account (0);
        for (int i = 0; i < 10; i++)
        {
            Thread t = new Thread(new ThreadStart(acc.DoTransactions));
            threads[i] = t;
        }
        for (int i = 0; i < 10; i++)
        {
            threads[i].Start();
        }
    }
}
```

Type Keywords

The C# typing system contains the following categories:

- Value types

- Reference types

- A.2 Pointer types

Variables of the value types store data, while those of the reference types store references to the actual data. Reference types are also referred to as objects. Pointer types can be used only in unsafe mode.

It is possible to convert a value type to a reference type and vice versa, by using boxing and unboxing.

This section also introduces the void type.

See Also

Types Reference Tables (pg. 161)

Value Types

The value types consist of two main categories:

- Struct type
- Enumeration type

The struct types contain the user-defined struct types and the following built-in simple types:

- Numeric types
  - Integral types
  - Floating-point types
  - decimal
- bool

In addition to explaining each category of the value types, the following topics are discussed in this section:

- Main Features of Value Types
- Main Features of Simple Types
- Initializing Value Types

Main Features of Value Types

A variable of a value type always contains a value of that type. The assignment to a variable of a value type creates a copy of the assigned value, while the assignment to a variable of a reference type creates a copy of the reference but not of the referenced object.

All value types are derived implicitly from the Object class.

Unlike reference types, it is not possible to derive a new type from a value type. However, like reference types, structs can implement interfaces.

Unlike reference types, it is not possible for a value type to contain the **null** value.

Each value type has an implicit default constructor that initializes the default value of that type. For information on default values of value types, see "Default Values Table" on page 164.

Main Features of Simple Types

All of the simple types are aliases of the .NET Framework System types. For example, **int** is an alias of **System.Int32**. For a complete list of aliases, see "Built-in Types Table" on page 162.

Constant expressions, whose operands are all simple type constants, are evaluated at compilation time.

Simple types can be initialized using literals. For example, 'A' is a literal of the type **char** and 2001 is a literal of the type **int**.

Initializing Value Types

Local variables in C# must be initialized before being used. Therefore, if you declare a local variable without initialization like this:

```
int myInt;
```

you cannot use it before you initialize it. You can initialize it using the following statement:

```
myInt = new int();  // Invoke the default constructor for the type int
```

which is equivalent to:

```
myInt = 0;          // Assign an initial value, 0 in this example
```

You can, of course, have the declaration and the initialization in the same statement like this:

```
int myInt = new int();
```

-or-

```
int myInt = 0;
```

Using the **new** operator calls the default constructor of the specific type and assigns the default value to the variable. In the preceding example, the default constructor assigned the value 0 to myInt. For more information on values assigned by calling default constructors, see "Default Values Table" on page 164.

With user-defined types, use **new** to invoke the default constructor. For example, the following statement invokes the default constructor of the Point struct:

```
Point p = new Point();   // Invoke the default constructor for the struct
```

After this call, the struct is considered to be definitely assigned; that is, all of its members are initialized to their default values.

For more information on the new operator, see the section "new" on page 65.

For information on formatting the output of numeric types, see "Formatting Numeric Results Table" on page 168.

See Also

Types Reference Tables (pg. 161), Reference Types (pg. 149)

bool

The **bool** keyword is an alias of **System.Boolean**. It is used to declare variables to store the Boolean values, true and false.

Literals

You can assign a Boolean value to a **bool** variable, for example:

```
bool MyVar = true;
```

You can also assign an expression that evaluates to **bool** to a **bool** variable, for example:

```
bool Alphabetic = (c > 64 && c < 123);
```

Conversions

In C++, a value of type **bool** can be converted to a value of type **int**; in other words, **false** is equivalent to zero and **true** is equivalent to nonzero values. In C#, there is no conversion between the **bool** type and other types. For example, the following **if** statement is illegal in C#, while it is legal in C++:

```
int x = 123;
if (x)    // Illegal in C#
{
    printf("The value of x is nonzero.");
}
```

To test a variable of the type **int**, you have to explicitly compare it to a value (for example, zero), that is:

```
int x = 123;
if (x != 0)    // The C# way
{
    Console.Write("The value of x is nonzero.");
}
```

Example

In this example, you enter a character from the keyboard and the program checks if the input character is a letter. If so, it checks if it is lowercase or uppercase. In each case, the proper message is displayed.

```
// keyword_bool.cs
// Character Tester
using System;
public class BoolTest
{
    public static void Main()
    {
        Console.Write("Enter a character: ");
        char c = (char) Console.Read();
        if (Char.IsLetter(c))
            if (Char.IsLower(c))
                Console.WriteLine("The character is lowercase.");
            else
                Console.WriteLine("The character is uppercase.");
        else
            Console.WriteLine("The character is not an alphabetic character.");
    }
}
```

Input

```
X
```

Sample Output

```
Enter a character: X
The character is uppercase.
```

Additional sample runs might look as follow:

```
Enter a character: x
The character is lowercase.
```

```
Enter a character: 2
The character is not an alphabetic character.
```

See Also

Default Values Table (pg. 164), Built-in Types Table (pg. 162)

byte

The **byte** keyword denotes an integral type that stores values as indicated in the following table.

Type	Range	Size	.NET Framework type
byte	0 to 255	Unsigned 8-bit integer	**System.Byte**

Literals

You can declare and initialize a **byte** variable like this example:

```
byte myByte = 255;
```

In the preceding declaration, the integer literal 255 is implicitly converted from **int** to **byte**. If the integer literal exceeds the range of **byte**, a compilation error will occur.

Conversions

There is a predefined implicit conversion from **byte** to **short**, **ushort**, **int**, **uint**, **long**, **ulong**, **float**, **double**, or **decimal**.

You cannot implicitly convert nonliteral numeric types of larger storage size to **byte** (for the storage sizes of integral types, see "Integral Types Table" on page 163). Consider, for example, the following two **byte** variables x and y:

```
byte x = 10, y = 20;
```

The following assignment statement will produce a compilation error, because the arithmetic expression on the right-hand side of the assignment operator evaluates to **int** by default.

```
byte z = x + y;   // Error: conversion from int to byte
```

To fix this problem, use a cast:

```
byte z = (byte)(x + y);   // OK: explicit conversion
```

It is possible though to use the following statements, where the destination variable has the same storage size or a larger storage size:

```
int x = 10, y = 20;
int m = x + y;
long n = x + y;
```

Also, there is no implicit conversion from floating-point types to **byte**. For example, the following statement generates a compiler error unless an explicit cast is used:

```
byte x = 3.0;       // Error: no implicit conversion from double
byte y = (byte)3.0;   // OK: explicit conversion
```

When calling overloaded methods, a cast must be used. Consider, for example, the following overloaded methods that use **byte** and **int** parameters:

```
public static void MyMethod(int i) {}
public static void MyMethod(byte b) {}
```

Using the **byte** cast guarantees that the correct type is called, for example:

```
MyMethod(5);        // Calling the method with the int parameter
MyMethod((byte)5);   // Calling the method with the byte parameter
```

For information on arithmetic expressions with mixed floating-point types and integral types, see the sections "float" on page 132 and "double" on page 128.

For more information on implicit numeric conversion rules, see "Implicit Numeric Conversions Table" on page 166.

See Also

Integral Types Table (pg. 163), Built-in Types Table (pg. 162), Implicit Numeric Conversions Table (pg. 166), Explicit Numeric Conversions Table (pg. 167)

char

The **char** keyword is used to declare a Unicode character in the range indicated in the following table. Unicode characters are 16-bit characters used to represent most of the known written languages throughout the world.

Type	Range	Size	.NET Framework type
char	U+0000 to U+ffff	Unicode 16-bit character	**System.Char**

Literals

Constants of the **char** type can be written as character literals, hexadecimal escape sequence, or Unicode representation. You can also cast the integral character codes. All of the following statements declare a **char** variable and initialize it with the character X:

```
char MyChar = 'X';      // Character literal
char MyChar = '\x0058'; // Hexadecimal
char MyChar = (char)88;  // Cast from integral type
char MyChar = '\u0058'; // Unicode
```

Conversions

A **char** can be implicitly converted to **ushort**, **int**, **uint**, **long**, **ulong**, **float**, **double**, or **decimal**. However, there are no implicit conversions from other types to the **char** type.

See Also

Integral Types Table (pg. 163), Built-in Types Table (pg. 162), Implicit Numeric Conversions Table (pg. 166), Explicit Numeric Conversions Table (pg. 167)

decimal

The **decimal** keyword denotes a 128-bit data type. Compared to floating-point types, the **decimal** type has a greater precision and a smaller range, which makes it suitable for financial and monetary calculations. The approximate range and precision for the **decimal** type are shown in the following table.

Type	Approximate Range	Precision	.NET Framework type
decimal	1.0×10^{-28} to 7.9×10^{28}	28–29 significant digits	**System.Decimal**

Literals

If you want a numeric real literal to be treated as **decimal**, use the suffix m or M, for example:

```
decimal myMoney = 300.5m;
```

Without the suffix m, the number is treated as a **double**, thus generating a compiler error.

Conversions

The integral types are implicitly converted to **decimal** and the result evaluates to **decimal**. Therefore you can initialize a decimal variable using an integer literal, without the suffix, for example:

```
decimal myMoney = 300;
```

There is no implicit conversion between floating-point types and the **decimal** type; therefore, a cast must be used to convert between these two types. For example:

```
decimal myMoney = 99.9m;
double x = (double) myMoney;
myMoney = (decimal) x;
```

You can also mix **decimal** and numeric integral types in the same expression. However, mixing **decimal** and floating-point types without a cast results in a compilation error.

For more information on implicit numeric conversions, see "Implicit Numeric Conversions Table" on page 166.

For more information on explicit numeric conversions, see "Explicit Numeric Conversions Table" on page 167.

Example 1

In this example, a **decimal** and an **int** are mixed in the same expression. The result evaluates to the **decimal** type.

```
// keyword_decimal.cs
// decimal conversion
using System;
public class TestDecimal {
   public static void Main ()
   {
      decimal d = 9.1m;
      int y = 3;
      Console.WriteLine(d + y);   // Result converted to decimal
   }
}
```

Output

```
12.1
```

In the preceding example, if you attempt to add the **double** and **decimal** variables by using a statement like this:

```
Console.WriteLine(d + x);   // error
```

you will get the following error:

```
Operator '+' cannot be applied to operands of type 'double' and 'decimal'
```

Formatting Decimal Output

You can format the results by using the **String.Format** method, or through the **Console.Write** method, which calls **String.Format()**. The currency format is specified using the standard currency format string "C" or "c", as shown in Example 2.

Example 2

In this example, the output is formatted using the currency format string. Notice that x is rounded because the decimal places exceed $0.99. The variable y, which represents the maximum exact digits, is displayed exactly in the proper format.

```
// keyword_decimal2.cs
// Decimal type formatting
using System;
public class TestDecimalFormat
{
   public static void Main ()
   {
      decimal x = 0.999m;
      decimal y = 99999999999999999999999999999m;
      Console.WriteLine("My amount = {0:C}", x);
      Console.WriteLine("Your amount = {0:C}", y);
   }
}
```

Output

```
My amount = $1.00
Your amount = $9,999,999,999,999,999,999,999,999,999.00
```

See Also

Default Values Table (pg. 164), Built-in Types Table (pg. 162), Floating-Point Types Table (pg. 164), Implicit Numeric Conversions Table (pg. 166), Explicit Numeric Conversions Table (pg. 167)

double

The **double** keyword denotes a simple type that stores 64-bit floating-point values. The following table shows the precision and approximate range for the **double** type.

Type	Approximate range	Precision	.NET Framework type
double	$\pm 5.0 \times 10^{-324}$ to $\pm 1.7 \times 10^{308}$	15–16 digits	**System.Double**

Literals

By default, a real numeric literal on the right-hand side of the assignment operator is treated as **double**. However, if you want an integer number to be treated as **double**, use the suffix d or D, for example:

```
double x = 3D;
```

Conversions

You can mix numeric integral types and floating-point types in an expression. In this case, the integral types are converted to floating-point types. The evaluation of the expression is performed according to the following rules:

- If one of the floating-point types is **double**, the expression evaluates to **double** (or **bool** in the case of relational or Boolean expressions).

- If there is no **double** type in the expression, it evaluates to **float** (or **bool** in the case of relational or Boolean expressions).

A floating-point expression can contain the following sets of values:

- Positive and negative zero

- Positive and negative infinity

- Not-a-Number value (NaN)

- The finite set of nonzero values

For more information on these values, refer to IEEE Standard for Binary Floating-Point Arithmetic, available on the Web site http://www.ieee.org/.

Example

In the following example, an **int**, a **short**, a **float**, and a **double** are added together giving a **double** result.

```
// keyword_double.cs
// Mixing types in expressions
using System;
class MixedTypes
{
    public static void Main()
    {
        int x = 3;
        float y = 4.5f;
        short z = 5;
        double w = 1.7E+3;
        Console.WriteLine("The sum is {0}", x + y + z + w);   // double result
    }
}
```

Output

```
The sum is 1712.5
```

See Also

Default Values Table (pg. 164), Built-in Types Table (pg. 162), Floating-Point Types Table (pg. 164), Implicit Numeric Conversions Table (pg. 166), Explicit Numeric Conversions Table (pg. 167)

enum

The **enum** keyword is used to declare an enumeration, a distinct type consisting of a set of named constants called the enumerator list. Every enumeration type has an underlying type, which can be any integral type except **char**. The declaration of an **enum** variable takes the form:

```
[attributes] [modifiers] enum identifier [:base-type] {enumerator-list};
```

where:

attributes (Optional)
> Additional declarative information. For more information on attributes and attribute classes, see "Attributes" on page 211.

modifiers (Optional)
> The allowed modifiers are new and the four access modifiers.

identifier
> The **enum** name.

base-type (Optional)
> The underlying type that specifies the storage allocated for each enumerator. It can be one of the integral types except **char**. The default is **int**.

enumerator-list
> The enumerators' identifiers separated by commas, optionally including a value assignment.

Remarks

The default underlying type of the enumeration elements is **int**. By default, the first enumerator has the value 0, and the value of each successive enumerator is increased by 1. For example:

```
enum Days {Sat, Sun, Mon, Tue, Wed, Thu, Fri};
```

In this enumeration, Sat is 0, Sun is 1, Mon is 2, and so forth. Enumerators can have initializers to override the default values. For example:

```
enum Days {Sat=1, Sun, Mon, Tue, Wed, Thu, Fri};
```

In this enumeration, the sequence of elements is forced to start from 1 instead of 0.

The default value of an **enum** E is the value produced by the expression (E)0.

The underlying type specifies how much storage is allocated for each enumerator. However, an explicit cast is needed to convert from **enum** type to an integral type. For example, the following statement assigns the enumerator Sun to a variable of the type **int** using a cast to convert from **enum** to **int**:

```
int x = (int) Days.Sun;
```

Example 1

In this example, an enumeration, Days, is declared. Two enumerators are explicitly converted to **int** and assigned to **int** variables.

```
// keyword_enum.cs
// enum initialization:
using System;
public class EnumTest
{
    enum Days {Sat=1, Sun, Mon, Tue, Wed, Thu, Fri};

    public static void Main()
    {
        int x = (int) Days.Sun;
        int y = (int) Days.Fri;
        Console.WriteLine("Sun = {0}", x);
        Console.WriteLine("Fri = {0}", y);
    }
}
```

Output

```
Sun = 2
Fri = 7
```

Notice that if you remove the initializer from Sat=1, the result will be:

```
Sun = 1
Fri = 6
```

Example 2

In this example, the *base-type* option is used to declare an **enum** whose members are of the type **long**. Notice that even though the underlying type of the enumeration is **long**, the enumeration members must still be explicitly converted to type **long** using a cast.

```
// keyword_enum2.cs
// Using long enumerators
using System;
public class EnumTest
{
    enum Range :long {Max = 2147483648L, Min = 255L};
    public static void Main()
    {
        long x = (long) Range.Max;
        long y = (long) Range.Min;
        Console.WriteLine("Max = {0}", x);
        Console.WriteLine("Min = {0}", y);
    }
}
```

Output

```
Max = 2147483648
Min = 255
```

See Also

Default Values Table (pg. 164), Built-in Types Table (pg. 162), Value Types (pg. 165)

float

The **float** keyword denotes a simple type that stores 32-bit floating-point values. The following table shows the precision and approximate range for the **float** type.

Type	Approximate range	Precision	.NET Framework type
float	$\pm1.5 \times 10^{-45}$ to $\pm3.4 \times 10^{38}$	7 digits	**System.Single**

Literals

By default, a real numeric literal on the right-hand side of the assignment operator is treated as **double**. Therefore, to initialize a float variable use the suffix f or F, for example:

```
float x = 3.5F;
```

If you don't use the suffix in the previous declaration, you will get a compilation error because you are attempting to store a **double** value into a **float** variable.

Conversions

You can mix numeric integral types and floating-point types in an expression. In this case, the integral types are converted to floating-point types. The evaluation of the expression is performed according to the following rules:

- If one of the floating-point types is **double**, the expression evaluates to **double** (or **bool** in the case of relational or Boolean expressions).

- If there is no **double** type in the expression, the expression evaluates to **float** (or **bool** in the case of relational or Boolean expressions).

A floating-point expression can contain the following sets of values:

- Positive and negative zero

- Positive and negative infinity

- Not-a-Number value (NaN)

- The finite set of nonzero values

For more information on these values, refer to IEEE Standard for Binary Floating-Point Arithmetic, available on the Web site http://www.ieee.org/.

Example

In the following example, an **int**, a **short**, and a **float** are included in a mathematical expression giving a **float** result (notice that there is no **double** in the expression).

```
// keyword_float.cs
// Mixing types in expressions
using System;
class MixedTypes
{
    public static void Main()
    {
        int x = 3;
        float y = 4.5f;
        short z = 5;
        Console.WriteLine("The result is {0}", x*y/z);
    }
}
```

Output

```
The result is 2.7
```

See Also

Default Values Table (pg. 164), Built-in Types Table (pg. 162), Floating-Point Types Table (pg. 165), Implicit Numeric Conversions Table (pg. 166), Explicit Numeric Conversions Table (pg. 167)

int

The **int** keyword denotes an integral type that stores values according to the size and range shown in the following table.

Type	Range	Size	.NET Framework type
int	–2,147,483,648 to 2,147,483,647	Signed 32-bit integer	**System.Int32**

Literals

You can declare and initialize a variable of the type **int** like this example:

```
int myInt = 123;
```

When an integer literal has no suffix, its type is the first of these types in which its value can be represented: **int**, **uint**, **long**, **ulong**. In this example, it is of the type **int**.

Conversions

There is a predefined implicit conversion from **int** to **long**, **float**, **double**, or **decimal**. For example:

```
float myFloat = 123;    // OK: implicit conversion to float
```

There is a predefined implicit conversion from **sbyte**, **byte**, **short**, **ushort**, or **char** to **int**. For example, if you have a **long** variable, myLong, the following assignment statement will produce a compilation error without a cast:

```
long myLong = 22;
int myInt = myLong;       // Error: no implicit conversion from long
int myInt = (int)myLong;  // OK: explicit conversion
```

Notice also that there is no implicit conversion from floating-point types to **int**. For example, the following statement generates a compiler error unless an explicit cast is used:

```
int x = 3.0;        // Error: no implicit conversion from double
int y = (int)3.0;   // OK: explicit conversion
```

For information on arithmetic expressions with mixed floating-point types and integral types, see the sections "float" on page 132 and "double" on page 128.

See Also

Integral Types Table (pg. 163), Built-in Types Table (pg. 162), Implicit Numeric Conversions Table (pg. 166), Explicit Numeric Conversions Table (pg. 167)

long

The **long** keyword denotes an integral type that stores values according to the size and range shown in the following table.

Type	Range	Size	.NET Framework type
long	−9,223,372,036,854,775,808 to 9,223,372,036,854,775,807	Signed 64-bit integer	**System.Int64**

Literals

You can declare and initialize a **long** variable like this example:

```
long myLong = 4294967296;
```

When an integer literal has no suffix, its type is the first of these types in which its value can be represented: **int**, **uint**, **long**, **ulong**. In the preceding example, it is of the type **long** because it exceeds the range of **uint** (for the storage sizes of integral types, see "Integral Types Table" on page 163).

You can also use the suffix L with the **long** type like this:

```
long myLong = 4294967296L;
```

When you use the suffix L, the type of the literal integer is determined to be either **long** or **ulong** according to its size. In the case it is **long** because it less than the range of **ulong**.

A common use of the suffix is with calling overloaded methods. Consider, for example, the following overloaded methods that use **long** and **int** parameters:

```
public static void MyMethod(int i) {}
public static void MyMethod(long l) {}
```

Using the suffix L guarantees that the correct type is called, for example:

```
MyMethod(5);    // Calling the method with the int parameter
MyMethod(5L);   // Calling the method with the long parameter
```

You can use the **long** type with other numeric integral types in the same expression, in which case the expression is evaluated as **long** (or **bool** in the case of relational or Boolean expressions). For example, the following expression evaluates as **long**:

```
898L + 88
```

> **Note** You can also use the lowercase letter "l" as a suffix. However, this generates a compiler warning because the letter "l" is easily confused with the digit "1." Use "L" for clarity.

For information on arithmetic expressions with mixed floating-point types and integral types, see the sections "float" on page 132 and "double" on page 128.

Conversions

There is a predefined implicit conversion from **long** to **float**, **double**, or **decimal**. Otherwise a cast must be used. For example, the following statement will produce a compilation error without an explicit cast:

```
int x = 8L;         // Error: no implicit conversion from long to int
int x = (int)8L;    // OK: explicit conversion to int
```

There is a predefined implicit conversion from **sbyte**, **byte**, **short**, **ushort**, **int**, **uint**, or **char** to **long**.

Notice also that there is no implicit conversion from floating-point types to **long**. For example, the following statement generates a compiler error unless an explicit cast is used:

```
long x = 3.0;         // Error: no implicit conversion from double
long y = (long)3.0;   // OK: explicit conversion
```

See Also

Integral Types Table (pg. 163), Built-in Types Table (pg. 162), Implicit Numeric Conversions Table (pg. 166), Explicit Numeric Conversions Table (pg. 167)

sbyte

The **sbyte** keyword denotes an integral type that stores values according to the size and range shown in the following table.

Type	Range	Size	.NET Framework type
sbyte	−128 to 127	Signed 8-bit integer	**System.SByte**

Literals

You can declare and initialize an **sbyte** variable like this example:

```
sbyte mySbyte = 127;
```

In the preceding declaration, the integer literal 127 is implicitly converted from **int** to **sbyte**. If the integer literal exceeds the range of **sbyte**, a compilation error will occur.

A cast must be used when calling overloaded methods. Consider, for example, the following overloaded methods that use **sbyte** and **int** parameters:

```
public static void MyMethod(int i) {}
public static void MyMethod(sbyte b) {}
```

Using the **sbyte** cast guarantees that the correct type is called, for example:

```
MyMethod(5);         // Calling the method with the int parameter
MyMethod((sbyte)5);  // Calling the method with the sbyte parameter
```

Conversions

There is a predefined implicit conversion from **sbyte** to **short**, **int**, **long**, **float**, **double**, or **decimal**.

You cannot implicitly convert nonliteral numeric types of larger storage size to **sbyte** (for the storage sizes of integral types, see "Integral Types Table" on page 163). Consider, for example, the following two **sbyte** variables x and y:

```
sbyte x = 10, y = 20;
```

The following assignment statement will produce a compilation error, because the arithmetic expression on the right-hand side of the assignment operator evaluates to **int** by default.

```
sbyte z = x + y;   // Error: conversion from int to sbyte
```

To fix this problem, use a cast:

```
sbyte z = (byte)(x + y);   // OK: explicit conversion
```

It is possible though to use the following statements, where the destination variable has the same storage size or a larger storage size:

```
sbyte x = 10, y = 20;
int m = x + y;
long n = x + y;
```

Notice also that there is no implicit conversion from floating-point types to **sbyte**. For example, the following statement generates a compiler error unless an explicit cast is used:

```
sbyte x = 3.0;          // Error: no implicit conversion from double
sbyte y = (sbyte)3.0;   // OK: explicit conversion
```

For information on arithmetic expressions with mixed floating-point types and integral types, see the sections "float" on page 132 and "double" on page 128.

For more information on implicit numeric conversion rules, see "Implicit Numeric Conversions Table" on page 167.

See Also

Integral Types Table (pg. 163), Built-in Types Table (pg. 162), Implicit Numeric Conversions Table (pg. 166), Explicit Numeric Conversions Table (pg. 167)

short

The **short** keyword denotes an integral data type that stores values according to the size and range shown in the following table.

Type	Range	Size	.NET Framework type
short	−32,768 to 32,767	Signed 16-bit integer	**System.Int16**

Literals

You can declare and initialize a **short** variable like this example:

```
short x = 32767;
```

In the preceding declaration, the integer literal 32767 is implicitly converted from **int** to **short**. If the integer literal does not fit into a **short** storage location, a compilation error will occur.

A cast must be used when calling overloaded methods. Consider, for example, the following overloaded methods that use **short** and **int** parameters:

```
public static void MyMethod(int i) {}
public static void MyMethod(short s) {}
```

Using the **short** cast guarantees that the correct type is called, for example:

```
MyMethod(5);        // Calling the method with the int parameter
MyMethod((short)5); // Calling the method with the short parameter
```

Conversions

There is a predefined implicit conversion from **short** to **int**, **long**, **float**, **double**, or **decimal**.

You cannot implicitly convert nonliteral numeric types of larger storage size to **short** (for the storage sizes of integral types, see "Integral Types Table" on page 163). Consider, for example, the following two **short** variables x and y:

```
short x = 5, y = 12;
```

The following assignment statement will produce a compilation error, because the arithmetic expression on the right-hand side of the assignment operator evaluates to **int** by default.

```
short z = x + y;    // Error: no conversion from int to short
```

To fix this problem, use a cast:

```
short z = (short)(x + y);    // OK: explicit conversion
```

It is possible though to use the following statements, where the destination variable has the same storage size or a larger storage size:

```
int m = x + y;
long n = x + y;
```

There is no implicit conversion from floating-point types to **short**. For example, the following statement generates a compiler error unless an explicit cast is used:

```
short x = 3.0;         // Error: no implicit conversion from double
short y = (short)3.0;  // OK: explicit conversion
```

For information on arithmetic expressions with mixed floating-point types and integral types, see the sections "float" on page 132 and "double" on page 128.

For more information on implicit numeric conversion rules, see "Implicit Numeric Conversions Table" on page 166.

See Also

Integral Types Table (pg. 163), Built-in Types Table (pg. 162), Implicit Numeric Conversions Table (pg. 166), Explicit Numeric Conversions Table (pg. 167)

struct

Structs are similar to classes in that they represent data structures that can contain data members and function members. Unlike classes, structs are value types and do not require heap allocation. A variable of a struct type directly contains the data of the struct, whereas a variable of a class type contains a reference to the data, the latter known as an object.

Structs are particularly useful for small data structures that have value semantics. Complex numbers, points in a coordinate system, or key-value pairs in a dictionary are all good examples of structs. Key to these data structures is that they have few data members, that they do not require use of inheritance or referential identity, and that they can be conveniently implemented using value semantics where assignment copies the value instead of the reference.

As described in "Value Types," the simple types provided by C#, such as `int`, `double`, and `bool`, are in fact all struct types. Just as these predefined types are structs, so it is possible to use structs and operator overloading to implement new "primitive" types in the C# language.

A **struct** type is a value type that can contain constructors, constants, fields, methods, properties, indexers, operators, and nested types. The declaration of a **struct** takes the following form:

```
[attributes] [modifiers] struct identifier [:interfaces] body [;]
```

where:

attributes (Optional)
Additional declarative information. For more information on attributes and attribute classes, see "Attributes" on page 211.

modifiers (Optional)
The allowed modifiers are new and the four access modifiers.

identifier
The **struct** name.

interfaces (Optional)
A list that contains the interfaces implemented by the struct, all separated by commas.

body
The struct body that contains member declarations.

Remarks

The **struct** type is suitable for representing lightweight objects such as Point, Rectangle, and Color. Although it is possible to represent a point as a class, a struct is more efficient in some scenarios. For example, if you declare an array of 1000 Point objects, you will allocate additional memory for referencing each object. In this case, the struct is less expensive.

It is an error to declare a default (parameterless) constructor for a struct. A default constructor is always provided to initialize the struct members to their default values.

It is an error to initialize an instance field in a struct.

When you create a struct object using the **new** operator, it gets created and the appropriate constructor is called. Unlike classes, structs can be instantiated without using the **new** operator. If you do not use **new**, the fields will remain unassigned and the object cannot be used until all of the fields are initialized.

There is no inheritance for structs as there is for classes. A struct cannot inherit from another struct or class, and it cannot be the base of a class. Structs, however, inherit from the base class **Object**. A struct can implement interfaces, and it does that exactly as classes do.

Unlike C++, you cannot declare a class using the keyword **struct**. In C#, classes and structs are semantically different. A struct is a value type, while a class is a reference type. For more information on the features of value types, see "Value Types" on page 121.

Unless you need reference type semantics, a class that is smaller than 16 bytes may be more efficiently handled by the system as a struct.

In Managed Extensions for C++, the equivalents to a C# class and a C# struct are as follows:

C#	Managed Extensions for C++	For more information
Class	__gc struct -or- __gc class	__gc keyword
Struct	__value struct -or- __value class	__value keyword

Example 1

This example demonstrates **struct** initialization using both default and parameterized constructors.

```
// keyword_struct.cs
// struct declaration and initialization
using System;
public struct Point
{
   public int x, y;

   public Point(int p1, int p2)
   {
      x = p1;
      y = p2;
   }
}

class MainClass
{
   public static void Main()
   {
      // Initialize:
      Point myPoint = new Point();
      Point yourPoint = new Point(10,10);

      // Display results:
      Console.Write("My Point:   ");
      Console.WriteLine("x = {0}, y = {1}", myPoint.x, myPoint.y);
      Console.Write("Your Point: ");
      Console.WriteLine("x = {0}, y = {1}", yourPoint.x, yourPoint.y);
   }
}
```

Output

```
My Point:    x = 0, y = 0
Your Point: x = 10, y = 10
```

Example 2

This example demonstrates a feature that is unique to structs. It creates a Point object without using the **new** operator. If you replace the word **struct** with the word **class**, the program won't compile.

```
// keyword_struct2.cs
// Declare a struct object without "new"
using System;
public struct Point
{
   public int x, y;

   public Point(int x, int y)
   {
      this.x = x;
      this.y = y;
   }
}

class MainClass
{
   public static void Main()
   {
      // Declare an object:
      Point myPoint;

      // Initialize:
      myPoint.x = 10;
      myPoint.y = 20;

      // Display results:
      Console.WriteLine("My Point:");
      Console.WriteLine("x = {0}, y = {1}", myPoint.x, myPoint.y);
   }
}
```

Output

```
My Point:
x = 10, y = 20
```

See Also

Default Values Table (pg. 164), Built-in Types Table (pg. 162), class (pg. 149), interface (pg. 155)

uint

The **uint** keyword denotes an integral type that stores values according to the size and range shown in the following table.

Type	Range	Size	.NET Framework type
uint	0 to 4,294,967,295	Unsigned 32-bit integer	**System.UInt32**

Literals

You can declare and initialize a variable of the type **uint** like this example:

```
uint myUint = 4294967290;
```

When an integer literal has no suffix, its type is the first of these types in which its value can be represented: **int**, **uint**, **long**, **ulong**. In this example, it is **uint**.

You can also use the suffix u or U, like this:

```
uint myUint = 123U;
```

When you use the suffix U or u, the literal type is determined to be either **uint** or **ulong** according to its size. In this example, it is **uint**.

Conversions

There is a predefined implicit conversion from **uint** to **long**, **ulong**, **float**, **double**, or **decimal**. For example:

```
float myFloat = 4294967290;    // OK: implicit conversion to float
```

There is a predefined implicit conversion from **byte**, **ushort**, or **char** to **uint**. Otherwise you must use a cast. For example, if you have a **long** variable, `myLong`, the following assignment statement will produce a compilation error without a cast:

```
long myLong = 22;
uint myUint = myLong;        // Error: no implicit conversion from long
uint myUint = (uint)myLong;  // OK: explicit conversion
```

Notice also that there is no implicit conversion from floating-point types to **uint**. For example, the following statement generates a compiler error unless an explicit cast is used:

```
uint x = 3.0;        // Error: no implicit conversion from double
uint y = (uint)3.0;  // OK: explicit conversion
```

For information on arithmetic expressions with mixed floating-point types and integral types, see the sections "float" on page 132 and "double" on page 128.

For more information on implicit numeric conversion rules, see "Implicit Numeric Conversions Table" on page 166.

See Also

Integral Types Table (pg. 163), Built-in Types Table (pg. 162), Implicit Numeric Conversions Table (pg. 166), Explicit Numeric Conversions Table (pg. 167)

ulong

The **ulong** keyword denotes an integral type that stores values according to the size and range shown in the following table.

Type	Range	Size	.NET Framework type
ulong	0 to 18,446,744,073,709,551,615	Unsigned 64-bit integer	**System.UInt64**

Literals

You can declare and initialize a **ulong** variable like this example:

```
ulong myUlong = 9223372036854775808;
```

When an integer literal has no suffix, its type is the first of these types in which its value can be represented: **int**, **uint**, **long**, **ulong**. In this example, it is of the type **ulong**.

You can also use suffixes to specify the type of the literal according to the following rules:

- If you use L or l, the type of the literal integer will be either **long** or **ulong** according to its size.

  > **Note**   You can use the lowercase letter "l" as a suffix. However, this generates a compiler warning because the letter "l" is easily confused with the digit "1." Use "L" for clarity.

- If you use U or u, the type of the literal integer will be either **uint** or **ulong** according to its size.

- If you use UL, ul, Ul, uL, LU, lu, Lu, or lU, the type of the literal integer will be **ulong**.

  For example, the output of the following three statements will be the system type **UInt64**, which corresponds to the alias **ulong**:

  ```
  Console.WriteLine(9223372036854775808L.GetType());
  Console.WriteLine(123UL.GetType());
  Console.WriteLine((123UL + 456).GetType());
  ```

A common use of the suffix is with calling overloaded methods. Consider, for example, the following overloaded methods that use **ulong** and **int** parameters:

```
public static void MyMethod(int i) {}
public static void MyMethod(ulong l) {}
```

Using a suffix with the **ulong** parameter guarantees that the correct type is called, for example:

```
MyMethod(5);    // Calling the method with the int parameter
MyMethod(5UL);  // Calling the method with the ulong parameter
```

Conversions

There is a predefined implicit conversion from **ulong** to **float**, **double**, or **decimal**.

There is no implicit conversion from **ulong** to any integral type. For example, the following statement will produce a compilation error without an explicit cast:

```
long myLong = 8UL;   // Error: no implicit conversion from ulong
```

There is a predefined implicit conversion from **byte, ushort**, **uint**, or **char** to **ulong**.

Also, there is no implicit conversion from floating-point types to **ulong**. For example, the following statement generates a compiler error unless an explicit cast is used:

```
ulong x = 3.0;        // Error: no implicit conversion from double
ulong y = (ulong)3.0; // OK: explicit conversion
```

For information on arithmetic expressions with mixed floating-point types and integral types, see the sections "float" on page 132 and "double" on page 128.

For more information on implicit numeric conversion rules, see "Implicit Numeric Conversions Table" on page 166.

See Also

Integral Types Table (pg. 163), Built-in Types Table (pg. 162), Implicit Numeric Conversions Table (pg. 166), Explicit Numeric Conversions Table (pg. 167)

ushort

The **ushort** keyword denotes an integral data type that stores values according to the size and range shown in the following table.

Type	Range	Size	.NET Framework type
ushort	0 to 65,535	Unsigned 16-bit integer	**System.UInt16**

Literals

You can declare and initialize a **ushort** variable like this example:

```
ushort myShort = 65535;
```

In the preceding declaration, the integer literal 65535 is implicitly converted from **int** to **ushort**. If the integer literal exceeds the range of **ushort**, a compilation error will occur.

A cast must be used when calling overloaded methods. Consider, for example, the following overloaded methods that use **ushort** and **int** parameters:

```
public static void MyMethod(int i) {}
public static void MyMethod(ushort s) {}
```

Using the **ushort** cast guarantees that the correct type is called, for example:

```
MyMethod(5);          // Calling the method with the int parameter
MyMethod((ushort)5);  // Calling the method with the ushort parameter
```

Conversions

There is a predefined implicit conversion from **ushort** to **int, uint, long, ulong, float, double,** or **decimal**.

There is a predefined implicit conversion from **byte** or **char** to **ushort**. Otherwise a cast must be used to perform an explicit conversion. Consider, for example, the following two **ushort** variables x and y:

```
ushort x = 5, y = 12;
```

The following assignment statement will produce a compilation error, because the arithmetic expression on the right-hand side of the assignment operator evaluates to **int** by default.

```
ushort z = x + y;    // Error: conversion from int to ushort
```

To fix this problem, use a cast:

```
ushort z = (ushort)(x + y);    // OK: explicit conversion
```

It is possible though to use the following statements, where the destination variable has the same storage size or a larger storage size:

```
int m = x + y;
long n = x + y;
```

Notice also that there is no implicit conversion from floating-point types to **ushort**. For example, the following statement generates a compiler error unless an explicit cast is used:

```
ushort x = 3.0;            // Error: no implicit conversion from double
ushort y = (ushort)3.0;    // OK: explicit conversion
```

For information on arithmetic expressions with mixed floating-point types and integral types, see the sections "float" on page 132 and "double" on page 128.

For more information on implicit numeric conversion rules, see "Implicit Numeric Conversions Table" on page 166.

See Also

Integral Types Table (pg. 163), Built-in Types Table (pg. 162), Implicit Numeric Conversions Table (pg. 166), Explicit Numeric Conversions Table (pg. 167)

Boxing and Unboxing

Boxing and unboxing enable value types to be treated as objects. Value types, including both struct types and built-in types, such as **int**, can be converted to and from the type **object**.

See Also

Reference Types (pg. 149), Value Types (pg. 165)

Boxing Conversion

Boxing is an implicit conversion of a value type to the type **object** or to any interface type implemented by this value type. Boxing a value of a value allocates an object instance and copies the value into the new object.

Consider the following declaration of a value-type variable:

```
int i = 123;
```

The following statement implicitly applies the boxing operation on the variable i:

```
object o = i;
```

The result of this statement is creating an object o, on the stack, that references a value of the type **int**, on the heap. This value is a copy of the value-type value assigned to the variable i. The difference between the two variables, i and o, is illustrated in the following figure.

On the stack   **On the heap**

i

```
    123
```
int i=123;

o   **(i boxed)**

```
                            int
                            123
```
object o=i;

It also possible, but never needed, to perform the boxing explicitly as in the following example:

```
int i = 123;
object o = (object) i;
```

Example

This example converts an integer variable i to an object o via boxing. Then the value stored in the variable i is changed from 123 to 456. The example shows that the object keeps the original copy of the contents, 123.

```
// boxing.cs
// Boxing an integer variable
using System;
class TestBoxing
{
    public static void Main()
    {
        int i = 123;
        object o = i;   // Implicit boxing
        i = 456;        // Change the contents of i
        Console.WriteLine("The value-type value = {0}", i);
        Console.WriteLine("The object-type value = {0}", o);
    }
}
```

Output

```
The value-type value = 456
The object-type value = 123
```

See Also

Unboxing Conversion (pg. 147)

Unboxing Conversion

Unboxing is an explicit conversion from the type **object** to a value type or from an interface type to a value type that implements the interface. An unboxing operation consists of:

- Checking the object instance to make sure it is a boxed value of the given value type.

- Copying the value from the instance into the value-type variable.

The following statements demonstrate both boxing and unboxing operations:

```
int i = 123;          // A value type
object box = i;       // Boxing
int j = (int)box;     // Unboxing
```

The following figure demonstrates the result of the preceding statements.

On the stack

On the heap

i

```
   123
```

int i=123;

o

(i boxed)

```
   int
```
```
   123
```

object o=i;

j

```
   123
```

int j=(int) o;

For an unboxing conversion to a given value type to succeed at run time, the value of the source argument must be a reference to an object that was previously created by boxing a value of that value type. If the source argument is **null** or a reference to an incompatible object, an **InvalidCastException** is thrown.

Example

The following example demonstrates a case of invalid unboxing, of how incorrect unboxing leads to InvalidCastException. By using **try** and **catch**, an error message is displayed when the error occurs.

```csharp
using System;
public class UnboxingTest
{
    public static void Main()
    {
        int intI = 123;

        // Boxing
        object o = intI;

        // Reference to incompatible object produces InvalidCastException
        try
        {
            int intJ = (short) o;
            Console.WriteLine("Unboxing OK.");
        }

        catch (InvalidCastException e)
        {
            Console.WriteLine("{0} Error: Incorrect unboxing.",e);
        }
    }
}
```

Output

```
System.InvalidCastException
    at UnboxingTest.Main() Error: Incorrect unboxing.
```

If you change the statement:

```
int intJ = (short) o;
```

to:

```
int intJ = (int) o;
```

the conversion will be performed, and you will get the output Unboxing OK.

See Also

Boxing Conversion (pg. 146)

Reference Types

Variables of reference types, referred to as objects, store references to the actual data. This section introduces the following keywords used to declare reference types:

- class
- interface
- delegate

This section also introduces the following built-in reference types:

- object
- string

See Also

Value Types (pg. 121)

class

A class is a data structure that may contain data members (constants and fields), function members (methods, properties, events, indexers, operators, instance constructors, destructors, and static constructors), and nested types. Class types support inheritance, a mechanism whereby a derived class can extend and specialize a base class.

Classes are declared using the keyword **class**. The declaration takes the form:

```
[attributes] [modifiers] class identifier [:base-list] { class-body }[;]
```

where:

attributes (Optional)
> Additional declarative information. For more information on attributes and attribute classes, see "Attributes" on page 211.

modifiers (Optional)
> The allowed modifiers are new, abstract, sealed, and the four access modifiers.

identifier
> The class name.

base-list (Optional)
> A list that contains the one base class and any implemented interfaces, all separated by commas.

class-body
> Declarations of the class members.

Remarks

Unlike C++, only single inheritance is allowed in C#. In other words, a class can inherit implementation from one base class only. However, a class can implement more that one interface. The following table shows examples of class inheritance and interface implementation:

Inheritance	Example
None	`class ClassA { }`
Single	`class DerivedClass: BaseClass { }`
None, implements two interfaces	`class ImplClass: IFace1, IFace2 { }`
Single, implements one interface	`class ImplDerivedClass: BaseClass, IFace1 { }`

The access levels protected and private are only allowed on nested classes.

A class can contain declarations of the following members:

- Constructors (see "Instance Constructors" on page 261)
- Destructors (see "Destructors" on page 270)
- Constants
- Fields
- Methods
- Properties (see "Properties" on page 283)
- Indexers (see "Indexers" on page 272)
- Operators (see "Operators" on page 169)

In Managed Extensions for C++, the equivalents to a C# class and a C# struct are as follows:

C#	Managed Extensions for C++	For more information
class	__gc struct -or- __gc class	__gc keyword
struct	__value struct -or- __value class	__value keyword

Example

The following example demonstrates declaring class fields, constructors, and methods. It also demonstrates object instantiation and printing instance data. In this example, two classes are declared, the Kid class, which contains two private fields (name and age) and two public methods. The second class is MainClass, used for data processing.

```
// keyword_class.cs
// class example
using System;
public class Kid
{
    private int age;
    private string name;

    // Default constructor:
    public Kid()
    {
        name = "N/A";
    }

    // Constructor:
    public Kid(string name, int age)
    {
        this.name = name;
        this.age = age;
    }

    // Printing method:
    public void PrintKid()
    {
        Console.WriteLine("{0}, {1} years old.", name, age);
    }
}
```

(continued)

(continued)

```
public class MainClass
{
    public static void Main()
    {
        // Create objects
        // Objects must be created using the new operator:
        Kid kid1 = new Kid("Craig", 11);
        Kid kid2 = new Kid("Sally", 10);

        // Create an object using the default constructor:
        Kid kid3 = new Kid();

        // Display results:
        Console.Write("Kid #1: ");
        kid1.PrintKid();
        Console.Write("Kid #2: ");
        kid2.PrintKid();
        Console.Write("Kid #3: ");
        kid3.PrintKid();
    }
}
```

Output

```
Kid #1: Craig, 11 years old.
Kid #2: Sally, 10 years old.
Kid #3: N/A, 0 years old.
```

Notice, in the preceding example, that the private fields (name and age) can only be accessed through the public methods of the Kid class. For example, you cannot print the kid's name, from the Main method, using a statement like this:

```
Console.Write(kid1.name);    // Error
```

However, it is possible to do that if the Main method is a member of the Kid class.

Notice also that the **private** modifier is the default modifier for class members. If you remove the modifier, you still get private members. For more information on access level modifiers, see "Access Modifiers" on page 21.

Notice also that for the object created using the default constructor (kid3), the age field was initialized to zero.

For more information on classes, see "class" on page 149.

See Also

interface (pg. 155), struct (pg. 138)

delegate

A **delegate** declaration defines a reference type that can be used to encapsulate a method with a specific signature. A delegate instance encapsulates a static or an instance method. Delegates are roughly similar to function pointers in C++; however, delegates are type-safe and secure.

The delegate declaration takes the form:

```
[attributes] [modifiers] delegate result-type identifier ([formal-parameters]);
```

where:

attributes (Optional)
> Additional declarative information. For more information on attributes and attribute classes, see "Attributes" on page 211.

modifiers (Optional)
> The allowed modifiers are new and the four access modifiers.

result-type
> The result type, which matches the return type of the method.

identifier
> The delegate name.

formal-parameters (Optional)
> Parameter list. If a parameter is a pointer, the delegate must be declared with the unsafe modifier.

Remarks

A delegate lets you pass a function as a parameter. The type safety of delegates requires the function you pass as a delegate to have the same signature as the delegate declaration.

The Delegates Tutorial shows how to compose delegates, that is, create delegates from other delegates. A delegate that contains an out parameter cannot be composed.

Delegates are the basis for events.

For more information on delegates, see "delegate" on page 153 and "Delegates Tutorial" on page 321.

Example 1

The following is a simple example of declaring and using a delegate.

```
// keyword_delegate.cs
// delegate declaration
delegate void MyDelegate(int i);

class Program
{
    public static void Main()
    {
        TakesADelegate(new MyDelegate(DelegateFunction));
    }

    public static void TakesADelegate(MyDelegate SomeFunction)
    {
        SomeFunction(21);
    }

    public static void DelegateFunction(int i)
    {
        System.Console.WriteLine("Called by delegate with number: {0}.", i);
    }
}
```

Output

```
Called by delegate with number: 21.
```

Example 2

In the following example, one delegate is mapped to both static and instance methods and returns specific information from each.

```
// keyword_delegate2.cs
// Calling both static and instance methods from delegates
using System;

// delegate declaration
delegate void MyDelegate();

public class MyClass
{
    public void InstanceMethod()
    {
        Console.WriteLine("A message from the instance method.");
    }
```

```
    static public void StaticMethod()
    {
        Console.WriteLine("A message from the static method.");
    }
}

public class MainClass
{
    static public void Main()
    {
        MyClass p = new MyClass();

        // Map the delegate to the instance method:
        MyDelegate d = new MyDelegate(p.InstanceMethod);
        d();

        // Map to the static method:
        d = new MyDelegate(MyClass.StaticMethod);
        d();
    }
}
```

Output

```
A message from the instance method.
A message from the static method.
```

See Also

Delegates Tutorial (pg. 321)

interface

An interface defines a contract. A class or struct that implements an interface must adhere to its contract. An interface may inherit from multiple base interfaces, and a class or struct may implement multiple interfaces.

Interfaces can contain methods, properties, events, and indexers. The interface itself does not provide implementations for the members that it defines. The interface merely specifies the members that must be supplied by classes or interfaces that implement the interface.

The **interface** keyword declares a reference type that has abstract members. The interface declaration takes the form:

```
[attributes] [modifiers] interface identifier [:base-list] {interface-body}[;]
```

where:

attributes (Optional)

Additional declarative information. For more information on attributes and attribute classes, see "Attributes" on page 211.

modifiers (Optional)

    The allowed modifiers are new and the four access modifiers.

identifier

    The interface name.

base-list (Optional)

    A list that contains one or more explicit base interfaces separated by commas.

interface-body

    Declarations of the interface members.

Remarks

An interface can be a member of a namespace or a class and can contain signatures of the following members:

- Methods
- Properties
- Indexers

An interface can inherit from one or more base interfaces. In the following example, the interface IMyInterface inherits from two base interfaces, IBase1 and IBase2:

```
interface IMyInterface: IBase1, IBase2
{
    void MethodA();
    void MethodB();
}
```

Interfaces can be implemented by classes. The identifier of the implemented interface appears in the class base list. For example:

```
class Class1: Iface1, Iface2
{
    // class members
}
```

When a class base list contains a base class and interfaces, the base class comes first in the list. For example:

```
class ClassA: BaseClass, Iface1, Iface2
{
    // class members
}
```

For more information on properties and indexers, see "Property Declaration" on page 284 and "Indexer Declaration" on page 273.

Example

The following example demonstrates interface implementation. In this example, the interface
IPoint contains the property declaration, which is responsible for setting and getting the values
of the fields. The class MyPoint contains the property implementation.

```
// keyword_interface.cs
// Interface implementation
using System;
interface IPoint
{
   // Property signatures:
   int x
   {
      get;
      set;
   }

   int y
   {
      get;
      set;
   }
}

class MyPoint : IPoint
{
   // Fields:
   private int myX;
   private int myY;

   // Constructor:
   public MyPoint(int x, int y)
   {
      myX = x;
      myY = y;
   }

   // Property implementation:
   public int x
   {
      get
      {
         return myX;
      }
```

(continued)

(continued)

```csharp
         set
         {
            myX = value;
         }
      }

      public int y
      {
         get
         {
            return myY;
         }
         set
         {
            myY = value;
         }
      }
   }

class MainClass
{
   private static void PrintPoint(IPoint p)
   {
      Console.WriteLine("x={0}, y={1}", p.x, p.y);
   }

   public static void Main()
   {
      MyPoint p = new MyPoint(2,3);
      Console.Write("My Point: ");
      PrintPoint(p);
   }
}
```

Output

```
My Point: x=2, y=3
```

See Also

Properties (pg. 283), Indexers (pg. 272), class (pg. 149), struct (pg. 138)

object

The **object** type is based on **System.Object** in the .NET Framework. You can assign values of any type to variables of type **object**.

All data types, predefined and user-defined, inherit from the **System.Object** class. The **object** data type is the type to and from which objects are boxed.

Example

The following sample shows how variables of type **object** can accept values of any data type and how variables of type **object** can use methods on **System.Object** from the .NET Framework.

```
// keyword_object.cs
using System;
public class MyClass1
{
    public int i = 10;
}

public class MyClass2
{
    public static void Main()
    {
        object a;
        a = 1;    // an example of boxing
        Console.WriteLine(a);
        Console.WriteLine(a.GetType());
        Console.WriteLine(a.ToString());
        Console.WriteLine();

        a = new MyClass1 ();
        MyClass1 ref_MyClass1;
        ref_MyClass1 = (MyClass1)a;
        Console.WriteLine(ref_MyClass1.i);
    }
}
```

Output

```
1
System.Int32
1

10
```

See Also

Value Types (pg. 121)

string

The **string** type represents a string of Unicode characters. **string** is an alias for System.String in the .NET Framework.

Although **string** is a reference type, the equality operators (== and !=) are defined to compare the *values* of **string** objects, not references. This makes testing for string equality more intuitive.

```
string a = "hello";
string b = "h";
b += "ello"; // append to b
Console.WriteLine( a == b );             // output: True -- same value
Console.WriteLine( (object)a == b );  // False -- different objects
```

The + operator concatenates strings:

```
string a = "good " + "morning";
```

The [] operator accesses individual characters of a **string**:

```
char x = "test"[2];   // x = 's';
```

String literals are of type **string** and can be written in two forms, quoted and @-quoted. Quoted string literals are enclosed in double quotation marks (" "):

```
"good morning"  // a string literal
```

and can contain any character literal, including escape sequences:

```
string a = "\\\u0066\n";  // backslash, letter f, new line
```

> **Note** The escape code \u*dddd* (where *dddd* is a four-digit number) represents the Unicode character U+*dddd*. Eight-digit Unicode escape codes are also recognized: \u*dddd*\u*dddd*.

@-quoted string literals start with @ and are enclosed in double quotation marks. For example:

```
@"good morning"  // a string literal
```

The advantage of @-quoting is that escape sequences are *not* processed, which makes it easy to write, for example, a fully qualified file name:

```
@"c:\Docs\Source\a.txt"  // rather than "c:\\Docs\\Source\\a.txt"
```

To include a double quotation mark in an @-quoted string, double it:

```
@"""Ahoy!""" cried the captain." // "Ahoy!" cried the captain.
```

Another use of the @ symbol is to use referenced (/reference) identifiers that happen to be C# keywords.

Example

```
// keyword_string.cs
using System;
class test
{
    public static void Main( String[] args )
    {
        string a = "\u0068ello ";
        string b = "world";
        Console.WriteLine( a + b );
        Console.WriteLine( a + b == "hello world" );
    }
}
```

Output

```
hello world
True
```

See Also

Value Types (pg. 121)

void

When used as the return type for a method, **void** specifies that the method does not return a value.

void is not allowed in a method's parameter list. A method that takes no parameters and returns no value is declared as follows:

```
void MyMethod();
```

See Also

Value Types (pg. 121)

Types Reference Tables

The following reference tables summarize the C# types:

- Built-in types
- Integral types
- Floating-point types
- Default values
- Value types
- Implicit numeric conversions
- Explicit numeric conversions

For information on formatting the output of numeric types, see "Formatting Numeric Results Table" on page 168.

See Also

Reference Types (pg. 149), Value Types (pg. 121)

Built-in Types Table

The following table shows the keywords for built-in C# types, which are aliases of predefined types in the **System** namespace.

C# Type	.NET Framework type
bool	**System.Boolean**
byte	**System.Byte**
sbyte	**System.SByte**
char	**System.Char**
decimal	**System.Decimal**
double	**System.Double**
float	**System.Single**
int	**System.Int32**
uint	**System.UInt32**
long	**System.Int64**
ulong	**System.UInt64**
object	**System.Object**
short	**System.Int16**
ushort	**System.UInt16**
string	**System.String**

Remarks

All of the types in the table, except **object** and **string**, are referred to as simple types.

The C# type keywords and their aliases are interchangeable. For example, you can declare an integer variable by using either of the following declarations:

```
int x = 123;
System.Int32 x = 123;
```

To display the actual type for any C# type use the system method `GetType()`. For example, the following statement displays the system alias that represents the type of `myVariable`:

```
Console.WriteLine(myVariable.GetType());
```

You can also use the typeof operator

See Also

Value Types (pg. 121), Default Values Table (pg. 164), Formatting Numeric Results Table (pg. 168), Types Reference Tables (pg. 161)

Integral Types Table

The following table shows the sizes and ranges of the integral types, which constitute a subset of simple types.

Type	Range	Size
sbyte	−128 to 127	Signed 8-bit integer
byte	0 to 255	Unsigned 8-bit integer
char	U+0000 to U+ffff	Unicode 16-bit character
short	−32,768 to 32,767	Signed 16-bit integer
ushort	0 to 65,535	Unsigned 16-bit integer
int	−2,147,483,648 to 2,147,483,647	Signed 32-bit integer
uint	0 to 4,294,967,295	Unsigned 32-bit integer
long	−9,223,372,036,854,775,808 to 9,223,372,036,854,775,807	Signed 64-bit integer
ulong	0 to 18,446,744,073,709,551,615	Unsigned 64-bit integer

Remarks

If the value represented by an integer literal exceeds the range of **ulong**, a compilation error will occur.

See Also

Built-in Types Table (pg. 162), Floating-Point Types Table (pg. 164), Default Values Table (pg. 164), Formatting Numeric Results Table (pg. 168)

Floating-Point Types Table

The following table shows the precision and approximate ranges for the floating-point types.

Type	Approximate range	Precision
float	$\pm1.5 \times 10^{-45}$ to $\pm3.4 \times 10^{38}$	7 digits
double	$\pm5.0 \times 10^{-324}$ to $\pm1.7 \times 10^{308}$	15–16 digits

See Also

Default Values Table (pg. 164), Built-in Types Table (pg. 162), Integral Types Table (pg. 163), Formatting Numeric Results Table (pg. 168), decimal (pg. 126)

Default Values Table

The following table shows the default values of value types returned by the default constructors. Default constructors are invoked by using the **new** operator, for example:

```
int myInt = new int();
```

The preceding statement has the same effect as the following statement:

```
int myInt = 0;
```

Remember that using uninitialized variables in C# is not allowed.

Value type	Default value
bool	**false**
byte	0
char	'\0'
decimal	0.0M
double	0.0D
enum	The value produced by the expression (E)0, where E is the enum identifier.
float	0.0F
int	0
long	0L
sbyte	0
short	0

Value type	Default value
struct	The value produced by setting all value-type fields to their default values and all reference-type fields to **null**.
uint	0
ulong	0
ushort	0

See Also

Value Types (pg. 121), Built-in Types Table (pg. 162)

Value Types Table

The following table lists the C# value types by category.

Value type	Category
bool	Boolean
byte	Unsigned, numeric, integral
char	Unsigned, numeric, integral
decimal	Numeric, decimal
double	Numeric, floating-point
enum	Enumeration
float	Numeric, floating-point
int	Signed, numeric, integral
long	Signed, numeric, integral
sbyte	Signed, numeric, integral
short	Signed, numeric, integral
struct	User-defined structure
uint	Unsigned, numeric, integral
ulong	Unsigned, numeric, integral
ushort	Unsigned, numeric, integral

See Also

Value Types (pg. 121), Formatting Numeric Results Table (pg. 168)

Implicit Numeric Conversions Table

The following table shows the predefined implicit numeric conversions. Implicit conversions might occur in many situations, including method invoking and assignment statements.

From	To
sbyte	**short**, **int**, **long**, **float**, **double**, or **decimal**
byte	**short**, **ushort**, **int**, **uint**, **long**, **ulong**, **float**, **double**, or **decimal**
short	**int**, **long**, **float**, **double**, or **decimal**
ushort	**int**, **uint**, **long**, **ulong**, **float**, **double**, or **decimal**
int	**long**, **float**, **double**, or **decimal**
uint	**long**, **ulong**, **float**, **double**, or **decimal**
long	**float**, **double**, or **decimal**
char	**ushort**, **int**, **uint**, **long**, **ulong**, **float**, **double**, or **decimal**
float	**double**
ulong	**float**, **double**, or **decimal**

Remarks

- The conversions from **int**, **uint**, or **long** to **float** and from **long** to **double** may cause a loss of precision, but not a loss of magnitude.

- There are no implicit conversions to the **char** type.

- There are no implicit conversions between floating-point types and the **decimal** type.

- A constant expression of type **int** can be converted to **sbyte**, **byte**, **short**, **ushort**, **uint**, or **ulong**, provided the value of the constant expression is within the range of the destination type.

For more information on implicit conversion, see the section "implicit" on page 11.

See Also

Integral Types Table (pg. 163), Built-in Types Table (pg. 162), Explicit Numeric Conversions Table (pg. 167)

Explicit Numeric Conversions Table

Explicit numeric conversion is used to convert any numeric type to any other numeric type, for which there is no implicit conversion, by using a cast expression. The following table shows these conversions.

From	To
sbyte	**byte**, **ushort**, **uint**, **ulong**, or **char**
byte	**sbyte** or **char**
short	**sbyte**, **byte**, **ushort**, **uint**, **ulong**, or **char**
ushort	**sbyte**, **byte**, **short**, or **char**
int	**sbyte**, **byte**, **short**, **ushort**, **uint**, **ulong**, or **char**
uint	**sbyte**, **byte**, **short**, **ushort**, **int**, or **char**
long	**sbyte**, **byte**, **short**, **ushort**, **int**, **uint**, **ulong**, or **char**
ulong	**sbyte**, **byte**, **short**, **ushort**, **int**, **uint**, **long**, or **char**
char	**sbyte**, **byte**, or **short**
float	**sbyte**, **byte**, **short**, **ushort**, **int**, **uint**, **long**, **ulong**, **char**, or **decimal**
double	**sbyte**, **byte**, **short**, **ushort**, **int**, **uint**, **long**, **ulong**, **char**, **float**, or **decimal**
decimal	**sbyte**, **byte**, **short**, **ushort**, **int**, **uint**, **long**, **ulong**, **char**, **float**, or **double**

Remarks

- The explicit numeric conversion may cause loss of precision or result in throwing exceptions.
- When you convert a **float**, **double**, or **decimal** value to an integral type, this value is rounded towards zero to the nearest integral value. If the resulting integral value is outside the range of the destination type, an **InvalidCastException** is thrown.
- When you convert **double** to **float**, the **double** value is rounded to the nearest **float** value. If the **double** value is too small or too large to fit into the destination type, the result will be zero or infinity.
- When you convert **float** or **double** to **decimal**, the source value is converted to **decimal** representation and rounded to the nearest number after the 28th decimal place if required. Depending on the value of the source value, one of the following results may occur:
  - If the source value is too small to be represented as a **decimal**, the result becomes zero.
  - If the source value is NaN (not a number), infinity, or too large to be represented as a **decimal**, an **InvalidCastException** is thrown.
- When you convert **decimal** to **float** or **double**, the **decimal** value is rounded to the nearest **double** or **float** value.

For more information on explicit conversion, see the section "explicit" on page 9.

See Also

Integral Types Table (pg. 163), Built-in Types Table (pg. 162), Implicit Numeric Conversions Table (pg. 166)

Formatting Numeric Results Table

You can format numeric results by using the **String.Format** method, or through the **Console.Write** method, which calls **String.Format**. The format is specified using format strings. The following table contains the supported standard format strings. The format string takes the form *Axx*, where *A* is the *format specifier* and *xx* is the *precision specifier*. The format specifier controls the type of formatting applied to the numerical value, and the precision specifier controls the number of significant digits or decimal places of the formatted output.

Character	Description	Examples	Output
C or c	Currency	Console.Write("{0:C}", 2.5); Console.Write("{0:C}", –2.5);	$2.50 ($2.50)
D or d	Decimal	Console.Write("{0:D5}", 25);	00025
E or e	Scientific	Console.Write("{0:E}", 250000);	2.500000E+005
F or f	Fixed-point	Console.Write("{0:F2}", 25); Console.Write("{0:F0}", 25);	25.00 25
G or g	General	Console.Write("{0:G}", 2.5);	2.5
N or n	Number	Console.Write("{0:N}", 2500000);	2,500,000.00
X or x	Hexadecimal	Console.Write("{0:X}", 250); Console.Write("{0:X}", 0xffff);	FA FFFF

See Also

string (pg. 160)

PART 3

C# Features

Operators

C# provides a large set of operators, which are symbols that specify which operations to perform in an expression. C# predefines the usual arithmetic and logical operators, as well as a variety of others as shown in the following table. In addition, many operators can be overloaded by the user, thus changing their meaning when applied to a user-defined type.

Operator category	Operators
Arithmetic	+ - * / %
Logical (boolean and bitwise)	& | ^ ! ~ && || true false
String concatenation	+
Increment, decrement	++ --
Shift	<< >>
Relational	== != < > <= >=
Assignment	= += -= *= /= %= &= |= ^= <<= >>=
Member access	.
Indexing	[]
Cast	()
Conditional	?:
Delegate concatenation and removal	+ -
Object creation	new
Type information	is sizeof typeof
Overflow exception control	checked unchecked
Indirection and Address	* -> [] &

Arithmetic Overflow

The arithmetic operators (+, -, *, /) can produce results that are outside the range of possible values for the numeric type involved. You should refer to the *C# Language Reference* section on a particular operator for details, but in general:

- Integer arithmetic overflow either throws an OverflowException or discards the most significant bits of the result (see below). Integer division by zero always throws a DivideByZeroException.

- Floating-point arithmetic overflow or division by zero never throws an exception, because floating-point types are based on IEEE 754 and so have provisions for representing infinity and NaN (Not a Number).

- Decimal arithmetic overflow always throws an OverflowException. **Decimal** division by zero always throws a DivideByZeroException.

When integer overflow occurs, what happens depends on the execution context, which can be checked or unchecked. In a checked context, an OverflowException is thrown. In an unchecked context, the most significant bits of the result are discarded and execution continues. Thus, C# gives you the choice of handling or ignoring overflow.

In addition to the arithmetic operators, integral-type to integral-type casts can cause overflow (for example, casting a long to an int) and are subject to checked or unchecked execution. Also note that bitwise operators and shift operators never cause overflow.

See Also

Overloadable Operators (pg. 170), C# Keywords (pg. 3)

Overloadable Operators

C# allows user-defined types to overload operators by defining static member functions using the operator keyword. Not all operators can be overloaded, however, and others have restrictions, as listed in this table:

Operators	Overloadability
+, -, !, ~, ++, --, true, false	These unary operators can be overloaded.
+, -, *, /, %, &, |, ^, <<, >>	These binary operators can be overloaded.
==, !=, <, >, <=, >=	The comparison operators can be overloaded (but see note below).
&&, ||	The conditional logical operators cannot be overloaded, but they are evaluated using **&** and **|**, which can be overloaded.
[]	The array indexing operator cannot be overloaded, but you can define indexers.

Operators	Overloadability
()	The cast operator cannot be overloaded, but you can define new conversion operators (see the sections "explicit" on page 9 and "implicit" on page 11.
+=, -=, *=, /=, %=, &=, |=, ^=, <<=, >>=	Assignment operators cannot be overloaded, but +=, for example, is evaluated using +, which can be overloaded.
=, ., ?:, ->, new, is, sizeof, typeof	These operators cannot be overloaded.

Note   The comparison operators, if overloaded, must be overloaded in pairs; that is, if == is overloaded, != must also be overloaded. The reverse is also true, and similar for < and >, and for <= and >=.

[] Operator

Square brackets ([]) are used for arrays, indexers, and attributes. They can also be used with pointers.

```
type []
array [ indexexpr ]
```

Where:

type
   A type.

array
   An array.

indexexpr
   An index expression.

Remarks

An array type is a type followed by []:

```
int[] fib; // fib is of type int[], "array of int"
fib = new int[100]; // create a 100-element int array
```

To access an element of an array, the index of the desired element is enclosed in brackets:

```
fib[0] = fib[1] = 1;
for( int i=2; i<100; ++i ) fib[i] = fib[i-1] + fib[i-2];
```

An exception is thrown if an array index is out of range.

The array indexing operator cannot be overloaded; however, types can define indexers, properties that take one or more parameters. Indexer parameters are enclosed in square brackets, just like array indices, but indexer parameters can be declared to be of any type (unlike array indices, which must be integral).

For example, the .NET Framework defines a Hashtable type which associates keys and values of arbitrary type:

```
Collections.Hashtable h =  new Collections.Hashtable();
h["a"] = 123; // note: using a string as the index
```

Square brackets are also used to specify attributes:

```
[attribute(AllowMultiple=true)]
public class Attr {
}
```

You can use square brackets to index off a pointer:

```
unsafe fixed ( int* p = fib )   // p points to fib from earlier example
{
    p[0] = p[1] = 1;
    for( int i=2; i<100; ++i ) p[i] = p[i-1] + p[i-2];
}
```

No bounds checking is performed.

See Also

Arrays (pg. 248), Indexers (pg. 272), unsafe (pg. 50), fixed (pg. 116)

() Operator

In addition to being used to specify the order of operations in an expression, parentheses are used to specify casts (type conversions):

```
( type ) expr
```

Where:

type
> The name of the type to which *expr* is to be converted.

expr
> An expression.

Remarks

A cast explicitly invokes the conversion operator from *expr*'s type to *type*; the cast will fail if no such conversion operator is defined. To define a conversion operator, see the sections "explicit" on page 9 and "implicit" on page 11.

Example

The following program casts a **double** to an **int**. The program won't compile without the cast.

```
// cs_operator_parentheses.cs
using System;
class Test
{
   public static void Main()
   {
      double x = 1234.7;
      int a;
      a = (int)x; // cast double to int
      Console.WriteLine(a);
   }
}
```

Output

```
1234
```

. Operator

The dot operator is used for member access.

```
name1 . name2
```

Where:

name1
    A name.

name2
    A name.

Remarks

For example, consider the following class:

```
class Simple
{
   public int a;
   public void b()
   {
   }
}
Simple s = new Simple();
```

The variable s has two members, a and b; to access them, use the dot operator:

```
s.a = 6;    // assign to field a;
s.b();      // invoke member function b;
```

The dot is also used to form qualified names, names that specify the namespace or interface (for example) to which they belong.

```
System.Console.WriteLine("hello"); // class Console in namespace System
```

The using directive makes some name qualification optional:

```
using System;
...
System.Console.WriteLine("hello");
Console.WriteLine("hello");    // same thing
```

But when an identifier is ambiguous, it must be qualified:

```
using System;
using OtherSystem; // a namespace containing another Console class
...
System.Console.WriteLine( "hello" ); // must qualify Console
```

+ Operator

The + operator can function as either a unary or a binary operator.

```
+ expr

expr1 + expr2
```

Where:

expr
>   An expression.

expr1
>   An expression.

expr2
>   An expression.

Remarks

Unary + operators are predefined for all numeric types. The result of a unary + operation on a numeric type is simply the value of the operand.

Binary + operators are predefined for numeric and string types. For numeric types, + computes the sum of its two operands. When one or both operands are of type string, + concatenates the string representations of the operands.

Delegate types also provide a binary + operator, which performs delegate concatenation.

User-defined types can overload the unary + and binary + operators (see the section "operator" on page 12).

Example

```
// cs_operator_plus.cs
using System;
class Test
{
   public static void Main()
   {
      Console.WriteLine(+5);        // unary plus
      Console.WriteLine(5 + 5);     // addition
      Console.WriteLine(5 + .5);    // addition
      Console.WriteLine("5" + "5"); // string concatenation
      Console.WriteLine(5.0 + "5"); // string concatenation
      // note automatic conversion from double to string
   }
}
```

Output

```
5
10
5.5
55
55
```

- Operator

The - operator can function as either a unary or a binary operator.

```
- expr
expr1 - expr2
```

Where:

expr
> An expression.

expr1
> An expression.

expr2
> An expression.

Remarks

Unary - operators are predefined for all numeric types. The result of a unary - operation on a numeric type is the negation of the operand.

Binary - operators are predefined for all numeric and enumeration types to subtract the second operand from the first.

Delegate types also provide a binary - operator, which performs delegate removal.

User-defined types can overload the unary - and binary - operators (see the section "operator" on page 12).

Example

```
// cs_operator_minus.cs
using System;
class Test
{
    public static void Main()
    {
        int a = 5;
        Console.WriteLine(-a);
        Console.WriteLine(a - 1);
        Console.WriteLine(a - .5);
    }
}
```

Output

```
-5
4
4.5
```

* Operator

The multiplication operator (*) computes the product of its operands. All numeric types have predefined multiplication operators.

```
expr1 * expr2
```

Where:

expr1
    An expression.

expr2
    An expression.

Remarks

The * operator is also used to declare pointer types and to dereference pointers.

User-defined types can overload the * operator (see the section "operator" on page 12).

Example

```
// cs_operator_mult.cs
using System;
class Test
{
   public static void Main()
   {
      Console.WriteLine(5 * 2);
      Console.WriteLine(-.5 * .2);
      Console.WriteLine(-.5m * .2m); // decimal type
   }
}
```

Output

```
10
-0.1
-0.1
```

/ Operator

The division operator (/) divides its first operand by its second. All numeric types have predefined division operators.

> *expr1* **/** *expr2*

Where:

expr1
   An expression.

expr2
   An expression.

Remarks

User-defined types can overload the / operator (see the section "operator" on page 12).

Example

```
// cs_operator_division.cs
using System;
class Test
{
   public static void Main()
   {
      Console.WriteLine(-5/2);
      Console.WriteLine(-5.0/2);
   }
}
```

Output

```
-2
-2.5
```

% Operator

The modulus operator (%) computes the remainder after dividing its first operand by its second. All numeric types have predefined modulus operators.

```
expr1 % expr2
```

Where:

expr1
    An expression.

expr2
    An expression.

Remarks

User-defined types can overload the % operator (see the section "operator" on page 12).

Example

```
// cs_operator_modulus.cs
using System;
class Test
{
    public static void Main()
    {
        Console.WriteLine(5 % 2);       // int
        Console.WriteLine(-5 % 2);      // int
        Console.WriteLine(5.0 % 2.2);   // double
        Console.WriteLine(5.0m % 2.2m); // decimal
        Console.WriteLine(-5.2 % 2.0);  // double
    }
}
```

Output

```
1
-1
0.6
0.6
-1.2
```

Note the round-off errors associated with the double type.

& Operator

The & operator can function as either a unary or a binary operator.

```
& expr
expr1 & expr2
```

Where:

expr
>   An expression.

expr1
>   An expression.

expr2
>   An expression.

Remarks

The unary & operator returns the address of its operand (requires unsafe context).

Binary & operators are predefined for the integral types and **bool**. For integral types, & computes the bitwise AND of its operands. For **bool** operands, & computes the logical AND of its operands; that is, the result is **true** if and only if both its operands are **true**.

User-defined types can overload the binary & operator (see the section "operator" on page 12).

Example

```
// cs_operator_ampersand.cs
using System;
class Test
{
   public static void Main()
   {
      Console.WriteLine(true & false); // logical and
      Console.WriteLine(true & true);  // logical and
      Console.WriteLine("0x{0:x}", 0xf8 & 0x3f);  // bitwise and
   }
}
```

Output

```
False
True
0x38
```

| Operator

Binary | operators are predefined for the integral types and **bool**. For integral types, | computes the bitwise OR of its operands. For **bool** operands, | computes the logical OR of its operands; that is, the result is **false** if and only if both its operands are **false**.

```
expr1 | expr2
```

Where:

expr1
    An expression.

expr2
    An expression.

Remarks

User-defined types can overload the | operator (see the section "operator" on page 12).

Example

```
// cs_operator_OR.cs
using System;
class Test
{
   public static void Main()
   {
      Console.WriteLine(true | false);  // logical or
      Console.WriteLine(false | false); // logical or
      Console.WriteLine("0x{0:x}", 0xf8 | 0x3f);   // bitwise or
   }
}
```

Output

```
True
False
0xff
```

^ Operator

Binary ^ operators are predefined for the integral types and **bool**. For integral types, ^ computes the bitwise exclusive-OR of its operands. For **bool** operands, ^ computes the logical exclusive-or of its operands; that is, the result is **true** if and only if exactly one of its operands is **true**.

```
expr1 ^ expr2
```

Where:

expr1
    An expression.

expr2
    An expression.

Remarks

User-defined types can overload the ^ operator (see the section "operator" on page 12).

Example

```
// cs_operator_bitwise_OR.cs
using System;
class Test
{
    public static void Main()
    {
        Console.WriteLine(true ^ false);  // logical exclusive-or
        Console.WriteLine(false ^ false); // logical exclusive-or
        Console.WriteLine("0x{0:x}", 0xf8 ^ 0x3f);   // bitwise exclusive-or
    }
}
```

Output

```
True
False
0xc7
```

! Operator

The logical negation operator (!) is a unary operator that negates its operand. It is defined for **bool** and returns **true** if and only if its operand is **false**.

```
! expr
```

Where:

expr
>   An expression.

Remarks

User-defined types can overload the ! operator (see the section "operator" on page 12).

Example

```
// cs_operator_negation.cs
using System;
class Test
{
    public static void Main()
{
        Console.WriteLine(!true);
        Console.WriteLine(!false);
    }
}
```

Output

```
False
True
```

~ **Operator**

The ~ operator performs a bitwise complement operation on its operand. Bitwise complement operators are predefined for **int**, **uint**, **long**, and **ulong**.

```
~ expr
```

Where:

expr
    An expression.

Remarks

User-defined types can overload the ~ operator (see the section "operator" on page 12).

Example

```
// cs_operator_bitwise_compl.cs
using System;
class Test
{
    public static void Main()
    {
        Console.WriteLine("!0x{0:x8} = 0x{1:x8}", 8, ~8);
        Console.WriteLine("!0x{0:x8} = 0x{1:x8}", -8, ~-8);
    }
}
```

Output

```
!0x00000008 = 0xfffffff7
!0xfffffff8 = 0x00000007
```

= Operator

The assignment operator (=) stores the value of its right-hand operand in the storage location, property, or indexer denoted by its left-hand operand and returns the value as its result. The operands must be of the same type (or the right-hand operand must be implicitly convertible to the type of the left-hand operand).

```
lhs = expr
```

Where:

lhs

  A storage location, property, or indexer.

expr

  An expression.

Remarks

The assignment operator cannot be overloaded.

Example

```
// cs_operator_assignment.cs
using System;
class Test
{
    public static void Main()
    {
        double x;
        int i;
        i = 5; // int to int assignment
        x = i; // implicit conversion from int to double
        i = (int)x; // needs cast
        Console.WriteLine("i is {0}, x is {1}", i, x);
        object obj = i;
        Console.WriteLine("boxed value = {0}, type is {1}",
            obj, obj.GetType());
        i = (int)obj;
        Console.WriteLine("unboxed: {0}", i);
    }
}
```

Output

```
i is 5, x is 5
boxed value = 5, type is System.Int32
unboxed: 5
```

< Operator

All numeric and enumeration types define a "less than" relational operator (<) that returns **true** if the first operand is less than the second, **false** otherwise.

```
expr1 < expr2
```

Where:

expr1
   An expression.

expr2
   An expression.

Remarks

User-defined types can overload the < operator (see the section "operator" on page 12). If < is overloaded, > must also be overloaded.

Example

```
// cs_operator_less_than.cs
using System;
class Test
{
   public static void Main()
   {
      Console.WriteLine(1 < 1.1);
      Console.WriteLine(1.1 < 1.1);
   }
}
```

Output

```
True
False
```

> Operator

All numeric and enumeration types define a "greater than" relational operator (>) that returns **true** if the first operand is greater than the second, **false** otherwise.

```
expr1 > expr2
```

Where:

expr1
    An expression.

expr2
    An expression.

Remarks

User-defined types can overload the > operator (see the section "operator" on page 12). If > is overloaded, < must also be overloaded.

Example

```
// cs_operator_greater_than.cs
using System;
class Test
{
    public static void Main()
    {
        Console.WriteLine(1.1 > 1);
        Console.WriteLine(1.1 > 1.1);
    }
}
```

Output

```
True
False
```

?: Operator

The conditional operator (?:) returns one of two values depending on a third value. The conditional operator is used in an expression of the following form:

```
cond-expr ? expr1 : expr2
```

Where:

cond-expr
    An expression of type **bool**.

expr1
    An expression.

expr2
    An expression.

Remarks

If *cond-expr* is **true**, *expr1* is evaluated and becomes the result; if *cond-expr* is **false**, *expr2* is evaluated and becomes the result. Only one of *expr1* and *expr2* is ever evaluated.

Calculations that might otherwise require an if-else construction can be expressed more concisely and elegantly with the conditional operator. For example, to avoid a division by zero in the calculation of the sinc function you could write either

```
if(x != 0.0) s = Math.Sin(x)/x; else s = 1.0;
```

or, using the conditional operator,

```
s = x != 0.0 ? Math.Sin(x)/x : 1.0;
```

The conditional operator is right-associative, so an expression of the form

```
a ? b : c ? d : e
```

is evaluated as

```
a ? b : (c ? d : e)
```

not

```
(a ? b : c) ? d : e
```

The conditional operator cannot be overloaded.

Example

```
// cs_operator_conditional.cs
using System;
class Test
{
    public static double sinc(double x)
    {
        return x != 0.0 ? Math.Sin(x)/x : 1.0;
    }

    public static void Main()
    {
        Console.WriteLine(sinc(0.2));
        Console.WriteLine(sinc(0.1));
        Console.WriteLine(sinc(0.0));
    }
}
```

Output

```
0.993346653975306
0.998334166468282
1
```

++ Operator

The increment operator (++) increments its operand by 1. The increment operator can appear before or after its operand:

```
++ var
var ++
```

Where:

var

    An expression that denotes a storage location or a property or an indexer.

Remarks

The first form is a prefix increment operation. The result of the operation is the value of the operand after it has been incremented.

The second form is a postfix increment operation. The result of the operation is the value of the operand *before* it has been incremented.

Numeric and enumeration types have predefined increment operators. User-defined types can overload the ++ operator (see the section "operator" on page 12).

Example

```
// cs_operator_increment.cs
using System;
class Test
{
   public static void Main()
   {
      double x;
      x = 1.5;
      Console.WriteLine(++x);
      x = 1.5;
      Console.WriteLine(x++);
      Console.WriteLine(x);
   }
}
```

Output

```
2.5
1.5
2.5
```

-- Operator

The decrement operator (--) decrements its operand by 1. The decrement operator can appear before or after its operand:

```
-- var
var --
```

Where:

var
>   An expression that denotes a storage location or a property or an indexer.

Remarks

The first form is a prefix decrement operation. The result of the operation is the value of the operand *after* it has been decremented.

The second form is a postfix decrement operation. The result of the operation is the value of the operand *before* it has been decremented.

Numeric and enumeration types have predefined decrement operators. User-defined types can overload the -- operator (see the section "operator" on page 12).

Example

```
// cs_operator_decrement.cs
using System;
class Test
{
    public static void Main()
    {
        double x;
        x = 1.5;
        Console.WriteLine(--x);
        x = 1.5;
        Console.WriteLine(x--);
        Console.WriteLine(x);
    }
}
```

Output

```
0.5
1.5
0.5
```

&& Operator

The conditional-AND operator (&&) performs a logical-AND of its bool operands, but only evaluates its second operand if necessary.

```
expr1 && expr2
```

Where:

expr1
    An expression.

expr2
    An expression.

Remarks

The operation

```
x && y
```

corresponds to the operation

```
x & y
```

except that if x is false, y is not evaluated (because the result of the AND operation is false no matter what the value of y may be). This is known as "short-circuit" evaluation.

The conditional-AND operator cannot be overloaded, but overloads of the regular logical operators and operators true and false are, with certain restrictions, also considered overloads of the conditional logical operators.

Example

In the following example, observe that the expression using && evaluates only the first operand.

```
// cs_operator_logical_and.cs
using System;
class Test
{
    static bool fn1()
    {
        Console.WriteLine("fn1 called");
        return false;
    }

    static bool fn2()
    {
        Console.WriteLine("fn2 called");
        return true;
    }

    public static void Main()
    {
        Console.WriteLine("regular AND:");
        Console.WriteLine("result is {0}", fn1() & fn2());
        Console.WriteLine("short-circuit AND:");
        Console.WriteLine("result is {0}", fn1() && fn2());
    }
}
```

Output

```
regular AND:
fn1 called
fn2 called
result is False
short-circuit AND:
fn1 called
result is False
```

|| Operator

The conditional-OR operator (||) performs a logical-OR of its bool operands, but only evaluates its second operand if necessary.

```
expr1 || expr2
```

Where:

expr1
   An expression.

expr2
   An expression.

Remarks

The operation

```
x || y
```

corresponds to the operation

```
x | y
```

except that if x is true, y is not evaluated (because the result of the OR operation is true no matter what the value of y might be). This is known as "short-circuit" evaluation.

The conditional-OR operator cannot be overloaded, but overloads of the regular logical operators and operators true and false are, with certain restrictions, also considered overloads of the conditional logical operators.

Example

In the following example, observe that the expression using || evaluates only the first operand.

```
// cs_operator_short_circuit_OR.cs
using System;
class Test
{
   static bool fn1()
   {
      Console.WriteLine("fn1 called");
      return true;
   }

   static bool fn2()
   {
      Console.WriteLine("fn2 called");
      return false;
   }
```

```
public static void Main()
{
    Console.WriteLine("regular OR:");
    Console.WriteLine("result is {0}", fn1() | fn2());
    Console.WriteLine("short-circuit OR:");
    Console.WriteLine("result is {0}", fn1() || fn2());
}
}
```

Output

```
regular OR:
fn1 called
fn2 called
result is True
short-circuit OR:
fn1 called
result is True
```

<< Operator

The left-shift operator (<<) shifts its first operand left by the number of bits specified by its second operand.

```
expr << count
```

Where:

expr
> An expression of type **int**, **uint**, **long**, or **ulong**; the value to be shifted.

count
> An expression of type **int**; the shift count.

Remarks

If *expr* is an **int** or **uint** (32-bit quantity), the shift count is given by the low-order five bits of *count* (*count* & 0x1f).

If *expr* is a **long** or **ulong** (64-bit quantity), the shift count is given by the low-order six bits of *count* (*count* & 0x3f).

The high-order bits of *expr* are discarded and the low-order empty bits are zero-filled. Shift operations never cause overflows.

User-defined types can overload the << operator (see the section "operator" on page 12); the type of the first operand must be the user-defined type, and the type of the second operand must be **int**.

Example

```
// cs_operator_left_shift.cs
using System;
class Test
{
   public static void Main()
   {
      int i = 1;
      long lg = 1;
      Console.WriteLine("0x{0:x}", i << 1);
      Console.WriteLine("0x{0:x}", i << 33);
      Console.WriteLine("0x{0:x}", lg << 33);
   }
}
```

Output

```
0x2
0x2
0x200000000
```

Note that i<<1 and i<<33 give the same result, because 1 and 33 have the same low-order five bits.

>> Operator

The right-shift operator (>>) shifts its first operand right by the number of bits specified by its second operand.

```
expr >> count
```

Where:

expr
   An expression of type **int**, **uint**, **long**, or **ulong**; the value to be shifted.

count
   An expression of type **int**; the shift count.

Remarks

If *expr* is an **int** or **uint** (32-bit quantity), the shift count is given by the low-order five bits of *count* (*count* & 0x1f).

If *expr* is a **long** or **ulong** (64-bit quantity), the shift count is given by the low-order six bits of *count* (*count* & 0x3f).

If *expr* is an **int** or **long**, the right-shift is an arithmetic shift (high-order empty bits are set to the sign bit). If *expr* is of type **uint** or **ulong**, the right-shift is a logical shift (high-order bits are zero-filled).

User-defined types can overload the >> operator (see the section "operator" on page 12); the type of the first operand must be the user-defined type, and the type of the second operand must be **int**.

Example

```
// cs_operator_right_shift.cs
using System;
class Test
{
    public static void Main()
    {
        int i = -1000;
        Console.WriteLine(i >> 3);
    }
}
```

Output

```
-125
```

== Operator

For predefined value types, the equality operator (==) returns true if the values of its operands are equal, false otherwise. For reference types other than **string**, == returns true if its two operands refer to the same object. For the **string** type, == compares the values of the strings.

```
expr1 == expr2
```

Where:

expr1
    An expression.

expr2
    An expression.

Remarks

User-defined value types can overload the == operator (see the section "operator" on page 12). So can user-defined reference types, although by default == behaves as described above for both predefined and user-defined reference types. If == is overloaded, != must also be overloaded.

Example

```
// cs_operator_equality.cs
using System;
class Test
{
    public static void Main()
    {
        // Numeric equality: True
        Console.WriteLine((2 + 2) == 4);

        // Reference equality: different objects, same boxed value: False
        object s = 1;
        object t = 1;
        Console.WriteLine(s == t);

        // Define some string
        string a = "hello";
        string b = String.Copy(a);
        string c = "hello";

        // compare string values for a constant and an instance: True
        Console.WriteLine(a == b);

        // compare string references;
        // a is a constant but b is an instance: False
        Console.WriteLine((object)a == (object)b);

        // compare string references, both constants have the same value,
        // so string interning points to same reference: True
        Console.WriteLine((object)a == (object)c);
    }
}
```

Output

```
True
False
True
False
True
```

!= Operator

The inequality operator (!=) returns false if its operands are equal, true otherwise. Inequality operators are predefined for all types, including string and object. User-defined types can overload the != operator.

```
expr1 != expr2
```

Where:

expr1
> An expression.

expr2
> An expression.

Remarks

For predefined value types, the inequality operator (!=) returns true if the values of its operands are different, false otherwise. For reference types other than **string**, != returns true if its two operands refer to different objects. For the **string** type, != compares the values of the strings.

User-defined value types can overload the != operator (see the section "operator" on page 12). So can user-defined reference types, although by default != behaves as described above for both predefined and user-defined reference types. If != is overloaded, == must also be overloaded.

Example

```
// cs_operator_inequality.cs
using System;
class Test
{
    public static void Main()
    {
        // Numeric inequality:
        Console.WriteLine((2 + 2) != 4);

        // Reference equality: two objects, same boxed value
        object s = 1;
        object t = 1;
        Console.WriteLine(s != t);

        // String equality: same string value, same string objects
        string a = "hello";
        string b = "hello";

        // compare string values
        Console.WriteLine(a != b);

        // compare string references
        Console.WriteLine((object)a != (object)b);
    }
}
```

Output

```
False
True
False
False
```

<= Operator

All numeric and enumeration types define a "less than or equal" relational operator (<=) that returns **true** if the first operand is less than or equal to the second, **false** otherwise.

```
expr1 <= expr2
```

Where:

expr1
    An expression.

expr2
    An expression.

Remarks

User-defined types can overload the <= operator (see the section "operator" on page 12). If <= is overloaded, >= must also be overloaded.

Example

```
// cs_operator_less_than_or_equal.cs
using System;
class Test
{
    public static void Main()
    {
        Console.WriteLine(1 <= 1.1);
        Console.WriteLine(1.1 <= 1.1);
    }
}
```

Output

```
True
True
```

>= Operator

All numeric and enumeration types define a "greater than or equal" relational operator (>=) that returns **true** if the first operand is greater than or equal to the second, **false** otherwise.

```
expr1 >= expr2
```

Where:

expr1
> An expression.

expr2
> An expression.

Remarks

User-defined types can overload the >= operator (see the section "operator" on page 12). If >= is overloaded, <= must also be overloaded.

Example

```
// cs_operator_greater_than_or_equal.cs
using System;
class Test
{
    public static void Main()
    {
        Console.WriteLine(1.1 >= 1);
        Console.WriteLine(1.1 >= 1.1);
    }
}
```

Output

```
True
True
```

+= Operator

The addition assignment operator.

```
lhs += expr
```

Where:

lhs
> A storage location, property, or indexer.

expr
> An expression.

Remarks

An expression using the += assignment operator, such as

```
x += y
```

is equivalent to

```
x = x + y
```

except that x is only evaluated once. The meaning of the + operator is dependent on the types of x and y (addition for numeric operands, concatenation for string operands, and so forth).

The += operator cannot be overloaded directly, but user-defined types can overload the + operator (see the section "operator" on page 12).

Example

```
// cs_operator_addition_assignment.cs
using System;
class Test
{
    public static void Main()
    {
        int a = 5;
        a += 6;
        Console.WriteLine(a);
        string s = "Micro";
        s += "soft";
        Console.WriteLine(s);
    }
}
```

Output

```
11
Microsoft
```

-= Operator

The subtraction assignment operator.

```
lhs -= expr
```

Where:

lhs
> A storage location, property, or indexer.

expr
> An expression.

Remarks

An expression using the -= assignment operator, such as

```
x -= y
```

is equivalent to

```
x = x - y
```

except that x is only evaluated once. The meaning of the - operator is dependent on the types of x and y (subtraction for numeric operands, delegate removal for delegate operands, and so forth).

The -= operator cannot be overloaded directly, but user-defined types can overload the - operator (see the section "operator" on page 12).

Example

```
// cs_operator_subtraction_assignment.cs
using System;
class Test
{
    public static void Main()
    {
        int a = 5;
        a -= 6;
        Console.WriteLine(a);
    }
}
```

Output

```
-1
```

*= Operator

The multiplication assignment operator.

```
lhs *= expr
```

Where:

lhs
> A storage location, property, or indexer.

expr
> An expression.

Remarks

An expression using the *= assignment operator, such as

```
x *= y
```

is equivalent to

```
x = x * y
```

except that x is only evaluated once. The * operator is predefined for numeric types to perform multiplication.

The *= operator cannot be overloaded directly, but user-defined types can overload the * operator (see the section "operator" on page 12).

Example

```
// cs_operator_multiplication_assignment.cs
using System;
class Test
{
    public static void Main()
    {
        int a = 5;
        a *= 6;
        Console.WriteLine(a);
    }
}
```

Output

```
30
```

/= Operator

The division assignment operator.

```
lhs /= expr
```

Where:

lhs
> A storage location, property, or indexer.

expr
> An expression.

Remarks

An expression using the /= assignment operator, such as

```
x /= y
```

is equivalent to

```
x = x / y
```

except that x is only evaluated once. The / operator is predefined for numeric types to perform division.

The /= operator cannot be overloaded directly, but user-defined types can overload the / operator (see the section "operator" on page 12).

Example

```
// cs_operator_division_assignment.cs
using System;
class Test
{
    public static void Main()
    {
        int a = 5;
        a /= 6;
        Console.WriteLine(a);
        double b = 5;
        b /= 6;
        Console.WriteLine(b);
    }
}
```

Output

```
0
0.833333333333333
```

%= Operator

The modulus assigment operator.

```
lhs %= expr
```

Where:

lhs
>   A storage location, property, or indexer.

expr
>   An expression.

Remarks

An expression using the %= assignment operator, such as

```
x %= y
```

is equivalent to

```
x = x % y
```

except that x is only evaluated once. The % operator is predefined for numeric types to compute the remainder after division.

The %= operator cannot be overloaded directly, but user-defined types can overload the % operator (see the section "operator" on page 12).

Example

```
// cs_operator_modulus_assignment.cs
using System;
class Test
{
    public static void Main()
    {
        int a = 5;
        a %= 3;
        Console.WriteLine(a);
    }
}
```

Output

```
2
```

&= Operator

The AND assignment operator.

```
lhs &= expr
```

Where:

lhs
>   A storage location, property, or indexer.

expr
>   An expression.

Remarks

An expression using the &= assignment operator, such as

```
x &= y
```

is equivalent to

```
x = x & y
```

except that x is only evaluated once. The & operator performs a bitwise AND operation on integral operands and logical AND on bool operands.

The &= operator cannot be overloaded directly, but user-defined types can overload the & operator (see the section "operator" on page 12).

Example

```
// cs_operator_and_assignment.cs
using System;
class Test
{
   public static void Main()
   {
      int a = 0x0c;
      a &= 0x06;
      Console.WriteLine("0x{0:x8}", a);
      bool b = true;
      b &= false;
      Console.WriteLine(b);
   }
}
```

Output

```
0x00000004
False
```

|= Operator

The OR assignment operator.

```
lhs |= expr
```

Where:

lhs
>   A storage location, property, or indexer.

expr
>   An expression.

Remarks

An expression using the |= assignment operator, such as

```
x |= y
```

is equivalent to

```
x = x | y
```

except that x is only evaluated once. The | operator performs a bitwise OR operation on integral operands and logical OR on bool operands.

The |= operator cannot be overloaded directly, but user-defined types can overload the | operator (see the section "operator" on page 12).

Example

```
// cs_operator_or_assignment.cs
using System;
class Test
{
    public static void Main()
    {
        int a = 0x0c;
        a |= 0x06;
        Console.WriteLine("0x{0:x8}", a);
        bool b = true;
        b |= false;
        Console.WriteLine(b);
    }
}
```

Output

```
0x0000000e
True
```

^= Operator

The exclusive-OR assignment operator.

```
lhs ^= expr
```

Where:

lhs
A storage location, property, or indexer.

expr
An expression.

Remarks

An expression of the form

```
x ^= y
```

is evaluated as

```
x = x ^ y
```

except that x is only evaluated once. The ^ operator performs a bitwise exclusive-OR operation on integral operands and logical exclusive-OR on bool operands.

The ^= operator cannot be overloaded directly, but user-defined types can overload the ^ operator (see the section "operator" on page 12).

Example

```
// cs_operator_xor_assignment.cs
using System;
class Test
{
    public static void Main()
    {
        int a = 0x0c;
        a ^= 0x06;
        Console.WriteLine("0x{0:x8}", a);
        bool b = true;
        b ^= false;
        Console.WriteLine(b);
    }
}
```

Output

```
0x0000000a
True
```

<<= Operator

The left-shift assignment operator.

```
lhs <<= expr
```

Where:

lhs
> A storage location, property, or indexer.

expr
> An expression.

Remarks

An expression of the form

```
x <<= y
```

is evaluated as

```
x = x << y
```

except that x is only evaluated once. The << operator shifts x left by an amount specified by y.

The <<= operator cannot be overloaded directly, but user-defined types can overload the << operator (see the section "operator" on page 12).

Example

```
// cs_operator_left_shift_assignment.cs
using System;
class Test
{
    public static void Main()
    {
        int a = 1000;
        a <<= 4;
        Console.WriteLine(a);
    }
}
```

Output

```
16000
```

>>= Operator

The right-shift assignment operator.

```
lhs >>= expr
```

Where:

lhs
> A storage location, property, or indexer.

expr
> An expression.

Remarks

An expression of the form

```
x >>= y
```

is evaluated as

```
x = x >> y
```

except that x is only evaluated once. The >> operator shifts x right by an amount specified by y.

The >>= operator cannot be overloaded directly, but user-defined types can overload the >> operator (see the section "operator" on page 12).

Example

```
// cs_operator_right_shift_assignment.cs
using System;
class Test
{
    public static void Main()
    {
        int a = 1000;
        a >>= 4;
        Console.WriteLine(a);
    }
}
```

Output

```
62
```

-> Operator

The -> operator combines pointer dereferencing and member access.

```
expr1 -> expr2
```

Where:

expr1
    A pointer expression.

expr2
    An expression.

Remarks

An expression of the form

```
x->y
```

(where x is a pointer of type T∗ and y is a member of T) is equivalent to

```
(*x).y
```

The -> operator can be used only in unmanaged code.

The -> operator cannot be overloaded.

Example

```
// cs_operator_dereferencing.cs
// compile with: /unsafe
using System;
struct Point
{
    public int x, y;
}

class Test
{
    public unsafe static void Main()
    {
        Point pt = new Point();
        Point* pp = &pt;
        pp->x = 123;
        pp->y = 456;
        Console.WriteLine ( "{0} {1}", pt.x, pt.y );
    }
}
```

Output

```
123 456
```

Attributes

This section contains an introduction to attributes and descriptions of the following reserved attributes.

AttributeUsage	Describes how a custom attribute class can be used.
Conditional	Marks a conditional method, a method whose execution depends on a specified preprocessing identifier.
Obsolete	Marks a program entity that should not be used.

See Also

Attributes Tutorial (pg. 222), Introduction to Attributes (pg. 211)

Introduction to Attributes

C# provides a mechanism for defining declarative tags, called attributes, which you can place on certain entities in your source code to specify additional information. The information that attributes contain can be retrieved at run time through reflection. You can use predefined attributes or you can define your own custom attributes. This section provides a general introduction to attributes in C#.

- Using Attributes

- Attribute Targets and Global Attributes

- Creating Custom Attributes

- Retrieving Attribute Information

See Also

Attributes Tutorial (pg. 222)

Using Attributes

Attributes can be placed on most any declaration (though a specific attribute might restrict the types of declarations on which it is valid). Syntactically, an attribute is specified by placing the name of the attribute, enclosed in square brackets, in front of the declaration of the entity to which it applies. For example, a class with the attribute **DllImport** is declared like this:

```
[DllImport] public class MyDllimportClass { ... }
```

Many attributes have parameters, which can be either positional (unnamed) or named. Any positional parameters must be specified in a certain order and cannot be omitted; named parameters are optional and can be specified in any order. Positional parameters are specified first. For example, these three attributes are equivalent:

```
[DllImport("user32.dll", SetLastError=false, ExactSpelling=false)]
[DllImport("user32.dll", ExactSpelling=false, SetLastError=false)]
[DllImport("user32.dll")]
```

The first parameter, the DLL name, is positional and always comes first; the others are named. In this case, both named parameters default to false, so they can be omitted (refer to the individual attribute's documentation for information on default parameter values).

More than one attribute can be placed on a declaration, either separately or within the same set of brackets:

```
bool AMethod([In][Out]ref double x);
bool AMethod([Out][In]ref double x);
bool AMethod([In,Out]ref double x);
```

Some attributes can be specified more than once for a given entity. An example of such a multiuse attribute is Conditional:

```
[Conditional("DEBUG"), Conditional("TEST1")] void TraceMethod() {...}
```

See Also

Introduction to Attributes (pg. 211), Attribute Targets (pg. 212), Global Attributes (pg. 214), Creating Custom Attributes (pg. 215), Retrieving Attribute Information (pg. 216)

Attribute Targets

In certain situations, the target of an attribute (that is, the entity to which the attribute applies) appears to be ambiguous. For example, in the following method declaration, the SomeAttr attribute could apply to the method or to the method's return value:

```
[SomeAttr] int Method1( string s )
```

This sort of situation arises frequently when marshaling. To resolve the ambiguity, C# has a set of default targets for each kind of declaration, which can be overridden by explicitly specifying attribute targets.

```
[method: SomeAttr] int Method1( string s ) // applies to method
[return: SomeAttr] int Method1( string s ) // applies to return value
[SomeAttr] int Method1( string s ) // default: applies to method
```

Note that this is independent of the targets on which SomeAttr is defined to be valid (see "AttributeUsage" on page 218); that is, even if SomeAttr were defined to apply only to return values, the **return** target would still have to be specified. In other words, the compiler will not use **AttributeUsage** information to resolve ambiguous attribute targets.

The syntax for attribute targets is as follows:

```
[target : attribute-list]
```

where:

target
   One of the following: assembly, field, event, method, module, param, property, return, type.

attribute-list
   A list of applicable attributes.

The table below lists all declarations where attributes are allowed; for each declaration, the possible targets for attributes on the declaration are listed in the second column. Targets in bold are the defaults.

Declaration	Possible targets
assembly	assembly
module	module
class	**type**
struct	**type**
interface	**type**
enum	**type**
delegate	**type**, return
method	**method**, return
parameter	**param**
field	**field**
property—indexer	**property**
property—get accessor	**method**, return
property—set accessor	**method**, param, return
event—field	**event**, field, method
event—property	**event**, property
event—add	**method**, param
event—remove	**method**, param

Note that assembly- and module-level attributes have no default target. For more information, see "Global Attributes" on page 214.

Example

```
// cs_attribute_targets.cs
// compile with: /target:library
using System.Runtime.InteropServices;

[Guid("12345678-1234-1234-1234-123456789abc"),
InterfaceType(ComInterfaceType.InterfaceIsIUnknown)]
interface IMyInterface
{
    [DispId(17)]                    // set the DISPID of the method
    // the following attribute sets the marshaling on the return type
    [return : MarshalAs(UnmanagedType.Interface)]
    object MyInterfaceMethod();
}
```

See Also

Introduction to Attributes (pg. 211), Global Attributes (pg. 214), Creating Custom
Attributes (pg. 215), Retrieving Attribute Information (pg. 216)

Global Attributes

Most attributes are attached to specific language elements, such as classes or methods; however,
some attributes are global—they apply to an entire assembly or module. Assembly-level attributes
are specified as follows:

```
[assembly: attribute-list]
```

Module-level attributes are specified as follows:

```
[module: attribute-list]
```

where:

attribute-list
    A list of applicable global attributes.

Global attributes appear in the source code after any top-level using directives and before any type
or namespace declarations. Global attributes can appear in multiple source files in a single
compilation.

Of the .NET Framework assembly-level attributes, the following let you modify the information in
an assembly:

- System.Reflection.AssemblyConfigurationAttribute

- System.Reflection.AssemblyCultureAttribute

- System.Reflection.AssemblyDescriptionAttribute

- System.Reflection.AssemblyKeyFileAttribute

- System.Reflection.AssemblyKeyNameAttribute

- System.Reflection.AssemblyDelaySignAttribute

- System.Reflection.AssemblyTitleAttribute

- System.Reflection.AssemblyVersionAttribute

Use the file created by Strong Name Utility (SN.exe) as the parameter to **AssemblyKeyFileAttribute**, **AssemblyKeyNameAttribute**, or **AssemblyDelaySignAttribute** to sign (or give a strong name to) your assembly.

See the file AssemblyInfo.cs, which is added to all C# projects created in Visual Studio, to see those attributes in use.

Use /target:module to create an output file that does not contain an Assembly.

> **Note** Assembly-level attributes are ignored if you are not creating an assembly.

Example

The CLSCompliant attribute indicates whether all types defined in the assembly comply with the .NET Framework common language specification.

```
[assembly: System.CLSCompliant(true)]
```

See Also

Using Attributes (pg. 211), Attribute Targets (pg. 212), Creating Custom Attributes (pg. 215), Retrieving Attribute Information (pg. 216)

Creating Custom Attributes

You can create your own custom attributes by defining an attribute class, a class that derives directly or indirectly from **System.Attribute** (which makes identifying attribute definitions in metadata fast and easy). Suppose you want to tag classes and structs with the name of the programmer who wrote the class or struct. You might define a custom Author attribute class:

```
using System;
[AttributeUsage(AttributeTargets.Class|AttributeTargets.Struct)]
public class Author : Attribute
{
    public Author(string name) { this.name = name; version = 1.0; }
    public double version;
    string name;
}
```

The class name is the attribute's name, Author. It is derived from **System.Attribute**, so it is a custom attribute class. The constructor's parameters are the custom attribute's positional parameters (in this case, name), and any public read-write fields or properties are named parameters (in this case, version is the only named parameter). Note the use of the **AttributeUsage** attribute to make the Author attribute valid only on class and struct declarations.

You could use this new attribute as follows:

```
[Author("H. Ackerman", version=1.1)] class SomeClass{...}
```

AttributeUsage has a named parameter, **AllowMultiple**, with which you can make a custom attribute single-use or multiuse.

```
[AttributeUsage(AttributeTargets.Class|AttributeTargets.Struct,
    AllowMultiple=true)] // multiuse attribute
public class Author : Attribute
{
    ...
}
```

> **Note** To prevent namespace collisions, all attribute names implicitly end with "Attribute"; in the preceding example, Author and AuthorAttribute could be used interchangeably. The same applies to **AttributeUsage**, which is defined in the .NET Framework as **System.AttributeUsageAttribute**.

See Also

Using Attributes (pg. 211), Attribute Targets (pg. 212), Global Attributes (pg. 214), Retrieving Attribute Information (pg. 216), AttributeUsage (pg. 218)

Retrieving Attribute Information

The fact that you can define custom attributes and place them in your source code would be of little value without some way of retrieving that information and acting on it. Fortunately, C# has a reflection system that allows you to do just that. The key method is **GetCustomAttributes**, which returns an array of objects that are the run-time equivalents of the source code attributes.

An attribute specification such as:

```
[Author("H. Ackerman", version=1.1)] class AClass {...}
```

is conceptually equivalent to this:

```
Author anonymousAuthorObject = new Author("H. Ackerman");
anonymousAuthorObject.version = 1.1;
```

However, the code is not executed until AClass is queried for attributes. Calling **GetCustomAttributes** on AClass causes an Author object to be constructed and initialized as above. If the class has other attributes, other attribute objects are constructed similarly. **GetCustomAttributes** then returns the Author object and any other attribute objects in an array. You can then iterate over this array, determine what attributes were applied based on the type of each array element, and extract information from the attribute objects.

Example

Here is a complete example. A custom attribute is defined, applied to several entities, and retrieved via reflection.

```
// cs_attributes_retr.cs
using System;
[AttributeUsage(AttributeTargets.Class|AttributeTargets.Struct,
    AllowMultiple=true)]
public class Author : Attribute
{
    public Author(string name)
    {
        this.name = name; version = 1.0;
    }
    public double version;
    string name;
    public string GetName()
    {
        return name;
    }
}

[Author("H. Ackerman")]
class FirstClass
{
    /*...*/
}

class SecondClass  // no Author attribute
{
    /*...*/
}

[Author("H. Ackerman"), Author("M. Knott", version=1.1)]
class Steerage
{
    /*...*/
}

class AuthorInfo
{
    public static void Main()
    {
        PrintAuthorInfo(typeof(FirstClass));
        PrintAuthorInfo(typeof(SecondClass));
        PrintAuthorInfo(typeof(Steerage));
    }
```

(continued)

(continued)

```
public static void PrintAuthorInfo(Type t)
{
    Console.WriteLine("Author information for {0}", t);
    Attribute[] attrs = Attribute.GetCustomAttributes(t);
    foreach(Attribute attr in attrs)
    {
        if (attr is Author)
        {
            Author a = (Author)attr;
            Console.WriteLine("   {0}, version {1:f}",
a.GetName(), a.version);
        }
    }
}
}
```

Output
```
Author information for FirstClass
    H. Ackerman, version 1.00
Author information for SecondClass
Author information for Steerage
    H. Ackerman, version 1.00
    M. Knott, version 1.10
```

See Also
Introduction to Attributes (pg. 211)

AttributeUsage

Describes how a custom attribute class can be used.

```
[AttributeUsage(
    validon,
    AllowMultiple=allowmultiple,
    Inherited=inherited
)]
```

Parameters

validon
> Specifies the language elements on which the attribute can be placed; a combination of AttributeTargets values. Default value is **AttributeTargets.All**.

allowmultiple (optional)
> A bool; if **true**, the attribute is multiuse. Default is **false** (single-use).

inherited (optional)
> A **bool**; if **true**, the attribute is inherited by derived classes. Default is **false** (not inherited).

Applies To

Class declarations.

Remarks

The **AttributeUsage** attribute is a single-use attribute. **AttributeUsage** is an alias for **System.AttributeUsageAttribute**.

Example

See the example in "Retrieving Attribute Information" on page 216.

See Also

Attributes Tutorial (pg. 222)

Conditional

Marks a conditional method whose execution depends on a specified preprocessing identifier.

```
[Conditional(
    conditionalSymbol
)]
```

Parameters

conditionalSymbol
    A string representing the name of a preprocessing identifier.

Applies To

Method declarations.

Remarks

The **Conditional** attribute is a multiuse attribute. **Conditional** is an alias for **System.Diagnostics.ConditionalAttribute**.

Wherever a conditional method is called, the presence or absence of the preprocessing symbol specified by *conditionalSymbol* at the point of the call determines whether the call is included or omitted. If the symbol is defined, the call is included; otherwise, the call is omitted. Conditional methods provide a cleaner, more elegant alternative to enclosing the method call in #if *conditionalSymbol*...#endif preprocessor directives.

A conditional method must be a method in a class or struct declaration and must have a return type of void.

If a method has multiple **Conditional** attributes, a call to the method is included if at least one of the conditional symbols is defined (in other words, the symbols are logically ORed together).

```
[Conditional("A"), Conditional("B")] public static void IfAorB( )
{
    ...
}
```

To achieve the effect of logically ANDing symbols, you can define serial conditional methods:

```
[Conditional("A")] public static void IfAandB( )
{
    AandBPrivate( );
}
[Conditional("B")] static void AandBPrivate( )
{
    /* Code to execute when both A and B are defined... */
}
```

Call `IfAandB`; if both `A` and `B` are defined, `AandBPrivate` will execute.

Example

```
// cs_attribute_conditional.cs
#define DEBUG
using System;
using System.Diagnostics;
public class Trace
{
    [Conditional("DEBUG")] public static void Msg(string msg)
    {
        Console.WriteLine(msg);
    }
}
class Test
{
    static void A( )
    {
        Trace.Msg("Now in A.");
        B( );
    }
    static void B( )
    {
        Trace.Msg("Now in B.");
    }
    public static void Main( )
    {
        Trace.Msg("Now in Main.");
        A( );
        Console.WriteLine("Done.");
    }
}
```

Output

```
Now in Main.
Now in A.
Now in B.
Done.
```

If you compile the sample with first line omitted (or changed to #undef DEBUG), the output will be: Done.

See Also

Attributes (pg. 211), Conditional Methods Tutorial (pg. 318), Preprocessor Directives (pg. 240)

Obsolete

Marks a program entity that should not be used.

```
[Obsolete(
    message
)]
[Obsolete(
    message,
    iserror
)]
```

Parameters

message
> A string; ideally, a human-readable explanation of why the item is obsolete and what to use instead.

iserror
> A bool; if **true**, the compiler should treat the use of the item as an error. Default value is **false** (compiler generates a warning).

Applies To

Any declaration that allows attributes.

Remarks

The **Obsolete** attribute is a single-use attribute. **Obsolete** is an alias for **System.ObsoleteAttribute**.

When an entity marked **Obsolete** is used in a program, the compiler issues either an error or a warning (depending on *iserror*) and prints out *message*.

Example

```
// cs_attribute_obsolete.cs
// CS0619 expected
using System;
public class MyClass
{
   [Obsolete("Don't use OldWay; use NewWay instead", true)]
   static void OldWay( ) { Console.WriteLine("Silly me!"); }
   static void NewWay( ) { Console.WriteLine("D'oh!"); }
   public static void Main( )
   {
      OldWay( );
   }
}
```

Attributes Tutorial

This tutorial shows how to create custom attribute classes, use them in code, and query them through reflection.

Further Reading

• Attributes

• AttributeUsage

Tutorial

Attributes provide a powerful method of associating declarative information with C# code (types, methods, properties, and so forth). Once associated with a program entity, the attribute can be queried at run time and used in any number of ways.

Example usage of attributes includes:

• Associating help documentation with program entities (through a Help attribute).

• Associating value editors to a specific type in a GUI framework (through a ValueEditor attribute).

In addition to a complete example, this tutorial includes the following topics:

• Declaring an Attribute Class   The first thing you need to be able to do is declare an attribute.

• Using an Attribute Class   Once the attribute has been created, you then associate the attribute with a particular program element.

• Accessing Attributes via Reflection   Once the attribute has been associated with a program element, you use reflection to query its existence and its value.

Declaring an Attribute Class

Declaring an attribute in C# is simple—it takes the form of a class declaration that inherits from **System.Attribute** and has been marked with the **AttributeUsage** attribute as shown below:

```
using System;
[AttributeUsage(AttributeTargets.All)]
public class HelpAttribute : System.Attribute
{
    public readonly string Url;

    public string Topic              // Topic is a named parameter
    {
        get
        {
            return topic;
        }
        set
        {

            topic = value;
        }
    }

    public HelpAttribute(string url)  // url is a positional parameter
    {
        this.Url = url;
    }

    private string topic;
}
```

Code Discussion

- The attribute **AttributeUsage** specifies the language elements to which the attribute can be applied.

- Attributes classes are public classes derived from **System.Attribute** that have at least one public constructor.

- Attribute classes have two types of parameters:

    - *Positional parameters* must be specified every time the attribute is used. Positional parameters are specified as constructor arguments to the attribute class. In the example above, url is a positional parameter.

    - *Named parameters* are optional. If they are specified when the attribute is used, the name of the parameter must be used. Named parameters are defined by having a nonstatic field or property. In the example above, Topic is a named parameter.

- Attribute parameters are restricted to constant values of the following types:

    - Simple types (bool, byte, char, short, int, long, float, and double)

    - string

    - System.Type

    - enums

    - object (The argument to an attribute parameter of type object must be a constant value of one of the above types.)

    - One-dimensional arrays of any of the above types

Parameters for the AttributeUsage Attribute

The attribute **AttributeUsage** provides the underlying mechanism by which attributes are declared.

AttributeUsage has one positional parameter:

- **AllowOn**   Specifies the program elements that the attribute can be assigned to (class, method, property, parameter, and so on). Valid values for this parameter can be found in the **System.Attributes.AttributeTargets enumeration** in the .NET Framework. The default value for this parameter is all program elements (**AttributeElements.All**).

AttributeUsage has one named parameter:

- **AllowMultiple**   A Boolean value that indicates whether multiple attributes can be specified for one program element. The default value for this parameter is **False**.

Using an Attribute Class

Here's a simple example of using the attribute declared in the previous section:

```
[HelpAttribute("http://msvc/MyClassInfo")]
class MyClass
{
}
```

In this example, the HelpAttribute attribute is associated with MyClass.

Accessing Attributes Through Reflection

Once attributes have been associated with program elements, reflection can be used to query their existence and values. The main reflection methods to query attributes are contained in the **System.Reflection.MemberInfo** class (**GetCustomAttributes** family of methods). The following example demonstrates the basic way of using reflection to get access to attributes:

```
class MainClass
{
    public static void Main()
    {
        System.Reflection.MemberInfo info = typeof(MyClass);
        object[] attributes = info.GetCustomAttributes(true);
        for (int i = 0; i < attributes.Length; i ++)
        {
            System.Console.WriteLine(attributes[i]);
        }
    }
}
```

Example

The following is a complete example where all pieces are brought together.

```
// AttributesTutorial.cs
// This example shows the use of class and method attributes.

using System;
using System.Reflection;
using System.Collections;

// The IsTested class is a user-defined custom attribute class.
// It can be applied to any declaration including
//  - types (struct, class, enum, delegate)
//  - members (methods, fields, events, properties, indexers)
// It is used with no arguments.
public class IsTestedAttribute : Attribute
{
    public override string ToString()
    {
        return "Is Tested";
    }
}

// The AuthorAttribute class is a user-defined attribute class.
// It can be applied to classes and struct declarations only.
// It takes one unnamed string argument (the author's name).
// It has one optional named argument Version, which is of type int.
[AttributeUsage(AttributeTargets.Class | AttributeTargets.Struct)]
public class AuthorAttribute : Attribute
{
    // This constructor specifies the unnamed arguments to the attribute class.
    public AuthorAttribute(string name)
    {
        this.name = name;
        this.version = 0;
    }
```

(continued)

(continued)

```csharp
    // This property is readonly (it has no set accessor)
    // so it cannot be used as a named argument to this attribute.
    public string Name
    {
        get
        {
            return name;
        }
    }

    // This property is read-write (it has a set accessor)
    // so it can be used as a named argument when using this
    // class as an attribute class.
    public int Version
    {
        get
        {
            return version;
        }
        set
        {
            version = value;
        }
    }

    public override string ToString()
    {
        string value = "Author : " + Name;
        if (version != 0)
        {
            value += " Version : " + Version.ToString();
        }
        return value;
    }

    private string name;
    private int version;
}

// Here you attach the AuthorAttribute user-defined custom attribute to
// the Account class. The unnamed string argument is passed to the
// AuthorAttribute class's constructor when creating the attributes.
[Author("Joe Programmer")]
class Account
```

```
{
    // Attach the IsTestedAttribute custom attribute to this method.
    [IsTested]
    public void AddOrder(Order orderToAdd)
    {
        orders.Add(orderToAdd);
    }

    private ArrayList orders = new ArrayList();
}

// Attach the AuthorAttribute and IsTestedAttribute custom attributes
// to this class.
// Note the use of the 'Version' named argument to the AuthorAttribute.
[Author("Jane Programmer", Version = 2), IsTested()]
class Order
{
    // add stuff here ...
}

class MainClass
{
    private static bool IsMemberTested(MemberInfo member)
    {
        foreach (object attribute in member.GetCustomAttributes(true))
        {
            if (attribute is IsTestedAttribute)
            {
                return true;
            }
        }
        return false;
    }

    private static void DumpAttributes(MemberInfo member)
    {
        Console.WriteLine("Attributes for : " + member.Name);
        foreach (object attribute in member.GetCustomAttributes(true))
        {
            Console.WriteLine(attribute);
        }
    }

    public static void Main()
    {
        // display attributes for Account class
        DumpAttributes(typeof(Account));
```

(continued)

(continued)

```csharp
        // display list of tested members
        foreach (MethodInfo method in (typeof(Account)).GetMethods())
        {
            if (IsMemberTested(method))
            {
                Console.WriteLine("Member {0} is tested!", method.Name);
            }
            else
            {
                Console.WriteLine("Member {0} is NOT tested!", method.Name);
            }
        }
        Console.WriteLine();

        // display attributes for Order class
        DumpAttributes(typeof(Order));

        // display attributes for methods on the Order class
        foreach (MethodInfo method in (typeof(Order)).GetMethods())
        {
            if (IsMemberTested(method))
            {
                Console.WriteLine("Member {0} is tested!", method.Name);
            }
            else
            {
                Console.WriteLine("Member {0} is NOT tested!", method.Name);
            }
        }
        Console.WriteLine();
    }
}
```

Output

```
Attributes for : Account
Author : Joe Programmer
Member GetHashCode is NOT tested!
Member Equals is NOT tested!
Member ToString is NOT tested!
Member AddOrder is tested!
Member GetType is NOT tested!

Attributes for : Order
Author : Jane Programmer Version : 2
Is Tested
Member GetHashCode is NOT tested!
Member Equals is NOT tested!
Member ToString is NOT tested!
Member GetType is NOT tested!
```

Declarations

Declarations in a C# program define the constituent elements of the program. C# programs are organized using namespaces, which can contain type declarations and nested namespace declarations. For more information on namespaces, see "Namespace Keywords" on page 55.

Type declarations are used to define classes, structs, interfaces, enums, and delegates. The kinds of members permitted in a type declaration depend on the form of the type declaration. For instance, class declarations can contain declarations for constants, fields, methods, properties, events, indexers, operators, instance constructors, static constructors, destructors, and nested types.

A declaration defines a name in the declaration space to which the declaration belongs. Except for overloaded members, it is a compile-time error to have two or more declarations that introduce members with the same name in a declaration space. It is never possible for a declaration space to contain different kinds of members with the same name. For example, a declaration space can never contain a field and a method by the same name.

There are several different types of declaration spaces, as described in the following.

- Within all source files of a program, namespace-member-declarations with no enclosing namespace-declaration are members of a single combined declaration space called the global declaration space.

- Within all source files of a program, namespace-member-declarations within namespace-declarations that have the same fully qualified namespace name are members of a single combined declaration space.

- Each class, struct, or interface declaration creates a new declaration space. Names are introduced into this declaration space through class-member-declarations, struct-member-declarations, or interface-member-declarations. Except for overloaded instance constructor declarations and static constructor declarations, a class or struct member declaration cannot introduce a member by the same name as the class or struct. A class, struct, or interface permits the declaration of overloaded methods and indexers. Furthermore, a class or struct permits the declaration of overloaded instance constructors and overloaded operators. For example, a class, struct, or interface may contain multiple method declarations with the same name, provided these method declarations differ in their signature. Note that base classes do not contribute to the declaration space of a class, and base interfaces do not contribute to the declaration space of an interface. Thus, a derived class or interface is allowed to declare a member with the same name as an inherited member. Such a member is said to hide the inherited member.

- Each enumeration declaration creates a new declaration space. Names are introduced into this declaration space through enum-member-declarations.

- Each block or switch-block creates a different declaration space for local variables. Names are introduced into this declaration space through local-variable-declarations. If a block is the body of an instance constructor, static constructor, or method declaration, the parameters declared in the formal-parameter-list are members of the block's local variable declaration space. The local variable declaration space of a block includes any nested blocks. Thus, within a nested block it is not possible to declare a local variable with the same name as a local variable in an enclosing block.

- Each block or switch-block creates a separate declaration space for labels. Names are introduced into this declaration space through labeled-statements, and the names are referenced through go to statements. The label declaration space of a block includes any nested blocks. Thus, within a nested block it is not possible to declare a label with the same name as a label in an enclosing block.

The textual order in which names are declared is generally of no significance. In particular, textual order is not significant for the declaration and use of namespaces, constants, methods, properties, events, indexers, operators, instance constructors, destructors, types, static constructors, and types. Declaration order is significant in the following ways:

- Declaration order for field declarations and local variable declarations determines the order in which their initializers (if any) are executed.

- Local variables must be defined before they are used.

- Declaration order for enum member declarations is significant when constant-expression values are omitted.

The declaration space of a namespace is "open ended", and two namespace declarations with the same fully qualified name contribute to the same declaration space. For example:

```
namespace Megacorp.Data
{
    class Customer
    {
        ...
    }
}
namespace Megacorp.Data
{
    class Order
    {
        ...
    }
}
```

The two namespace declarations above contribute to the same declaration space, in this case declaring two classes with the fully qualified names `Megacorp.Data.Customer` and `Megacorp.Data.Order`. Because the two declarations contribute to the same declaration space, it would have caused a compile-time error if each contained a declaration of a class with the same name.

The declaration space of a block includes any nested blocks. Thus, in the following example, the F and G methods result in a compile-time error because the name i is declared in the outer block and cannot be redeclared in the inner block. However, the H and I methods are valid because the two is are declared in separate non-nested blocks.

```
class A
{
    void F() {
        int i = 0;
        if (true) {
            int i = 1;
        }
    }
    void G() {
        if (true) {
            int i = 0;
        }
        int i = 1;
    }
    void H() {
        if (true) {
            int i = 0;
        }
        if (true) {
            int i = 1;
        }
    }
    void I() {
        for (int i = 0; i < 10; i++)
            H();
        for (int i = 0; i < 10; i++)
            H();
    }
}
```

Members

Namespaces and types have members. The members of an entity are generally available through the use of a qualified name that starts with a reference to the entity, followed by a "." token, followed by the name of the member.

Members of a type are either declared in the type or inherited from the base class of the type. When a type inherits from a base class, all members of the base class, except instance constructors, destructors and static constructors, become members of the derived type. The declared accessibility of a base class member does not control whether the member is inherited—inheritance extends to any member that is not an instance constructor, static constructor, or destructor. However, an inherited member may not be accessible in a derived type, either because of its declared accessibility or because it is hidden by a declaration in the type itself. For more information on hiding with such a declaration, see "Hiding Through Inheritance" on page 307.

Namespace Members

Namespaces and types that have no enclosing namespace are members of the global namespace. This corresponds directly to the names declared in the global declaration space.

Namespaces and types declared within a namespace are members of that namespace. This corresponds directly to the names declared in the declaration space of the namespace.

Namespaces have no access restrictions. It is not possible to declare private, protected, or internal namespaces, and namespace names are always publicly accessible.

Struct Members

The members of a struct are the members declared in the struct and the members inherited from class `object`.

The members of a simple type correspond directly to the members of the struct type aliased by the simple type:

- The members of `sbyte` are the members of the `System.SByte` struct.

- The members of `byte` are the members of the `System.Byte` struct.

- The members of `short` are the members of the `System.Int16` struct.

- The members of `ushort` are the members of the `System.UInt16` struct.

- The members of `int` are the members of the `System.Int32` struct.

- The members of `uint` are the members of the `System.UInt32` struct.

- The members of `long` are the members of the `System.Int64` struct.

- The members of `ulong` are the members of the `System.UInt64` struct.

- The members of `char` are the members of the `System.Char` struct.

- The members of `float` are the members of the `System.Single` struct.

- The members of double are the members of the System.Double struct.

- The members of decimal are the members of the System.Decimal struct.

- The members of bool are the members of the System.Boolean struct.

Class Members

The members of a class are the members declared in the class and the members inherited from the base class (except for class object which has no base class). The members inherited from the base class include the constants, fields, methods, properties, events, indexers, operators, and types of the base class, but not the instance constructors, destructors and static constructors of the base class. Base class members are inherited without regard to their accessibility.

A class declaration may contain declarations of constants, fields, methods, properties, events, indexers, operators, instance constructors, destructors, static constructors and types.

The members of object and string correspond directly to the members of the class types they alias:

- The members of object are the members of the System.Object class.

- The members of string are the members of the System.String class.

Other Members

The following are other kinds of members:

Enumeration members. The members of an enumeration are the constants declared in the enumeration and the members inherited from class object.

Interface members. The members of an interface are the members declared in the interface and in all base interfaces of the interface, and the members inherited from class object.

Array members. The members of an array are the members inherited from class System.Array.

Delegate members. The members of a delegate are the members inherited from class System.Delegate.

Member Access

Declarations of members allow control over member access. The accessibility of a member is established by the declared accessibility of the member combined with the accessibility of the immediately containing type, if any.

When access to a particular member is allowed, the member is said to be accessible. Conversely, when access to a particular member is disallowed, the member is said to be inaccessible. Access to a member is permitted when the textual location in which the access takes place is included in the accessibility domain of the member.

Declared Accessibility

The declared accessibility of a member can be one of the following:

- Public, which is selected by including a `public` modifier in the member declaration. The intuitive meaning of `public` is "access not limited".

- Protected internal (meaning protected or internal), which is selected by including both a `protected` and an `internal` modifier in the member declaration. The intuitive meaning of `protected internal` is "access limited to this program or types derived from the containing class".

- Protected, which is selected by including a `protected` modifier in the member declaration. The intuitive meaning of `protected` is "access limited to the containing class or types derived from the containing class".

- Internal, which is selected by including an `internal` modifier in the member declaration. The intuitive meaning of `internal` is "access limited to this program".

- Private, which is selected by including a `private` modifier in the member declaration. The intuitive meaning of `private` is "access limited to the containing type".

Depending on the context in which a member declaration takes place, only certain types of declared accessibility are permitted. Furthermore, when a member declaration does not include any access modifiers, the context in which the declaration takes place determines the default declared accessibility.

- Namespaces implicitly have public declared accessibility. No access modifiers are allowed on namespace declarations.

- Types declared in compilation units or namespaces can have public or internal declared accessibility and default to internal declared accessibility.

- Class members can have any of the five kinds of declared accessibility and default to private declared accessibility. (Note that a type declared as a member of a class can have any of the five kinds of declared accessibility, whereas a type declared as a member of a namespace can have only public or internal declared accessibility.)

- Struct members can have public, internal, or private declared accessibility and default to private declared accessibility because structs are implicitly sealed. Struct members cannot have protected or protected internal declared accessibility. (Note that a type declared as a member of a struct can have public, internal, or private declared accessibility, whereas a type declared as a member of a namespace can have only `public` or `internal` declared accessibility.)

- Interface members implicitly have public declared accessibility. No access modifiers are allowed on interface member declarations.

- Enumeration members implicitly have public declared accessibility. No access modifiers are allowed on enumeration member declarations.

Accessibility Domains

The accessibility domain of a member consists of the (possibly disjoint) sections of program text in which access to the member is permitted. For purposes of defining the accessibility domain of a member, a member is said to be top-level if it is not declared within a type, and a member is said to be nested if it is declared within another type. Furthermore, the program text of a program is defined as all program text contained in all source files of the program, and the program text of a type is defined as all program text contained between the opening and closing "{" and "}" tokens in the class-body, struct-body, interface-body, or enum-body of the type (including, possibly, types that are nested within the type).

The accessibility domain of a predefined type (such as object, int, or double) is unlimited.

The accessibility domain of a top-level type T declared in a program P is defined as follows:

- If the declared accessibility of T is public, the accessibility domain of T is the program text of P and any program that references P.

- If the declared accessibility of T is internal, the accessibility domain of T is the program text of P.

From these definitions it follows that the accessibility domain of a top-level type is always at least the program text of the program in which the type is declared.

The accessibility domain of a nested member M declared in a type T within a program P is defined as follows (noting that M may itself possibly be a type):

- If the declared accessibility of M is public, the accessibility domain of M is the accessibility domain of T.

- If the declared accessibility of M is protected internal, the accessibility domain of M is the intersection of the accessibility domain of T with the program text of P and the program text of any type derived from T declared outside P.

- If the declared accessibility of M is protected, the accessibility domain of M is the intersection of the accessibility domain of T with the program text of T and any type derived from T.

- If the declared accessibility of M is internal, the accessibility domain of M is the intersection of the accessibility domain of T with the program text of P.

- If the declared accessibility of M is private, the accessibility domain of M is the program text of T.

From these definitions it follows that the accessibility domain of a nested member is always at least the program text of the type in which the member is declared. Furthermore, it follows that the accessibility domain of a member is never more inclusive than the accessibility domain of the type in which the member is declared.

In intuitive terms, when a type or member M is accessed, the following steps are evaluated to ensure that the access is permitted:

- First, if M is declared within a type (as opposed to a compilation unit or a namespace), a compile-time error occurs if that type is not accessible.

- Then, if M is public, the access is permitted.

- Otherwise, if M is protected internal, the access is permitted if it occurs within the program in which M is declared, or if it occurs within a class derived from the class in which M is declared and takes place through the derived class type. For more information on this kind of access, see "Protected Access for Instance Members" on page 238.

- Otherwise, if M is protected, the access is permitted if it occurs within the class in which M is declared, or if it occurs within a class derived from the class in which M is declared and takes place through the derived class type. For more information on this kind of access, see "Protected Access for Instance Members" on page 238.

- Otherwise, if M is internal, the access is permitted if it occurs within the program in which M is declared.

- Otherwise, if M is private, the access is permitted if it occurs within the type in which M is declared.

- Otherwise, the type or member is inaccessible, and a compile-time error occurs.

In the example

```
public class A
{
   public static int X;
   internal static int Y;
   private static int Z;
}
internal class B
{
   public static int X;
   internal static int Y;
   private static int Z;
   public class C
   {
      public static int X;
      internal static int Y;
      private static int Z;
   }
   private class D
   {
      public static int X;
      internal static int Y;
      private static int Z;
   }
}
```

the classes and members have the following accessibility domains:

- The accessibility domain of A and A.X is unlimited.

- The accessibility domain of A.Y, B, B.X, B.Y, B.C, B.C.X, and B.C.Y is the program text of the containing program.

- The accessibility domain of A.Z is the program text of A.

- The accessibility domain of B.Z and B.D is the program text of B, including the program text of B.C and B.D.

- The accessibility domain of B.C.Z is the program text of B.C.

- The accessibility domain of B.D.X, B.D.Y, and B.D.Z is the program text of B.D.

As the example illustrates, the accessibility domain of a member is never larger than that of a containing type. For example, even though all X members have public declared accessibility, all but A.X have accessibility domains that are constrained by a containing type.

All members of a base class, except for instance constructors, destructors and static constructors, are inherited by derived types. This includes even private members of a base class. However, the accessibility domain of a private member includes only the program text of the type in which the member is declared. For more information on inheritance of members of a base class, see "Members" on page 231.

In the example

```
class A
{
    int x;
    static void F(B b) {
        b.x = 1;      // Ok
    }
}
class B: A
{
    static void F(B b) {
        b.x = 1;      // Error, x not accessible
    }
}
```

the B class inherits the private member x from the A class. Because the member is private, it is only accessible within the *class-body* of A. Thus, the access to b.x succeeds in the A.F method, but fails in the B.F method.

Protected Access for Instance Members

When a `protected` instance member is accessed outside the program text of the class in which it is declared, and when a `protected internal` instance member is accessed outside the program text of the program in which it is declared, the access is required to take place through an instance of the derived class type in which the access occurs. Let B be a base class that declares a protected instance member M, and let D be a class that derives from B. Within the class-body of D, access to M can take one of the following forms:

- An unqualified type-name or primary-expression of the form M.

- A primary-expression of the form E.M, provided the type of E is D or a class derived from D.

- A primary-expression of the form base.M.

In addition to these forms of access, a derived class can access a protected instance constructor of a base class in a constructor-initializer.

In the example

```
public class A
{
   protected int x;
   static void F(A a, B b) {
      a.x = 1;       // Ok
      b.x = 1;       // Ok
   }
}
public class B: A
{
   static void F(A a, B b) {
      a.x = 1;       // Error, must access through instance of B
      b.x = 1;       // Ok
   }
}
```

within A, it is possible to access x through instances of both A and B, since in either case the access takes place through an instance of A or a class derived from A. However, within B, it is not possible to access x through an instance of A, since A does not derive from B.

Accessibility Constraints

Several constructs in the C# language require a type to be at least as accessible as a member or another type. A type T is said to be at least as accessible as a member or type M if the accessibility domain of T is a superset of the accessibility domain of M. In other words, T is at least as accessible as M if T is accessible in all contexts where M is accessible.

The following accessibility constraints exist:

- The direct base class of a class type must be at least as accessible as the class type itself.

- The explicit base interfaces of an interface type must be at least as accessible as the interface type itself.

- The return type and parameter types of a delegate type must be at least as accessible as the delegate type itself.

- The type of a constant must be at least as accessible as the constant itself.

- The type of a field must be at least as accessible as the field itself.

- The return type and parameter types of a method must be at least as accessible as the method itself.

- The type of a property must be at least as accessible as the property itself.

- The type of an event must be at least as accessible as the event itself.

- The type and parameter types of an indexer must be at least as accessible as the indexer itself.

- The return type and parameter types of an operator must be at least as accessible as the operator itself.

- The parameter types of an instance constructor must be at least as accessible as the instance constructor itself.

In the example

```
class A {...}
public class B: A {...}
the B class results in a compile-time error because A is not at least as accessible as B.
Likewise, in the example
class A {...}
public class B
{
    A F() {...}
    internal A G() {...}
    public A H() {...}
}
```

the H method in B results in a compile-time error because the return type A is not at least as accessible as the method.

Preprocessor Directives

This section discusses the C# language's preprocessor directives:

- #define
- #elif
- #else
- #endif
- #endregion
- #error
- #if
- #line
- #region
- #undef
- #warning

While the compiler does not have a separate preprocessor, the directives described in this section are processed as if there was one; these directives are used to aid in conditional compilation. Unlike C and C++ directives, you cannot use these directives to create macros.

A preprocessor directive must be the only instruction on a line.

See Also

Conditional Methods Tutorial (pg. 318)

#if

#if lets you begin a conditional directive, testing a symbol or symbols to see if they evaluate to **true**. If they do evaluate to **true**, the compiler evaluates all the code between the **#if** and the next directive.

```
#if symbol [operator symbol]...
```

where:

symbol

> The name of the symbol you want to test. You can also use **true** and **false**. *symbol* can be prefaced with the negation operator. For example, **!true** will evaluate to **false**.

operator (optional)

> You can use the following operators to evaluate multiple symbols:
>
> == (equality)
>
> != (inequality)
>
> && (and)
>
> || (or)

You can group symbols and operators with parentheses.

Remarks

#if, along with the **#else**, **#elif**, **#endif**, **#define**, and **#undef** directives, lets you include or exclude code based on the condition of one or more symbols. This can be most useful when compiling code for a debug build or when compiling for a specific configuration.

A conditional directive beginning with a **#if** directive must explicitly be terminated with a **#endif** directive.

Example

```
// preprocessor_if.cs
#define DEBUG
#define VC_V6
using System;
public class MyClass
{
    public static void Main()
    {

        #if (DEBUG && !VC_V6)
            Console.WriteLine("DEBUG is defined");
        #elif (!DEBUG && VC_V6)
            Console.WriteLine("VC_V6 is defined");
        #elif (DEBUG && VC_V6)
            Console.WriteLine("DEBUG and VC_V6 are defined");
        #else
            Console.WriteLine("DEBUG and VC_V6 are not defined");
        #endif
    }
}
```

Output

```
DEBUG and VC_V6 are defined
```

#else

#else lets you create a compound conditional directive, such that, if none of the expressions in the preceding #if or (optional) #elif directives did not evaluate to **true**, the compiler will evaluate all code between **#else** and the subsequent **#endif**.

```
#else
```

Remarks

#endif must be the next preprocessor directive after **#else**.

Example

For an example of how to use **#else**, see the section "#if" on page 240.

#elif

#elif lets you create a compound conditional directive. The **#elif** expression will be evaluated if neither the preceding #if nor any preceding (optional) #elif directive expressions evaluate to **true**. If a **#elif** expression evaluates to **true**, the compiler evaluates all the code between the **#elif** and the next directive.

```
#elif symbol [operator symbol]...
```

where:

symbol

> The name of the symbol you want to test. You can also use **true** and **false**. *symbol* can be prefaced with the negation operator. For example, **!true** will evaluate to **false**.

operator (optional)

> You can use the following operators to evaluate multiple symbols:
>
> == (equality)
>
> != (inequality)
>
> && (and)
>
> || (or)
>
> You can group symbols and operators with parentheses.

Remarks

#elif is equivalent to using:

```
#else
#if
```

But using **#elif** is simpler because each **#if** requires a #endif, whereas a **#elif** can be used without a matching **#endif**.

Example

For an example of how to use **#elif**, see the section "#if" on page 240.

#endif

#endif specifies the end of a conditional directive, which began with the #if directive.

```
#endif
```

Remarks

A conditional directive, beginning with a **#if** directive, must explicitly be terminated with a **#endif** directive.

Example

For an example of how to use **#endif**, see the section "#if" on page 240.

#define

#define lets you define a symbol, such that, by using the symbol as the expression passed to the #if directive, the expression will evaluate to **true**.

```
#define symbol
```

where:

symbol
    The name of the symbol to define.

Remarks

Symbols can be used to specify conditions for compilation. You can test for the symbol with either #if or #elif. You can also use the **conditional** attribute to perform conditional compilation.

You can define a symbol, but you cannot assign a value to a symbol. The **#define** directive must appear in the file before you use any instructions that are not also directives.

You can also define a symbol with the /define compiler option. You can undefine a symbol with undef.

A symbol that you define with /define or with **#define** does not conflict with a variable of the same name. That is, a variable name should not be passed to a preprocessor directive and a symbol can only be evaluated by a preprocessor directive.

The scope of a symbol created with **#define** is the file in which it was defined.

Example

For an example of how to use **#define**, see the section "#if" on page 240.

See Also

Conditional Methods Tutorial (pg. 318)

#undef

#undef lets you undefine a symbol, such that, by using the symbol as the expression in a **#if** directive, the expression will evaluate to **false**.

```
#undef symbol
```

where:

symbol
> The name of the symbol you want to undefine.

Remarks

A symbol can be defined either with the #define directive or the /define compiler option. The **#undef** directive must appear in the file before you use any statements that are not also directives.

Example

```
// preprocessor_undef.cs
// compile with: /d:DEBUG
#undef DEBUG
using System;
public class MyClass
{
    public static void Main()
    {
        #if DEBUG
            Console.WriteLine("DEBUG is defined");
        #else
            Console.WriteLine("DEBUG is not defined");
        #endif
    }
}
```

Output

```
DEBUG is not defined
```

#warning

#warning lets you generate a level one warning from a specific location in your code.

```
#warning text
```

where:

text
> The text of the warning that should appear in the compiler's output.

Remarks

A common use of **#warning** is in a conditional directive. It is also possible to generate a user-defined error with #error.

Example

```
// preprocessor_warning.cs
// CS1030 expected
#define DEBUG
public class MyClass
{
    public static void Main()
    {
        #if DEBUG
        #warning DEBUG is defined
        #endif
    }
}
```

#error

#error lets you generate an error from a specific location in your code.

```
#error text
```

where:

text
>   The text of the error that should appear in the compiler's output.

Remarks

A common use of **#error** is in a conditional directive. It is also possible to generate a user-defined warning with #warning.

Example

```
// preprocessor_error.cs
// CS1029 expected
#define DEBUG
public class MyClass
{
    public static void Main()
    {
        #if DEBUG
        #error DEBUG is defined
        #endif
    }
}
```

#line

#line lets you modify the compiler's line number and (optionally) the file name output for errors and warnings.

```
#line [ number ["file_name"] | default ]
```

where:

number
>   The number you want to specify for the following line in a source code file.

"file_name" (optional)
>   The file name you want to appear in the compiler output. By default, the actual name of the source code file is used. The file name must be in double quotation marks (" ").

default
>   Resets the line numbering in a file.

Remarks

#line might be used by an automated, intermediate step in the build process. For example, if the intermediate step removed lines from the original source code file, but if you still wanted the compiler to generate output based on the original line numbering in the file, you could remove lines and then simulate the original line numbering with **#line**.

A source code file can have any number of **#line** directives.

Example

```
// preprocessor_line.cs
public class MyClass2
{
    public static void Main()
    {
        #line 200
        int i;   // CS0168 on line 200
        #line default
        char c;   // CS0168 on line 8
    }
}
```

#region

#region lets you specify a block of code that you can expand or collapse when using the outlining feature of the Visual Studio Code Editor.

```
#region name
```

where:

name

>The name you want to give to the region, which will appear in the Visual Studio Code Editor.

Remarks

A **#region** block must be terminated with a #endregion directive.

A **#region** block cannot overlap with a #if block. However, a **#region** block can be nested in a **#if** block, and a **#if** block can be nested in a **#region** block.

Example

```
// preprocessor_region.cs
#region MyClass definition
public class MyClass
{
    public static void Main()
    {
    }
}
#endregion
```

#endregion

#endregion marks the end of a #region block.

```
#endregion
```

Example

For an example of how to use **#endregion**, see the section "#region" on page 247.

Arrays

An array is a data structure that contains a number of variables called the elements of the array. The array elements are accessed through computed indexes. C# arrays are zero indexed; that is, the array indexes start at zero. All of the array elements must be of the same type, which is called the element type of the array. Array elements can be of any type, including an array type. An array can be a single-dimensional array, or a multidimensional array. Array types are reference types derived from the abstract base type **System.Array**.

The following topics are discussed in this section:

- Single-Dimensional Arrays
- Multidimensional Arrays
- Jagged Arrays
- Passing Arrays Using ref and out

See Also
Reference Types (pg. 149)

Single-Dimensional Arrays

You can declare an array of five integers as in the following example:

```
int[] myArray = new int [5];
```

This array contains the elements from `myArray[0]` to `myArray[4]`. The **new** operator is used to create the array and initialize the array elements to their default values. In this example, all the array elements are initialized to zero.

An array that stores string elements can be declared in the same way. For example:

```
string[] myStringArray = new string[6];
```

Array Initialization

It is possible to initialize an array upon declaration, in which case, the rank specifier is not needed because it is already supplied by the number of elements in the initialization list. For example:

```
int[] myArray = new int[] {1, 3, 5, 7, 9};
```

A string array can be initialized in the same way. The following is a declaration of a string array where each array element is initialized by a name of a day:

```
string[] weekDays = new string[]
            {"Sun","Sat","Mon","Tue","Wed","Thu","Fri"};
```

When you initialize an array upon declaration, it is possible to use the following shortcuts:

```
int[] myArray = {1, 3, 5, 7, 9};
string[] weekDays = {"Sun","Sat","Mon","Tue","Wed","Thu","Fri"};
```

It is possible to declare an array variable without initialization, but you must use the **new** operator when you assign an array to this variable. For example:

```
int[] myArray;
myArray = new int[] {1, 3, 5, 7, 9};    // OK
myArray = {1, 3, 5, 7, 9};    // Error
```

Value Type and Reference Type Arrays

Consider the following array declaration:

```
MyType[] myArray = new MyType[10];
```

The result of this statement depends on whether MyType is a value type or a reference type. If it is a value type, the statement results in creating an array of 10 instances of the type MyType. If MyType is a reference type, the statement creates an array of 10 elements, each of which is initialized to a null reference.

For more information on value types and reference types, see "Type Keywords" on page 120.

Passing Arrays as Parameters

You can pass an initialized array to a method. For example:

```
PrintArray(myArray);
```

You can also initialize and pass a new array in one step. For example:

```
PrintArray(new int[] {1, 3, 5, 7, 9});
```

Example

In the following example, a string array is initialized and passed as a parameter to the PrintArray method, where its elements are displayed:

```
// cs_sd_arrays.cs
using System;
public class ArrayClass
{
   static void PrintArray(string[] w)
   {
      for (int i = 0 ; i < w.Length ; i++)
         Console.Write(w[i] + "{0}", i < w.Length - 1 ? " " : "");
      Console.WriteLine();
   }
```

(continued)

(continued)

```
public static void Main()
{
    // Declare and initialize an array:
    string[] WeekDays = new string []
        {"Sun","Sat","Mon","Tue","Wed","Thu","Fri"};

    // Pass the array as a parameter:
    PrintArray(WeekDays);
}
}
```

Output

```
Sun Sat Mon Tue Wed Thu Fri
```

See Also

Multidimensional Arrays (pg. 250), Jagged Arrays (pg. 252)

Multidimensional Arrays

Arrays can have more than one dimension. For example, the following declaration creates a two-dimensional array of four rows and two columns:

```
int[,] myArray = new int[4,2];
```

Also, the following declaration creates an array of three dimensions, 4, 2, and 3:

```
int[,,] myArray = new int [4,2,3];
```

Array Initialization

You can initialize the array upon declaration as shown in the following example:

```
int[,] myArray = new  int[,] {{1,2}, {3,4}, {5,6}, {7,8}};
```

You can also initialize the array without specifying the rank:

```
int[,] myArray = {{1,2}, {3,4}, {5,6}, {7,8}};
```

If you choose to declare an array variable without initialization, you must use the **new** operator to assign an array to the variable. For example:

```
int[,] myArray;
myArray = new int[,] {{1,2}, {3,4}, {5,6}, {7,8}};    // OK
myArray = {{1,2}, {3,4}, {5,6}, {7,8}};    // Error
```

You can also assign a value to an array element, for example:

```
myArray[2,1] = 25;
```

Passing Arrays as Parameters

You can pass an initialized array to a method. For example:

```
PrintArray(myArray);
```

You can also initialize and pass a new array in one step. For example:

```
PrintArray(new int[,] {{1,2}, {3,4}, {5,6}, {7,8}});
```

Example

In this example, a two-dimensional array is initialized and passed to the PrintArray method, where its elements are displayed.

```
// cs_td_arrays.cs
using System;
public class ArrayClass
{
   static void PrintArray(int[,] w)
   {
      // Display the array elements:
      for (int i=0; i < 4; i++)
         for (int j=0; j < 2; j++)
            Console.WriteLine("Element({0},{1})={2}", i, j, w[i,j]);
   }

   public static void Main()
   {
      // Pass the array as a parameter:
      PrintArray(new int[,] {{1,2}, {3,4}, {5,6}, {7,8}});
   }
}
```

Output

```
Element(0,0)=1
Element(0,1)=2
Element(1,0)=3
Element(1,1)=4
Element(2,0)=5
Element(2,1)=6
Element(3,0)=7
Element(3,1)=8
```

See Also

Single-Dimensional Arrays (pg. 248), Jagged Arrays (pg. 252)

Jagged Arrays

A jagged array is an array whose elements are arrays. The elements of a jagged array can be of different dimensions and sizes. A jagged array is sometimes called an "array-of-arrays." This topic contains examples of declaring, initializing, and accessing jagged arrays.

The following is a declaration of a single-dimensional array that has three elements, each of which is a single-dimensional array of integers:

```
int[][] myJaggedArray = new int[3][];
```

Before you can use myJaggedArray, its elements must be initialized. You can initialize the elements like this example:

```
myJaggedArray[0] = new int[5];
myJaggedArray[1] = new int[4];
myJaggedArray[2] = new int[2];
```

Each of the elements is a single-dimensional array of integers. The first element is an array of 5 integers, the second is an array of 4 integers, and the third is an array of 2 integers.

It is also possible to use initializers to fill the array elements with values, in which case you don't need the array size, for example:

```
myJaggedArray[0] = new int[] {1,3,5,7,9};
myJaggedArray[1] = new int[] {0,2,4,6};
myJaggedArray[2] = new int[] {11,22};
```

You can also initialize the array upon declaration like this:

```
int[][] myJaggedArray = new int [][]
                    {
                        new int[] {1,3,5,7,9},
                        new int[] {0,2,4,6},
                        new int[] {11,22}
                    };
```

You can use the following shortcut (notice that you cannot omit the **new** operator from the elements initialization because there is no default initialization for the elements):

```
int[][] myJaggedArray = {
                        new int[] {1,3,5,7,9},
                        new int[] {0,2,4,6},
                        new int[] {11,22}
                    };
```

You can access individual array elements like these examples:

```
// Assign 33 to the second element of the first array:
myJaggedArray[0][1] = 33;
// Assign 44 to the second element of the third array:
myJaggedArray[2][1] = 44;
```

It is possible to mix jagged and multidimensional arrays. The following is a declaration and initialization of a single-dimensional jagged array that contains two-dimensional array elements of different sizes:

```
int[][,] myJaggedArray = new int [3][,]
                    {
                        new int[,] { {1,3}, {5,7} },
                        new int[,] { {0,2}, {4,6}, {8,10} },
                        new int[,] { {11,22}, {99,88}, {0,9} }
                    };
```

You can access individual elements like this example, which displays the value of the element [1,0] of the first array (value 5):

```
Console.Write("{0}", myJaggedArray[0][1,0]);
```

Example

This example builds an array, myArray, whose elements are arrays. Each one of the array elements has a different size.

```
// cs_array_of_arrays.cs
using System;
public class ArrayTest
{
    public static void Main()
    {
        // Declare the array of two elements:
        int[][] myArray = new int[2][];

        // Initialize the elements:
        myArray[0] = new int[5] {1,3,5,7,9};
        myArray[1] = new int[4] {2,4,6,8};

        // Display the array elements:
        for (int i=0; i < myArray.Length; i++)
        {
            Console.Write("Element({0}): ", i);

            for (int j = 0 ; j < myArray[i].Length ; j++)
                Console.Write("{0}{1}", myArray[i][j],
                            j == (myArray[i].Length-1) ? "" : " ");

            Console.WriteLine();
        }
    }
}
```

Output

```
Element(0): 1 3 5 7 9
Element(1): 2 4 6 8
```

See Also

Single-Dimensional Arrays (pg. 248), Multidimensional Arrays (pg. 250)

Passing Arrays Using ref and out

Like all out parameters, an **out** parameter of an array type must be assigned before it is used; that is, it must be assigned by the callee. For example:

```
public static void MyMethod(out int[] arr)
{
   arr = new int[10];   // definite assignment of arr
}
```

Like all ref parameters, a **ref** parameter of an array type must be definitely assigned by the caller. Therefore, there is no need to be definitely assigned by the callee. A **ref** parameter of an array type may be altered as a result of the call. For example, the array can be assigned the **null** value or can be initialized to a different array. For example:

```
public static void MyMethod(ref int[] arr)
{
   arr = new int[10];   // arr initialized to a different array
}
```

The following two examples demonstrate the difference between **out** and **ref** when used in passing arrays to methods.

Example 1

In this example, the array myArray is declared in the caller (the Main method), and initialized in the FillArray method. Then, the array elements are returned to the caller and displayed.

```
// cs_array_ref_and_out.cs
using System;
class TestOut
{
   static public void FillArray(out int[] myArray)
   {
      // Initialize the array:
      myArray = new int[5] {1, 2, 3, 4, 5};
   }

   static public void Main()
   {
      int[] myArray; // Initialization is not required

      // Pass the array to the callee using out:
      FillArray(out myArray);
```

```
      // Display the array elements:
      Console.WriteLine("Array elements are:");
      for (int i=0; i < myArray.Length; i++)
         Console.WriteLine(myArray[i]);
   }
}
```

Output

```
Array elements are:
1
2
3
4
5
```

Example 2

In this example, the array myArray is initialized in the caller (the Main method), and passed to the FillArray method by using the **ref** parameter. Some of the array elements are updated in the FillArray method. Then, the array elements are returned to the caller and displayed.

```
// cs_array_ref_and_out2.cs
using System;
class TestRef
{
   public static void FillArray(ref int[] arr)
   {
      // Create the array on demand:
      if (arr == null)
         arr = new int[10];
      // Otherwise fill the array:
      arr[0] = 123;
      arr[4] = 1024;
   }

   static public void Main ()
   {
      // Initialize the array:
      int[] myArray = {1,2,3,4,5};

      // Pass the array using ref:
      FillArray(ref myArray);

      // Display the updated array:
      Console.WriteLine("Array elements are:");
      for (int i = 0; i < myArray.Length; i++)
         Console.WriteLine(myArray[i]);
   }
}
```

Output

```
Array elements are:
123
2
3
4
1024
```

Arrays Tutorial

This tutorial describes arrays and shows how they work in C#.

Further Reading

- Arrays

- foreach, in

Tutorial

This tutorial is divided into the following sections:

- Arrays in General

- Declaring Arrays

- Initializing Arrays

- Accessing Array Members

- Arrays are Objects

- Using foreach with Arrays

Arrays in General

C# arrays are zero indexed; that is, the array indexes start at zero. Arrays in C# work similarly to how arrays work in most other popular languages There are, however, a few differences that you should be aware of.

When declaring an array, the square brackets ([]) must come after the type, not the identifier. Placing the brackets after the identifier is not legal syntax in C#.

```
int[] table; // not int table[];
```

Another detail is that the size of the array is not part of its type as it is in the C language. This allows you to declare an array and assign any array of **int** objects to it, regardless of the array's length.

```
int[] numbers; // declare numbers as an int array of any size
numbers = new int[10]; // numbers is a 10-element array
numbers = new int[20]; // now it's a 20-element array
```

Declaring Arrays

C# supports single-dimensional arrays, multidimensional arrays (rectangular arrays), and array-of-arrays (jagged arrays). The following examples show how to declare different kinds of arrays:

Single-dimensional arrays:

```
int[] numbers;
```

Multidimensional arrays:

```
string[,] names;
```

Array-of-arrays (jagged):

```
byte[][] scores;
```

Declaring them (as shown above) does not actually create the arrays. In C#, arrays are objects (discussed later in this tutorial) and must be instantiated. The following examples show how to create arrays:

Single-dimensional arrays:

```
int[] numbers = new int[5];
```

Multidimensional arrays:

```
string[,] names = new string[5,4];
```

Array-of-arrays (jagged):

```
byte[][] scores = new byte[5][];
for (int x = 0; x < scores.Length; x++)
{
    scores[x] = new byte[4];
}
```

You can also have larger arrays. For example, you can have a three-dimensional rectangular array:

```
int[,,] buttons = new int[4,5,3];
```

You can even mix rectangular and jagged arrays. For example, the following code declares a single-dimensional array of three-dimensional arrays of two-dimensional arrays of type **int**:

```
int[][,,][,] numbers;
```

Example

The following is a complete C# program that declares and instantiates arrays as discussed above.

```
// arrays.cs
using System;
class DeclareArraysSample
{
    public static void Main()
    {
        // Single-dimensional array
        int[] numbers = new int[5];

        // Multidimensional array
        string[,] names = new string[5,4];

        // Array-of-arrays (jagged array)
        byte[][] scores = new byte[5][];

        // Create the jagged array
        for (int i = 0; i < scores.Length; i++)
        {
            scores[i] = new byte[i+3];
        }

        // Print length of each row
        for (int i = 0; i < scores.Length; i++)
        {
            Console.WriteLine("Length of row {0} is {1}", i, scores[i].Length);
        }
    }
}
```

Output

```
Length of row 0 is 3
Length of row 1 is 4
Length of row 2 is 5
Length of row 3 is 6
Length of row 4 is 7
```

Initializing Arrays

C# provides simple and straightforward ways to initialize arrays at declaration time by enclosing the initial values in curly braces ({}). It is important to note that array members are automatically initialized to the default initial value for the array type if the array is not initialized at the time it is declared.

The following examples show different ways to initialize different kinds of arrays.

Single-Dimensional Array

```
int[] numbers = new int[5] {1, 2, 3, 4, 5};
string[] names = new string[3] {"Matt", "Joanne", "Robert"};
```

You can omit the size of the array, like this:

```
int[] numbers = new int[] {1, 2, 3, 4, 5};
string[] names = new string[] {"Matt", "Joanne", "Robert"};
```

You can also omit the **new** statement if an initializer is provided, like this:

```
int[] numbers = {1, 2, 3, 4, 5};
string[] names = {"Matt", "Joanne", "Robert"};
```

Multidimensional Array

```
int[,] numbers = new int[3, 2] { {1, 2}, {3, 4}, {5, 6} };
string[,] siblings = new string[2, 2] { {"Mike","Amy"}, {"Mary","Albert"} };
```

You can omit the size of the array, like this:

```
int[,] numbers = new int[,] { {1, 2}, {3, 4}, {5, 6} };
string[,] siblings = new string[,] { {"Mike","Amy"}, {"Mary","Ray"} };
```

You can also omit the **new** statement if an initializer is provided, like this:

```
int[,] numbers = { {1, 2}, {3, 4}, {5, 6} };
string[,] siblings = { {"Mike", "Amy"}, {"Mary", "Albert"} };
```

Jagged Array (Array-of-Arrays)

You can initialize jagged arrays like this example:

```
int[][] numbers = new int[2][] { new int[] {2,3,4}, new int[] {5,6,7,8,9} };
```

You can also omit the size of the first array, like this:

```
int[][] numbers = new int[][] { new int[] {2,3,4}, new int[] {5,6,7,8,9} };
```

-or-

```
int[][] numbers = { new int[] {2,3,4}, new int[] {5,6,7,8,9} };
```

Notice that there is no initialization syntax for the elements of a jagged array.

Accessing Array Members

Accessing array members is straightforward and similar to how you access array members in C/C++. For example, the following code creates an array called numbers and then assigns a 5 to the fifth element of the array:

```
int[] numbers = {10, 9, 8, 7, 6, 5, 4, 3, 2, 1, 0};
numbers[4] = 5;
```

The following code declares a multidimensional array and assigns 5 to the member located at [1,"1]:

```
int[,] numbers = { {1, 2}, {3, 4}, {5, 6}, {7, 8}, {9, 10} };
numbers[1, 1] = 5;
```

The following is a declaration of a single-dimension jagged array that contains two elements. The first element is an array of two integers, and the second is an array of three integers:

```
int[][] numbers = new int[][] { new int[] {1, 2}, new int[] {3, 4, 5}
};
```

The following statements assign 58 to the first element of the first array and 667 to the second element of the second array:

```
numbers[0][0] = 58;
numbers[1][1] = 667;
```

Arrays are Objects

In C#, arrays are actually objects. **System.Array** is the abstract base type of all array types. You can use the properties, and other class members, that **System.Array** has. An example of this would be using the Length property to get the length of an array. The following code assigns the length of the numbers array, which is 5, to a variable called LengthOfNumbers:

```
int[] numbers = {1, 2, 3, 4, 5};
int LengthOfNumbers = numbers.Length;
```

The **System.Array** class provides many other useful methods/properties, such as methods for sorting, searching, and copying arrays.

Using foreach on Arrays

C# also provides the **foreach** statement. This statement provides a simple, clean way to iterate through the elements of an array. For example, the following code creates an array called numbers and iterates through it with the **foreach** statement:

```
int[] numbers = {4, 5, 6, 1, 2, 3, -2, -1, 0};
foreach (int i in numbers)
{
    System.Console.WriteLine(i);
}
```

Constructors and Destructors

This section explains the process of creation, initialization, and destruction of objects. It introduces the following topics:

- Class Constructors
- Struct Constructors
- Destructors

Class Constructors

In this section, three kinds of class constructors are discussed:

Type of class constructor	Comments
Instance	Used to create and initialize instances of the class.
Private	A special type of instance constructor that is not accessible outside the class. A class with a private constructor cannot be instantiated.
Static	Called automatically to initialize the class before the first instance is created or any static members are referenced. The constructor cannot be called directly.

Instance Constructors

Instance constructors are used to create and initialize instances. Constructors are declared using the following form:

```
[attributes] [modifiers] identifier([formal-parameter-list])
[initializer] { constructor-body }
```

where:

attributes (Optional)
Additional declarative information. For more information on attributes and attribute classes, see "Attributes" on page 211.

modifiers (Optional)
The allowed modifiers are extern and the four access modifiers.

identifier
The *identifier* is the same as the class name.

formal-parameter-list (Optional)
The optional parameters passed to the constructor. The parameters must be as accessible as the constructor itself.

initializer (Optional)

Invoked before the execution of the constructor body. The *initializer* can be one of the following with an optional *argument-list*:

: base (*argument-list*)

: this (*argument-list*)

constructor-body

The block that contains the statements that initialize the class instance.

Remarks

The class constructor is invoked when you create a new object, for example:

```
Point myPoint = new Point();
```

A class can have more than one constructor. For example, you can declare a constructor without arguments, such as `Point()`, and another constructor with arguments, such as `Point(int x, int y)`.

If the class does not have a constructor, a default parameterless constructor is automatically generated for you and the default values are used to initialize the object fields (for example, an **int** is initialized to 0). For more information on default values, see "Default Values Table" on page 164.

The class constructor can invoke the constructor of the base class through the initializer, for example:

```
public Cylinder(double radius, double height): base(radius, height)
{
}
```

In the preceding example, the fields, `radius` and `height`, are initialized through the base class constructor. This is analogous to the C++ initialization list.

The class constructor can also invoke another constructor from the same class by using the keyword **this**, for example:

```
public Point(): this(0,20)
{
}
```

In the preceding example, the parameterless constructor `Point()` is invoking another constructor that has two arguments to initialize the default position at (0, 20).

Example 1

The following example demonstrates a class with two class constructors, one without arguments and one with two arguments.

```csharp
// Constructor1.cs
using System;

class Point
{
    public int x, y;
    // Default constructor:
    public Point()
    {
        x = 0;
        y = 0;
    }
    // A constructor with two arguments:
    public Point(int x, int y)
    {
        this.x = x;
        this.y = y;
    }

    // Override the ToString method:
    public override string ToString()
    {
        return(String.Format("({0},{1})", x, y));
    }
}

class MainClass
{
    static void Main()
    {
        Point p1 = new Point();
        Point p2 = new Point(5,3);

        // Display the results using the overriden ToString method:
        Console.WriteLine("Point #1 at {0}", p1);
        Console.WriteLine("Point #2 at {0}", p2);
    }
}
```

Output

```
Point #1 at (0,0)
Point #2 at (5,3)
```

Example 2

In this example the class Person does not have any constructors, in which case, a default constructor is automatically provided and the fields are initialized to their default values.

```
// Constructor2.cs
using System;

public class Person
{
    public int age;
    public string name;
}

public class MainClass
{
    static void Main()
    {
        Person p = new Person();

        Console.Write("Name: {0}, Age: {1}",p.name, p.age);
    }
}
```

Output

```
Name: , Age: 0
```

Notice that the default value of age is 0 and the default value of name is **null**. For more information on default values, see "Default Values Table" on page 164.

Example 3

The following example demonstrates using the base class initializer. The Circle class is derived from the general class Shape, and the Cylinder class is derived from the Circle class. The constructor on each derived class is using its base class initializer.

```
// CtorInitializer.cs
using System;

abstract class Shape
{
    public const double pi = Math.PI;
    protected double x, y, z;

    public Shape (double x, double y, double z)
    {
        this.x = x;
        this.y = y;
        this.z = z;
    }
```

```
    public abstract double Area();
}

class Circle: Shape
{
    public Circle(double radius): base(radius,0,0)
    {
    }

    public override double Area()
    {
        return pi*x*x;
    }
}

class Cylinder: Circle
{
    public Cylinder(double radius, double height): base(radius)
    {
        y = height;
    }

    public override double Area()
    {
        return 2*(base.Area()) + 2*pi*x*y;
    }
}

class TestClass
{
    public static void Main()
    {
        double radius = 2.5, height = 3.0;
        Circle myCircle = new Circle(radius);
        Cylinder myCylinder = new Cylinder(radius, height);

        Console.WriteLine("Area of the circle   = {0:F2}",
                            myCircle.Area());
        Console.WriteLine("Area of the cylinder = {0:F2}",
                            myCylinder.Area());
    }
}
```

Output

```
Area of the circle   = 19.63
Area of the cylinder = 86.39
```

For more examples on invoking the base class constructors, see the sections "virtual" on page 51, "override" on page 44, and "base" on page 4.

See Also

Class Constructors (pg. 261)

Private Constructors

A private constructor is a special instance constructor. It is commonly used in classes that contain static members only. In such a case, other classes (except nested classes) are not allowed to create instances of this class. For example:

```
class NLog
{
    // Private Constructor:
    private NLog() {}

    public static double e = 2.71828;
}
```

The declaration of the empty constructor prevents the automatic generation of a default constructor. Note that if you don't use an access modifier with the constructor it will still be private by default. However, the **private** modifier is usually used explicitly to make it clear that the class cannot be instantiated.

Private constructors are useful to prevent creation of a class when there are no instance fields or methods, such as the Math class, or when a method is called to obtain an instance of a class.

Example

The following is an example of a class using a private constructor.

```
// PrivateCtor1.cs
using System;

public class MyClass
{
    private MyClass() {}
    public static int counter;
    public static int IncrementCounter()
    {
        return ++counter;
    }
}

class MainClass
{
    static void Main()
    {
        // If you uncomment the following statement, it will generate
        // an error because the constructor is inaccessible:
        // MyClass myObject = new MyClass();   // Error
```

```
        MyClass.counter = 100;
        MyClass.IncrementCounter();
        Console.WriteLine("New count: {0}", MyClass.counter);
    }
}
```

Output

```
New count: 101
```

Notice that if you uncomment the following statement from the example, it will generate an error because the constructor is inaccessible due to its protection level:

```
// MyClass myObject = new MyClass();    // error
```

See Also

static (pg. 48), Private Constructors (pg. 266), Class Constructors (pg. 261)

Static Constructors

A static constructor is used to initialize a class. It is called automatically to initialize the class before the first instance is created or any static members are referenced. It is declared using the following form:

```
[attributes] static identifier( ) { constructor-body }
```

where:

attributes (Optional)
> Additional declarative information. For more information on attributes and attribute classes, see "Attributes" on page 211.

identifier
> The *identifier* is the same as the class name.

constructor-body
> The block that contains the statements that initialize the class.

Remarks

A static constructor does not take access modifiers or have parameters.

A static constructor is called automatically to initialize the class before the first instance is created or any static members are referenced.

A static constructor cannot be called directly.

The user has no control on when the static constructor is executed in the program.

A typical use of static constructors is when the class is using a log file and the constructor is used to write entries to this file.

268 Part 3: C# Features

Example

In this example, the class `MyClass` has a static constructor and one static member, `MyMethod()`. When `MyMethod()` is called, the static constructor is invoked to initialize the class.

```
// StaticCtor1.cs
using System;
class MyClass
{
    // Static constructor:
    static MyClass()
    {
        Console.WriteLine("The static constructor invoked.");
    }

    public static void MyMethod()
    {
        Console.WriteLine("MyMethod invoked.");
    }
}

class MainClass
{
    static void Main()
    {
        MyClass.MyMethod();
    }
}
```

Output

```
The static constructor invoked.
MyMethod invoked.
```

See Also

static (pg. 48), Class Constructors (pg. 261)

Struct Constructors

Struct constructors are similar to class constructors, except for the following differences:

- Structs cannot contain explicit parameterless constructors. Struct members are automatically initialized to their default values.

- A struct cannot have an initializer in the form: **base** (*argument-list*).

Example

The following is an example of a constructor using two arguments for the `Point` struct.

```
// Structctor1.cs
using System;

public struct Point
{
    public int x, y;
    // Constructor:
    public Point(int x, int y)
    {
        this.x = x;
        this.y = y;
    }

    // Override the ToString method:
    public override string ToString()
    {
        return(String.Format("({0},{1})", x, y));
    }
}

class MainClass
{
    static void Main()
    {
        // Initialize two points:
        Point p1 = new Point();
        Point p2 = new Point(10,15);

        // Display the results using the overriden ToString method:
        Console.WriteLine("Point #1 (default initialization): {0}", p1);
        Console.WriteLine("Point #2 (explicit initialization): {0}", p2);
    }
}
```

Output

```
Point #1 (default initialization): (0,0)
Point #2 (explicit initialization): (10,15)
```

For more information on structs, see the section "struct" on page 138.

See Also

Class Constructors (pg. 261)

Destructors

Destructors are used to destruct instances of classes. A destructor is declared using the following form:

```
[attributes] ~ identifier( ) { destructor-body }
```

where:

attributes (Optional)
    Additional declarative information. For more information on attributes and attribute classes, see "Attributes" on page 211.

identifier
    The *identifier* is the same as the class name.

destructor-body
    The block that contains the statements that destruct the instance of the class.

Remarks

Note   Destructors cannot be used with structs. They are only used with classes.

A class can only have one destructor.

Destructors cannot be inherited or overloaded.

Destructors cannot be called. They are invoked automatically.

A destructor does not take modifiers or have parameters. For example, the following is a declaration of a destructor for the class MyClass:

```
~ MyClass()
{
   // Cleanup statements.
}
```

The destructor implicitly calls the Object.Finalize method on the object's base class. Therefore, the preceding destructor code is implicitly translated to:

```
protected override void Finalize()
{
   try
   {
      // Cleanup statements.
   }
   finally
   {
      base.Finalize();
   }
}
```

This means that the **Finalize** method is called recursively for all of the instances in the inheritance chain, from the most derived to the least derived.

The programmer has no control on when the destructor is called because this is determined by the garbage collector. The garbage collector checks for objects that are no longer being used by the application. It considers these objects eligible for destruction and reclaims their memory. Destructors are also called when the program exits.

> **Note** It is possible to force garbage collection by calling the GC.Collect method, but in most cases, this should be avoided because it may result in performance issues.

Example

The following example creates three classes that make a chain of inheritance. The class First is the base class, Second is derived from First, and Third is derived from Second. All three have destructors. In Main(), an instance of the most derived class is created. When the program runs, notice that the destructors for the three classes are called automatically, and in order, from the most derived to the least derived.

```
// Destructors1.cs
using System;

class First
{
    ~First()
    {
        Console.WriteLine("First's destructor is called");
    }
}

class Second: First
{
    ~Second()
    {
        Console.WriteLine("Second's destructor is called");
    }
}

class Third: Second
{
    ~Third()
    {
        Console.WriteLine("Third's destructor is called");
    }
}
```

(continued)

(continued)

```
public class MainClass
{
    public static void Main()
    {
        Third myObject = new Third();
    }
}
```

Output

```
Third's destructor is called
Second's destructor is called
First's destructor is called
```

Using Destructors to Release Resources

In general, you should not be as concerned about memory management as you would with C++. This is because the .NET Framework garbage collector implicitly manages the allocation and release of memory for your objects. However, when your application encapsulates unmanaged resources such as windows, files, and network connections, you should use destructors to free those resources. When the object is eligible for destruction, the garbage collector runs the object's **Finalize** method.

Explicit Release of Resources

If your application is using an expensive external resource, it is also recommended that you provide a way to explicitly release the resource before the garbage collector frees the object. You do this by implementing a **Dispose** method (from the IDisposable interface) that performs the necessary cleanup for the object. This can considerably improve the performance of the application. Even with this explicit control over resources, the destructor becomes a safeguard to clean up resources if the call to the **Dispose** method failed.

For more details on cleaning up resources, see "using Statement" on page 60.

See Also

using (pg. 57)

Indexers

Indexers permit instances of a class or struct to be indexed in the same way as arrays. Indexers are similar to properties except that their accessor take parameters.

In this section, the following topics are introduced:

- Indexer Declaration

- Comparison Between Properties and Indexers

- Interface Indexers

See Also
Properties (pg. 283)

Indexer Declaration

Indexers allow you to index a class or a struct instance in the same way as an array. To declare an indexer, use the following declaration:

```
[attributes] [modifiers] indexer-declarator {accessor-declarations}
```

The *indexer-declarator* takes one of the forms:

```
type this [formal-index-parameter-list]
type interface-type.this [formal-index-parameter-list]
```

The *formal-index-parameter* takes the form:

```
[attributes] type identifier
```

where:

attributes (Optional)

Additional declarative information. For more information on attributes and attribute classes, see "Attributes" on page 211.

modifiers (Optional)

Allowed modifiers are **new** and a valid combination of the four access modifiers.

indexer-declarator

Includes the *type* of the element introduced by the indexer, **this**, and the *formal-index-parameter-list*. If the indexer is an explicit interface member implementation, the *interface-type* is included.

type

A type name.

interface-type

The interface name.

formal-index-parameter-list

Specifies the parameters of the indexer. The parameter includes optional *attributes*, the index *type,* and the index *identifier*. At least one parameter must be specified. The parameter modifiers **out** and **ref** are not allowed.

accessor-declarations

The indexer accessors, which specify the executable statements associated with reading and writing indexer elements.

identifier

The parameter name.

The get Accessor

The **get** accessor body of an indexer is similar to a method body. It returns the type of the indexer. The **get** accessor uses the same *formal-index-parameter-list* as the indexer. For example:

```
get
{
    return myArray[index];
}
```

The set Accessor

The **set** accessor body of an indexer is similar to a method body. It uses the same *formal-index-parameter-list* as the indexer, in addition to the **value** implicit parameter. For example:

```
set
{
    myArray[index] = value;
}
```

Remarks

The type of an indexer and each of the types referenced in the *formal-index-parameter-list* must be at least as accessible as the indexer itself. For more information on accessibility levels, see "Access Modifiers" on page 21.

The signature of an indexer consists of the number and types of its formal parameters. It does not include the indexer type or the names of the formal parameters.

If you declare more than one indexer in the same class, they must have different signatures.

An indexer value is not classified as a variable; therefore, it is not possible to pass an indexer value as a **ref** or **out** parameter.

To provide the indexer a name that other languages can use for the default indexed property, use a name attribute in the declaration. For example:

```
[System.Runtime.CompilerServices.CSharp.IndexerName("MyItem")]
public int this [int index]    // indexer declaration
{
}
```

This indexer will have the name MyItem. Without providing the name attribute, the default name will be Item.

Example

This example declares a private array field myArray and an indexer. Using the indexer allows direct access to the instance b[i]. The alternative to using the indexer is to declare the array as a **public** member and access its members, myArray[i], directly.

```
// cs_keyword_indexers.cs
using System;
class IndexerClass
{
    private int [] myArray = new int[100];
    public int this [int index]    // indexer declaration
    {
        get
        {
            // Check the index limits
            if (index < 0 || index >= 100)
                return 0;
            else
                return myArray[index];
        }
        set
        {
            if (!(index < 0 || index >= 100))
                myArray[index] = value;
        }
    }
}

public class MainClass
{
    public static void Main()
    {
        IndexerClass b = new IndexerClass();
        // call the indexer to initialize the elements #3 and #5:
        b[3] = 256;
        b[5] = 1024;
        for (int i=0; i<=10; i++)
        {
            Console.WriteLine("Element #{0} = {1}", i, b[i]);
        }
    }
}
```

Output

```
Element #0 = 0
Element #1 = 0
Element #2 = 0
Element #3 = 256
Element #4 = 0
Element #5 = 1024
Element #6 = 0
Element #7 = 0
Element #8 = 0
Element #9 = 0
Element #10 = 0
```

Notice that when an indexer's access is evaluated (for example, in a **Console.Write** statement) the **get** accessor is invoked. Therefore, if no **get** accessor exists, a compile-time error occurs.

For an additional example, see the example in "Indexers" on page 272.

See Also

Properties (pg. 283), Accessors (pg. 286), Indexers Tutorial (pg. 279)

Comparison Between Properties and Indexers

Indexers are similar to properties. Except for the differences shown in the following table, all of the rules defined for property accessors apply to indexer accessors as well.

Property	Indexer
Identified by its name.	Identified by its signature.
Accessed through a simple name or a member access.	Accessed through an element access.
Can be a static or an instance member.	Must be an instance member.
A **get** accessor of a property has no parameters.	A **get** accessor of an indexer has the same formal parameter list as the indexer.
A **set** accessor of a property contains the implicit **value** parameter.	A **set** accessor of an indexer has the same formal parameter list as the indexer, in addition to the **value** parameter.

See Also

Properties (pg. 283), Accessors (pg. 286)

Interface Indexers

Indexers can be declared on interfaces. The declaration takes the following form:

```
[attributes] [new] type this [formal-index-parameter-list] {interface-accessors}
```

where:

attributes (Optional)
  Same as indexers on classes.

type
  Same as indexers on classes.

formal-index-parameter-list
  Same as indexers on classes.

interface-accessors
  The indexer accessors. See the Remarks below.

Remarks

Accessors of interface indexers differ from the accessors of class indexers as follows:

- Interface accessors don't use modifiers.

- The body of the accessor consists of a semicolon.

Thus, the purpose of the accessors is to indicate whether the indexer is read-write, read-only, or write-only.

The following is an example of an interface indexer accessor:

```
public interface IMyInterface
{
    ...
    // Indexer declaration:
    string this[int index]
    {
        get;
        set;
    }
}
```

The signature of an indexer must differ from the signatures of all other indexers declared in the same interface.

Example

The following example demonstrates implementation of interface indexers.

```csharp
// cs_interface_indexers.cs
using System;
// Indexer on an interface:
public interface IMyInterface
{
   // indexer declaration:
   int this[int index]
   {
      get;
      set;
   }
}

// Implementing the interface:
class IndexerClass : IMyInterface
{
   private int [] myArray = new int[100];
   public int this [int index]   // indexer declaration
   {
      get
      {
         // Check the index limits
         if (index < 0 || index >= 100)
            return 0;
         else
            return myArray[index];
      }
      set
      {
         if (!(index < 0 || index >= 100))
            myArray[index] = value;
      }
   }
}

public class MainClass
{
   public static void Main()
   {
      IndexerClass b = new IndexerClass();
      // call the indexer to initialize the elements #3 and #5:
      b[2] = 4;
      b[5] = 32;
      for (int i=0; i<=10; i++)
      {
         Console.WriteLine("Element #{0} = {1}", i, b[i]);
      }
   }
}
```

Output

```
Element #0 = 0
Element #1 = 0
Element #2 = 4
Element #3 = 0
Element #4 = 0
Element #5 = 32
Element #6 = 0
Element #7 = 0
Element #8 = 0
Element #9 = 0
Element #10 = 0
```

In the preceding example, you could use the explicit interface member implementation by using the fully qualified name of the interface member. For example:

```
public string IMyInterface.this
{
}
```

However, the fully qualified name is only needed to avoid ambiguity when the class is implementing more than one interface with the same indexer signature. For example, if the class Employee is implementing two interfaces, ICitizen and IEmployee, and both interfaces have the same indexer signature, the explicit interface member implementation will be necessary. That is, the following indexer declaration:

```
public string IEmployee.this
{
}
```

implements the indexer on the IEmployee interface, while the following declaration:

```
public string ICitizen.this
{
}
```

implements the indexer on the ICitizen interface.

See Also

interface (pg. 155)

Indexers Tutorial

This tutorial shows how C# classes can declare indexers to provide array-like access to the classes.

Further Reading

- Accessors
- Comparison Between Properties and Indexers

Tutorial

Defining an *indexer* allows you to create classes that act like "virtual arrays." Instances of that class can be accessed using the [] array access operator. Defining an indexer in C# is similar to defining operator [] in C++, but is considerably more flexible. For classes that encapsulate array- or collection-like functionality, using an indexer allows the users of that class to use the array syntax to access the class.

For example, suppose you want to define a class that makes a file appear as an array of bytes. If the file were very large, it would be impractical to read the entire file into memory, especially if you only wanted to read or change a few bytes. By defining a FileByteArray class, you could make the file appear similar to an array of bytes, but actually do file input and output when a byte was read or written.

In addition to the example below, an advanced topic on Creating an Indexed Property is discussed in this tutorial.

Example

In this example, the class FileByteArray makes it possible to access a file as if it were a byte array. The Reverse class reverses the bytes of the file. You can run this program to reverse the bytes of any text file including the program source file itself. To change the reversed file back to normal, run the program on the same file again.

```
// indexer.cs
// arguments: indexer.txt
using System;
using System.IO;

// Class to provide access to a large file
// as if it were a byte array.
public class FileByteArray
{
    Stream stream;       // Holds the underlying stream
                         // used to access the file.
// Create a new FileByteArray encapsulating a particular file.
    public FileByteArray(string fileName)
    {
        stream = new FileStream(fileName, FileMode.Open);
    }

    // Close the stream. This should be the last thing done
    // when you are finished.
    public void Close()
    {
        stream.Close();
        stream = null;
    }
```

```csharp
    // Indexer to provide read/write access to the file.
    public byte this[long index]    // long is a 64-bit integer
    {
        // Read one byte at offset index and return it.
        get
        {
            byte[] buffer = new byte[1];
            stream.Seek(index, SeekOrigin.Begin);
            stream.Read(buffer, 0, 1);
            return buffer[0];
        }
        // Write one byte at offset index and return it.
        set
        {
            byte[] buffer = new byte[1] {value};
            stream.Seek(index, SeekOrigin.Begin);
            stream.Write(buffer, 0, 1);
        }
    }

    // Get the total length of the file.
    public long Length
    {
        get
        {
            return stream.Seek(0, SeekOrigin.End);
        }
    }
}

// Demonstrate the FileByteArray class.
// Reverses the bytes in a file.
public class Reverse
{
    public static void Main(String[] args)
    {
        // Check for arguments.
        if (args.Length == 0)
        {
            Console.WriteLine("indexer <filename>");
            return;
        }

        FileByteArray file = new FileByteArray(args[0]);
        long len = file.Length;
```

```
        // Swap bytes in the file to reverse it.
        for (long i = 0; i < len / 2; ++i)
        {
            byte t;

            // Note that indexing the "file" variable invokes the
            // indexer on the FileByteStream class, which reads
            // and writes the bytes in the file.
            t = file[i];
            file[i] = file[len - i - 1];
            file[len - i - 1] = t;
        }

        file.Close();
    }
}
```

Input: indexer.txt

To test the program you can use the file Test.txt, which is included in the same folder with the sample (or create a new file to test). This is the text of the file:

```
public class Hello1
{
    public static void Main()
    {
        System.Console.WriteLine("Hello, World!");
    }
}
```

To reverse the bytes of this file, compile the program and then use the command line:

```
indexer indexer.txt
```

To display the reversed file, enter the command:

```
Type indexer.txt
```

Sample Output

```
}
}
;)"!dlroW ,olleH"(eniLetirW.elosnoC.metsyS
{
)(niaM diov citats cilbup
{
1olleH ssalc cilbup
```

Code Discussion

- Since an indexer is accessed using the [] operator, it does not have a name.

- In the example above, the indexer is of type byte and takes a single index of type long (64-bit integer). The Get accessor defines the code to read a byte from the file, while the Set accessor defines the code to write a byte to the file. Inside the Set accessor, the predefined parameter value has the value that is being assigned to the virtual array element.

- An indexer must have at least one parameter. Although it is comparatively rare, an indexer can have more than one parameter in order to simulate a multidimensional "virtual array." Although integral parameters are the most common, the indexer parameter can be of any type. For example, the standard Dictionary class provides an indexer with a parameter of type Object.

- Although indexers are a powerful feature, it is important to use them only when the array-like abstraction makes sense. Always carefully consider whether using regular method(s) would be just as clear. For example, the following is a bad use of an indexer:

```
class Employee
{
    // VERY BAD STYLE: using an indexer to access
    // the salary of an employee.
    public double this[int year]
    {
        get
        {
            // return employee's salary for a given year.
        }
    }
}
```

Although legal, an indexer with only a Get accessor is rarely good style. Strongly consider using a method in this case.

- Indexers can be overloaded.

Properties

Properties are named members of classes, structs, and interfaces. They provide a flexible mechanism to read, write, or compute the values of private fields through accessors.

In this section, the following topics are introduced:

- Property Declaration
- Accessors
- Interface Properties

See Also

Indexers (pg. 272)

Property Declaration

Properties are an extension of fields and are accessed using the same syntax. Unlike fields, properties do not designate storage locations. Instead, properties have accessors that read, write, or compute their values.

Property declaration takes one of the following forms:

```
[attributes] [modifiers] type identifier {accessor-declaration}
[attributes] [modifiers] type interface-type.identifier {accessor-declaration}
```

where:

attributes (Optional)
> Additional declarative information. For more information on attributes and attribute classes, see "Attributes" on page 211.

modifiers (Optional)
> The allowed modifiers are new, static, virtual, abstract, override, and a valid combination of the four access modifiers.

type
> The property type, which must be at least as accessible as the property itself. For more information on accessibility levels, see "Access Modifiers" on page 21.

identifier
> The property name. For more information on interface member implementation, see the section "interface" on page 155.

accessor-declaration
> Declaration of the property accessors, which are used to read and write the property.

interface-type
> The interface in a fully qualified property name. See "Interface Properties" on page 293.

Remarks

Unlike fields, properties are not classified as variables. Therefore, it is not possible to pass a property as a ref or out parameter.

A property declared using the **static** modifier is classified as a static property; otherwise, it is classified as an instance property. Like other static members, a static property is not associated with a specific instance and cannot be referenced through an instance. Instead, it is associated with the type and can only be referenced through the type name. For example, in the following statements:

```
Button okButton = new Button();
// Using an instance property:
string s = okButton.Caption;
```

the Caption property is associated with the instance okButton. If Caption is declared as a static property, the class name (Button) must be used instead:

```
// Using a static property:
string s = Button.Caption;
```

An instance of a class can be accessed using this in the accessors of an instance property, but it is an error to use **this** in the accessors of a static property.

It is an error to use a virtual, abstract, or override modifier on an accessor of a static property.

Example

This example demonstrates instance, static, and read-only properties. It accepts the name of the employee from the keyboard, increments numberOfEmployees by 1, and displays the Employee name and number.

```csharp
// property.cs
// Properties
using System;
public class Employee
{
    public static int numberOfEmployees;
    private static int counter;
    private string name;

    // A read-write instance property:
    public string Name
    {
        get
        {
            return name;
        }
        set
        {
            name = value;
        }
    }

    // A read-only static property:
    public static int Counter
    {
        get
        {
            return counter;
        }
    }
```

(continued)

(continued)

```
// Constructor:
public Employee()
{
    // Calculate the employee's number:
    counter = ++counter + numberOfEmployees;
}
}

public class MainClass
{
    public static void Main()
    {
        Employee.numberOfEmployees = 100;
        Employee e1 = new Employee();
        e1.Name = "Claude Vige";
        Console.WriteLine("Employee number: {0}", Employee.Counter);
        Console.WriteLine("Employee name: {0}", e1.Name);
    }
}
```

Output

```
Employee number: 101
Employee name: Claude Vige
```

See Also

Accessors (pg. 286), Indexers (pg. 272), Properties Tutorial (pg. 296)

Accessors

The accessor of a property contains the executable statements associated with getting (reading or computing) or setting (writing) the property. The accessor declarations can contain a **get** accessor, a **set** accessor, or both. The declarations take the following forms:

```
set {accessor-body}
get {accessor-body}
```

where:

accessor-body
    The block that contains the statements to be executed when the accessor is invoked.

The get Accessor

The body of the **get** accessor is similar to that of a method. It must return a value of the property type. The execution of the **get** accessor is equivalent to reading the value of the field. The following is a **get** accessor that returns the value of a private field `name`:

```
private string name;   // the name field
public string Name   // the Name property
{
   get
   {
      return name;
   }
}
```

When you reference the property, except as the target of an assignment, the **get** accessor is invoked to read the value of the property. For example:

```
Employee e1 = new Employee();
...
Console.Write(e1.Name);   // The get accessor is invoked here
```

The **get** accessor must terminate in a **return** or **throw** statement, and control cannot flow off the accessor body.

The set Accessor

The **set** accessor is similar to a method that returns **void**. It uses an implicit parameter called **value**, whose type is the type of the property. In the following example, a **set** accessor is added to the `Name` property:

```
public string Name
{
   get
   {
      return name;
   }
   set
   {
      name = value;
   }
}
```

When you assign a value to the property, the **set** accessor is invoked with an argument that provides the new value. For example:

```
e1.Name = "Joe";   // The set accessor is invoked here
```

It is an error to use the implicit parameter name (**value**) for a local variable declaration in a **set** accessor.

Remarks

A property is classified according to the accessors used as follows:

- A property with a **get** accessor only is called a read-only property. You cannot assign a value to a read-only property.

- A property with a **set** accessor only is called a write-only property. You cannot reference a write-only property except as a target of an assignment.

- A property with both **get** and **set** accessors is a read-write property.

In a property declaration, both the **get** and **set** accessors must be declared inside the body of the property.

It is a bad programming style to change the state of the object by using the **get** accessor. For example, the following accessor produces the side effect of changing the state of the object each time the number field is accessed.

```
public int Number
{
   get
   {
      return number++;    // Don't do this
   }
}
```

The **get** accessor can either be used to return the field value or to compute it and return it. For example:

```
public string Name
{
   get
   {
      return name != null ? name : "NA";
   }
}
```

In the preceding code segment, if you don't assign a value to the Name property, it will return the value NA.

Example 1

This example demonstrates how to access a property in a base class that is hidden by another property with the same name in a derived class.

```
// property_hiding.cs
// Property hiding
using System;
public class BaseClass
{
   private string name;
   public string Name
   {
      get
      {
         return name;
      }
      set
      {
         name = value;
      }
   }
}

public class DerivedClass : BaseClass
{
   private string name;
   public new string Name    // Notice the use of the new modifier
   {
      get
      {
         return name;
      }
      set
      {
         name = value;
      }
   }
}

public class MainClass
{
   public static void Main()
   {
      DerivedClass d1 = new DerivedClass();
      d1.Name = "John";  // Derived class property
      Console.WriteLine("Name in the derived class is: {0}",d1.Name);
      ((BaseClass)d1).Name = "Mary"; // Base class property
      Console.WriteLine("Name in the base class is: {0}",
         ((BaseClass)d1).Name);
   }
}
```

```
Name in the derived class is: John
Name in the base class is: Mary
```

The following are important points shown in the preceding example:

- The property Name in the derived class hides the property Name in the base class. In such a case, the **new** modifier is used in the declaration of the property in the derived class:

  ```
  public new string Name
  {
  ...
  ```

- The cast (BaseClass) is used to access the hidden property in the base class:

  ```
  ((BaseClass)d1).Name = "Mary";
  ```

For more information on hiding members, see the section "new" on page 65.

Example 2

In this example, two classes, Cube and Square, implement an abstract class, Shape, and override its abstract Area property. Note the use of the override modifier on the properties. The program accepts the side as an input and calculates the areas for the square and cube. It also accepts the area as an input and calculates the corresponding side for the square and cube.

```
// overridding_properties.cs
// Overriding properties
using System;
abstract class Shape
{
    public abstract double Area
    {
        get;
        set;
    }
}

class Square: Shape
{
        public double side;

        // Constructor:
        public Square(double s)
        {
            side = s;
        }
```

```
    // The Area property
    public override double Area
    {
        get
        {
            return side*side ;
        }
        set
        {
            // Given the area, compute the side
            side = Math.Sqrt(value);
        }
    }
}

class Cube: Shape
{
        public double side;

        // Constructor:
        public Cube(double s)
        {
            side = s;
        }

        // The Area property
        public override double Area
        {
            get
            {
                return 6*side*side;
            }
            set
            {
                // Given the area, compute the side
                side = Math.Sqrt(value/6);
            }
        }
}

public class MainClass
{
    public static void Main()
    {
        // Input the side:
        Console.Write("Enter the side: ");
        string sideString = Console.ReadLine();
        double side = double.Parse(sideString);
```

(continued)

(continued)

```
// Compute areas:
Square s = new Square(side);
Cube c = new Cube(side);

// Display results:
Console.WriteLine("Area of a square = {0:F2}",s.Area);
Console.WriteLine("Area of a cube = {0:F2}", c.Area);

// Input the area:
Console.Write("Enter the area: ");
string areaString = Console.ReadLine();
double area = double.Parse(areaString);

// Compute sides:
s.Area = area;
c.Area = area;

// Display results:
Console.WriteLine("Side of a square = {0:F2}", s.side);
Console.WriteLine("Side of a cube = {0:F2}", c.side);
    }
}
```

Input

```
4
24
```

Sample Output

```
Enter the side: 4
Area of a square = 16.00
Area of a cube = 96.00
Enter the area: 24
Side of a square = 4.90
Side of a cube = 2.00
```

See Also

virtual (pg. 51), override (pg. 44), abstract (pg. 31), base (pg. 4), Indexers (pg. 272), new (pg. 65), Properties Tutorial (pg. 296), Indexers Tutorial (pg. 279)

Interface Properties

Properties can be declared on interfaces. The declaration takes the following form:

```
[attributes] [new] type identifier {interface-accessors}
```

where:

attributes (Optional)
>   Same as properties on classes.

type
>   Same as properties on classes.

identifier
>   The property name.

interface-accessors
>   The property accessors. See the Remarks below.

Remarks

The body of the accessor of an interface property consists of a semicolon.

Thus, the purpose of the accessors is to indicate whether the property is read-write, read-only, or write-only.

The following is an example of an interface indexer accessor:

```
public interface IMyInterface
{
    // Property declaration:
    string Name
    {
        get;
        set;
    }
}
```

Example

In this example, the interface IEmployee has a read-write property, Name, and a read-only property, Counter. The class Employee implements the IEmployee interface and uses these two properties. The program reads the name of a new employee and the current number of employees and displays the employee name and the computed employee number.

```
// cs_interface_properties.cs
// Interface Properties
using System;
interface IEmployee
```

(continued)

(continued)

```
{
    string Name
    {
        get;
        set;
    }

    int Counter
    {
        get;
    }
}

public class Employee: IEmployee
{
    public static int numberOfEmployees;
    private int counter;
    private string name;
    // Read-write instance property:
    public string Name
    {
        get
        {
            return name;
        }
        set
        {
            name = value;
        }
    }
    // Read-only instance property:
    public int Counter
    {
        get
        {
            return counter;
        }
    }
    // Constructor:
    public Employee()
    {
        counter = ++counter + numberOfEmployees;
    }
}
```

```
public class MainClass
{
    public static void Main()
    {
        Console.Write("Enter number of employees: ");
        string s = Console.ReadLine();
        Employee.numberOfEmployees = int.Parse(s);
        Employee e1 = new Employee();
        Console.Write("Enter the name of the new employee: ");
        e1.Name = Console.ReadLine();
        Console.WriteLine("The employee information:");
        Console.WriteLine("Employee number: {0}", e1.Counter);
        Console.WriteLine("Employee name: {0}", e1.Name);
    }
}
```

Input
```
210
Hazem Abolrous
```

Sample Output
```
Enter number of employees: 201
Enter the name of the new employee: Hazem Abolrous
The employee information:
Employee number: 202
Employee name: Hazem Abolrous
```

In the preceding example, you could use the fully qualified name of the property, which references the interface in which the member is declared. For example:

```
public string IEmployee.Name
{
}
```

However, the fully qualified name is only needed to avoid ambiguity when the class is implementing more than one interface with the same property signature. For example, if the class Employee is implementing two interfaces ICitizen and IEmployee and both interfaces have the Name property, the explicit interface member implementation will be necessary. That is, the following property declaration:

```
public string IEmployee.Name
{
}
```

implements the Name property on the IEmployee interface, while the following declaration:

```
public string ICitizen.Name
{
}
```

implements the Name property on the ICitizen interface.

See Also

Accessors (pg. 286), Comparison Between Properties and Indexers (pg. 276)

Properties Tutorial

This tutorial shows how properties are an integral part of the C# programming language. It demonstrates how properties are declared and used.

Further Reading

Comparison Between Properties and Indexers

Tutorial

This tutorial includes two examples. The first example shows how to declare and use read/write properties. The second example demonstrates abstract properties and shows how to override these properties in subclasses.

Example 1

This sample shows a `Person` class that has two properties: `Name` (string) and `Age` (int). Both properties are read/write.

```
// person.cs
using System;
class Person
{
    private string myName ="N/A";
    private int myAge = 0;

    // Declare a Name property of type string:
    public string Name
    {
        get
        {
            return myName;
        }
        set
        {
            myName = value;
        }
    }
```

```
    // Declare an Age property of type int:
    public int Age
    {
        get
        {
            return myAge;
        }
        set
        {
            myAge = value;
        }
    }

    public override string ToString()
    {
        return "Name = " + Name + ", Age = " + Age;
    }

    public static void Main()
    {
        Console.WriteLine("Simple Properties");

        // Create a new Person object:
        Person person = new Person();

        // Print out the name and the age associated with the person:
        Console.WriteLine("Person details - {0}", person);

        // Set some values on the person object:
        person.Name = "Joe";
        person.Age = 99;
        Console.WriteLine("Person details - {0}", person);

        // Increment the Age property:
        person.Age += 1;
        Console.WriteLine("Person details - {0}", person);
    }
}
```

Output

```
Simple Properties
Person details - Name = N/A, Age = 0
Person details - Name = Joe, Age = 99
Person details - Name = Joe, Age = 100
```

Code Discussion

- Notice the way that the properties are declared, for example, consider the `Name` property:

```csharp
public string Name
{
    get
    {
        return myName;
    }
    set
    {
        myName = value;
    }
}
```

The Set and Get methods of a property are contained inside the property declaration. You can control whether a property is read/write, read-only, or write-only by controlling whether a Get or Set method is included.

- Once the properties are declared, they can be used as if they were fields of the class. This allows for a very natural syntax when both getting and setting the value of a property, as in the following statements:

```csharp
person.Name = "Joe";
person.Age = 99;
```

- Note that in a property Set method a special `value` variable is available. This variable contains the value that the user specified, for example:

```csharp
myName = value;
```

- Notice the clean syntax for incrementing the `Age` property on a `Person` object:

```csharp
person.Age += 1;
```

If separate Set and Get methods were used to model properties, the equivalent code might look like this:

```csharp
person.SetAge(person.GetAge() + 1);
```

- The ToString method is overridden in this example:

```csharp
public override string ToString()
{
    return "Name = " + Name + ", Age = " + Age;
}
```

Notice that ToString is not explicitly used in the program. It is invoked by default by the WriteLine calls.

Example 2

The following example shows how to define abstract properties. An abstract property declaration does not provide an implementation of the property accessors. The example demonstrates how to override these properties in subclasses. It consists of three files that must be compiled together:

- abstractshape.cs: The Shape class that contains an abstract Area property.

- shapes.cs: The subclasses of the Shape class.

- shapetest.cs: A test program to display the areas of some Shape-derived objects.

To compile the example, use the command line:

csc abstractshape.cs shapes.cs shapetest.cs

This will create the executable file shapetest.exe.

File 1—abstractshape.cs

This file declares the Shape class that contains the Area property of the type double.

```
// abstractshape.cs
// compile with: /target:library
// csc /target:library abstractshape.cs
using System;

public abstract class Shape
{
   private string myId;

   public Shape(string s)
   {
      Id = s;   // calling the set accessor of the Id property
   }

   public string Id
   {
      get
      {
         return myId;
      }

      set
      {
         myId = value;
      }
   }
}
```

(continued)

(continued)

```
// Area is a read-only property - only a get accessor is needed:
public abstract double Area
{
    get;
}

public override string ToString()
{
    return Id + " Area = " + string.Format("{0:F2}",Area);
}
}
```

Code Discussion

- Modifiers on the property are placed on the property declaration itself, for example:

  ```
  public abstract double Area
  ```

- When declaring an abstract property (such as Area in this example), you simply indicate what property accessors are available, but do not implement them. In this example, only a Get accessor is available, so the property is read-only.

File 2—shapes.cs

The following code shows three subclasses of Shape and how they override the Area property to provide their own implementation.

```
// shapes.cs
// compile with: /target:library /reference:abstractshape.dll
public class Square : Shape
{
    private int mySide;

    public Square(int side, string id) : base(id)
    {
        mySide = side;
    }

    public override double Area
    {
        get
        {
            // Given the side, return the area of a square:
            return mySide * mySide;
        }
    }
}
```

```
public class Circle : Shape
{
    private int myRadius;

    public Circle(int radius, string id) : base(id)
    {
        myRadius = radius;
    }

    public override double Area
    {
        get
        {
            // Given the radius, return the area of a circle:
            return myRadius * myRadius * System.Math.PI;
        }
    }
}

public class Rectangle : Shape
{
    private int myWidth;
    private int myHeight;

    public Rectangle(int width, int height, string id) : base(id)
    {
        myWidth  = width;
        myHeight = height;
    }

    public override double Area
    {
        get
        {
            // Given the width and height, return the area of a rectangle:
            return myWidth * myHeight;
        }
    }
}
```

File 3—shapetest.cs

The following code shows a test program that creates a number of Shape-derived objects and prints out their areas.

```
// shapetest.cs
// compile with: /reference:abstractshape.dll;shapes.dll
public class TestClass
{
    public static void Main()
    {
        Shape[] shapes =
            {
                new Square(5, "Square #1"),
                new Circle(3, "Circle #1"),
                new Rectangle( 4, 5, "Rectangle #1")
            };

        System.Console.WriteLine("Shapes Collection");
        foreach(Shape s in shapes)
        {
            System.Console.WriteLine(s);
        }

    }
}
```

Output

```
Shapes Collection
Square #1 Area = 25.00
Circle #1 Area = 28.27
Rectangle #1 Area = 20.00
```

Signatures and Overloading

Methods, instance constructors, indexers, and operators are characterized by their signatures:

- The signature of a method consists of the name of the method and the type and kind (value, reference, or output) of each of its formal parameters. The signature of a method specifically does not include the return type, nor does it include the params modifier that may be specified for the right-most parameter.

- The signature of an instance constructor consists of the type and kind (value, reference, or output) of each of its formal parameters. The signature of an instance constructor specifically does not include the params modifier that may be specified for the right-most parameter.

- The signature of an indexer consists of the type of each of its formal parameters. The signature of an indexer specifically does not include the element type.

- The signature of an operator consists of the name of the operator and the type of each of its formal parameters. The signature of an operator specifically does not include the result type.

Signatures are the enabling mechanism for overloading of members in classes, structs, and interfaces:

- Overloading of methods permits a class, struct, or interface to declare multiple methods with the same name, provided their signatures are unique.

- Overloading of instance constructors permits a class or struct to declare multiple instance constructors, provided their signatures are unique.

- Overloading of indexers permits a class, struct, or interface to declare multiple indexers, provided their signatures are unique.

- Overloading of operators permits a class or struct to declare multiple operators with the same name, provided their signatures are unique.

The following example shows a set of overloaded method declarations along with their signatures.

```
interface ITest
{
    void F();                   // F()
    void F(int x);               // F(int)
    void F(ref int x);          // F(ref int)
    void F(out int x);          // F(out int)
    void F(int x, int y);       // F(int, int)
    int F(string s);             // F(string)
    int F(int x);                // F(int)        error
    void F(string[] a);          // F(string[])
    void F(params string[] a);   // F(string[])   error
}
```

Note that any ref and out parameter modifiers are part of a signature. Thus, F(int), F(ref int), and F(out int) are all unique signatures. Also, note that the return type and the params modifier are not part of a signature, so it is not possible to overload solely based on return type or on the inclusion or exclusion of the params modifier. Because of these restrictions, the declarations of the methods F(int) and F(params string[]) in the example above result in a compile-time error. For more information about the ref and out parameter modifiers, see "Method Parameter Keywords" on page 17.

Scopes

The scope of a name is the region of program text within which it is possible to refer to the entity declared by the name without qualification of the name. Scopes can be nested, and an inner scope may redeclare the meaning of a name from an outer scope. (This does not, however, remove the restriction that within a nested block it is not possible to declare a local variable with the same name as a local variable in an enclosing block. For more information about this restriction, see "Declarations" on page 229.) The name from the outer scope is then said to be hidden in the region of program text covered by the inner scope, and access to the outer name is only possible by qualifying the name.

General Rules for Scopes

You should note the following characteristics of scopes:

- The scope of a namespace member declared by a *namespace-member-declaration* with no enclosing namespace-declaration is the entire program text.

- The scope of a namespace member declared by a namespace-member-declaration within a namespace-declaration whose fully qualified name is N is the namespace-body of every namespace-declaration whose fully qualified name is N or starts with the same sequence of identifiers as N.

- The scope of a name defined or imported by a using-directive extends over the namespace-member-declarations of the compilation-unit or namespace-body in which the using-directive occurs. A using-directive may make zero or more namespace or type names available within a particular compilation-unit or namespace-body, but does not contribute any new members to the underlying declaration space. In other words, a using-directive is not transitive but rather affects only the compilation-unit or namespace-body in which it occurs. For more information about using directives, see the section "using Directive" on page 57.

- The scope of a member declared by a class-member-declaration is the class-body in which the declaration occurs. In addition, the scope of a class member extends to the *class-body* of those derived classes that are included in the accessibility domain of the member. For more information on accessibility domains, see "Accessibility Domain" on page 23.

- The scope of a member declared by a struct-member-declaration is the struct-body in which the declaration occurs.

- The scope of a member declared by an enum-member-declaration is the enum-*body* in which the declaration occurs. For more information about enumerations, see the section "enum" on page 130.

- The scope of a parameter declared in a method-declaration is the method-body of that method-declaration.

- The scope of a parameter declared in an indexer-declaration is the accessor-declarations of that indexer-declaration. For more information about indexers, see "Indexers" on page 272.

- The scope of a parameter declared in an operator-declaration is the block of that operator-declaration. For more information about operators, see "Operators" on page 169.

- The scope of a parameter declared in a constructor-declaration is the constructor-initializer and block of that constructor-declaration. For more information about constructor-initializers, see "Instance Constructors" on page 261.

- The scope of a label declared in a labeled-statement is the block in which the declaration occurs.

- The scope of a local variable declared in a local-variable-declaration is the block in which the declaration occurs. It is a compile-time error to refer to a local variable in a textual position that precedes its variable-declarator.

- The scope of a local variable declared in a switch-block of a switch statement is the switch-block. For more information on switch statements, see the section "switch" on page 80.

- The scope of a local variable declared in a for-initializer of a for statement is the for-initializer, the for-condition, the for-iterator, and the contained statement of the for statement. For more information on for statements, see the section "for" on page 84.

- The scope of a local constant declared in a local-constant-declaration is the block in which the declaration occurs. It is a compile-time error to refer to a local constant in a textual position that precedes its constant-declarator.

Within the scope of a namespace, class, struct, or enumeration member it is possible to refer to the member in a textual position that precedes the declaration of the member. For example

```
class A
{
    void F() {
        i = 1;
    }
    int i = 0;
}
```

Here, it is valid for F to refer to i before it is declared.

Within the scope of a local variable, it is a compile-time error to refer to the local variable in a textual position that precedes the variable-declarator of the local variable. For example

```
class A
{
    int i = 0;
    void F() {
        i = 1;                  // Error, use precedes declaration
        int i;
        i = 2;
    }
    void G() {
        int j = (j = 1);        // Valid
    }
    void H() {
        int a = 1, b = ++a;     // Valid
    }
}
```

In the F method above, the first assignment to i specifically does not refer to the field declared in the outer scope. Rather, it refers to the local variable and it results in a compile-time error because it textually precedes the declaration of the variable. In the G method, the use of j in the initializer for the declaration of j is valid because the use does not precede the variable-declarator. In the H method, a subsequent variable-declarator refers to a local variable declared in an earlier variable-declarator within the same local-variable-declaration.

The scoping rules for local variables are designed to guarantee that the meaning of a name used in an expression context is always the same within a block. If the scope of a local variable was to extend only from its declaration to the end of the block, then in the example above, the first assignment would assign to the instance variable and the second assignment would assign to the local variable, possibly leading to compile-time errors if the statements of the block were later to be rearranged.

The meaning of a name within a block may differ based on the context in which the name is used. In the example

```
class A {}
class Test
{
    static void Main() {
        string A = "hello, world";
        string s = A;                  // expression context
        Type t = typeof(A);            // type context
        Console.WriteLine(s);          // writes "hello, world"
        Console.WriteLine(t);          // writes "A"
    }
}
```

the name A is used in an expression context to refer to the local variable A and in a type context to refer to the class A.

Name Hiding

The scope of an entity typically encompasses more program text than the declaration space of the entity. In particular, the scope of an entity may include declarations that introduce new declaration spaces containing entities of the same name. Such declarations cause the original entity to become hidden. Conversely, an entity is said to be visible when it is not hidden.

Name hiding occurs when scopes overlap through nesting and when scopes overlap through inheritance. The characteristics of the two types of hiding are described in the following sections.

Hiding Through Nesting

Name hiding through nesting can occur as a result of nesting namespaces or types within namespaces, as a result of nesting types within classes or structs, and as a result of parameter and local variable declarations.

In the example

```
class A
{
    int i = 0;
    void F() {
        int i = 1;
    }
    void G() {
        i = 1;
    }
}
```

within the F method, the instance variable i is hidden by the local variable i, but within the
G method, i still refers to the instance variable.

When a name in an inner scope hides a name in an outer scope, it hides all overloaded occurrences
of that name. In the example

```
class Outer
{
    static void F(int i) {}
    static void F(string s) {}
    class Inner
    {
        void G() {
            F(1);           // Invokes Outer.Inner.F
            F("Hello");     // Error
        }
        static void F(long l) {}
    }
}
```

the call F(1) invokes the F declared in Inner because all outer occurrences of F are hidden by the
inner declaration. For the same reason, the call F("Hello") results in a compile-time error.

Hiding Through Inheritance

Name hiding through inheritance occurs when classes or structs redeclare names that were
inherited from base classes. This type of name hiding takes one of the following forms:

- A constant, field, property, event, or type introduced in a class or struct hides all base class
  members with the same name.

- A method introduced in a class or struct hides all non-method base class members with the
  same name, and all base class methods with the same signature (method name and parameter
  count, modifiers, and types).

- An indexer introduced in a class or struct hides all base class indexers with the same signature
  (parameter count and types).

The rules governing operator declarations make it impossible for a derived class to declare an operator with the same signature as an operator in a base class. Thus, operators never hide one another. For more information on operators, see "Operators" on page 169.

Contrary to hiding a name from an outer scope, hiding an accessible name from an inherited scope causes a warning to be reported. In the example

```
class Base
{
    public void F() {}
}
class Derived: Base
{
    public void F() {}       // Warning, hiding an inherited name
}
```

the declaration of F in Derived causes a warning to be reported. Hiding an inherited name is specifically not an error, since that would preclude separate evolution of base classes. For example, the above situation might have come about because a later version of Base introduced an F method that wasn't present in an earlier version of the class. Had the above situation been an error, then *any* change made to a base class in a separately versioned class library could potentially cause derived classes to become invalid.

The warning caused by hiding an inherited name can be eliminated through use of the new modifier:

```
class Base
{
    public void F() {}
}
class Derived: Base
{
    new public void F() {}
}
```

The new modifier indicates that the F in Derived is "new" and that it is indeed intended to hide the inherited member.

A declaration of a new member hides an inherited member only within the scope of the new member.

```
class Base
{
    public static void F() {}
}
class Derived: Base
{
    new private static void F() {}    // Hides Base.F in Derived only
}
class MoreDerived: Derived
{
    static void G() { F(); }          // Invokes Base.F
}
```

In the example above, the declaration of F in Derived hides the F that was inherited from Base, but since the new F in Derived has private access, its scope does not extend to MoreDerived. Thus, the call F() in MoreDerived.G is valid and will invoke Base.F.

Passing Parameters

In C#, parameters can be passed either by value or by reference. Passing parameters by reference allows function members (methods, properties, indexers, operators, and constructors) to change the value of the parameters and have that change persist. To pass a parameter by reference, use the **ref** or **out** keyword. For simplicity, only the **ref** keyword is used in the examples of this topic. For information on the difference between **ref** and **out**, see "ref" on page 18, "out" on page 19, and "Passing Arrays Using ref and out" on page 254.

This topic includes the following sections:

- Passing Value-Type Parameters
- Passing Reference-Type Parameters

It also includes the following examples:

Example	Demonstrates	Uses ref or out
1	Passing value types by value	No
2	Passing value types by reference	Yes
3	Swapping value types (two integers)	Yes
4	Passing reference types by value	No
5	Passing reference types by reference	Yes
6	Swapping reference types (two strings)	Yes

Passing Value-Type Parameters

A value-type variable contains its data directly as opposed to a reference-type variable, which contains a reference to its data. Therefore, passing a value-type variable to a method means passing a copy of the variable to the method. Any changes to the parameter that take place inside the method have no affect on the original data stored in the variable. If you want the called method to change the value of the parameter, you have to pass it by reference, using the **ref** or **out** keyword. For simplicity, the following examples use **ref**.

Example 1: Passing Value Types by Value

The following example demonstrates passing value-type parameters by value. The variable myInt is passed by value to the method SquareIt. Any changes that take place inside the method have no affect on the original value of the variable.

```
// PassingParams1.cs
using System;
class PassingValByVal
{
    static void SquareIt(int x)
    // The parameter x is passed by value.
    // Changes to x will not affect the original value of myInt.
    {
        x *= x;
        Console.WriteLine("The value inside the method: {0}", x);
    }
    public static void Main()
    {
        int myInt = 5;
        Console.WriteLine("The value before calling the method: {0}",
            myInt);
        SquareIt(myInt);    // Passing myInt by value.
        Console.WriteLine("The value after calling the method: {0}",
            myInt);
    }
}
```

Output

```
The value before calling the method: 5
The value inside the method: 25
The value after calling the method: 5
```

Code Discussion

The variable myInt, being a value type, contains its data (the value 5). When SquareIt is invoked, the contents of myInt are copied into the parameter x, which is squared inside the method. In Main, however, the value of myInt is the same, before and after calling the SquareIt method. In fact, the change that takes place inside the method only affects the local variable x.

Example 2: Passing Value Types by Reference

The following example is the same as Example 1, except for passing the parameter using the **ref** keyword. The value of the parameter is changed after calling the method.

```
// PassingParams2.cs
using System;
class PassingValByRef
{
    static void SquareIt(ref int x)
    // The parameter x is passed by reference.
    // Changes to x will affect the original value of myInt.
    {
        x *= x;
        Console.WriteLine("The value inside the method: {0}", x);
    }
    public static void Main()
    {
        int myInt = 5;
        Console.WriteLine("The value before calling the method: {0}",
            myInt);
        SquareIt(ref myInt);    // Passing myInt by reference.
        Console.WriteLine("The value after calling the method: {0}",
            myInt);
    }
}
```

Output

```
The value before calling the method: 5
The value inside the method: 25
The value after calling the method: 25
```

Code Discussion

In this example, it is not the value of myInt that is passed; rather, a reference to myInt is passed. The parameter x is not an **int**; it is a reference to an **int** (in this case, a reference to myInt). Therefore, when x is squared inside the method, what actually gets squared is what x refers to: myInt.

Example 3: Swapping Value Types

A common example of changing the values of the passed parameters is the Swap method, where you pass two variables, x and y, and have the method swap their contents. You must pass the parameters to the Swap method by reference; otherwise, you will be dealing with a local copy of the parameters inside the method. The following is an example of the Swap method that uses reference parameters:

```
static void SwapByRef(ref int x, ref int y)
{
    int temp = x;
    x = y;
    y = temp;
}
```

When you call this method, use the **ref** keyword in the call, like this:

```
SwapByRef (ref i, ref j);
```

Passing Reference-Type Parameters

A variable of a reference type does not contain its data directly; it contains a reference to its data. When you pass a reference-type parameter by value, it is possible to change the data pointed to by the reference, such as the value of a class member. However, you cannot change the value of the reference itself; that is, you cannot use the same reference to allocate memory for a new class and have it persist outside the block. To do that, pass the parameter using the **ref** (or **out**) keyword. For simplicity, the following examples use **ref**.

Example 4: Passing Reference Types by Value

The following example demonstrates passing a reference-type parameter, myArray, by value, to a method, Change. Because the parameter is a reference to myArray, it is possible to change the values of the array elements. However, the attempt to reassign the parameter to a different memory location only works inside the method and does not affect the original variable, myArray.

```
// PassingParams4.cs
// Passing an array to a method without the ref keyword.
// Compare the results to those of Example 5.
using System;
class PassingRefByVal
{
    static void Change(int[] arr)
    {
        arr[0]=888;    // This change affects the original element.
        arr = new int[5] {-3, -1, -2, -3, -4};    // This change is local.
        Console.WriteLine("Inside the method, the first element is: {0}", arr[0]);
    }

    public static void Main()
    {
        int[] myArray = {1,4,5};
        Console.WriteLine("Inside Main, before calling the method, the first element is: {0}",
myArray [0]);
        Change(myArray);
        Console.WriteLine("Inside Main, after calling the method, the first element is: {0}",
myArray [0]);
    }
}
```

Output

```
Inside Main, before calling the method, the first element is: 1
Inside the method, the first element is: -3
Inside Main, after calling the method, the first element is: 888
```

Code Discussion

In the preceding example, the array, myArray, which is a reference type, is passed to the method without the **ref** parameter. In such a case, a copy of the reference, which points to myArray, is passed to the method. The output shows that it is possible for the method to change the contents of an array element (from 1 to 888). However, allocating a new portion of memory by using the **new** operator inside the Change method makes the variable arr reference a new array. Thus, any changes after that will not affect the original array, MyArray, which is created inside Main. In fact, two arrays are created in this example, one inside Main and one inside the Change method.

Example 5: Passing Reference Types by Reference

This example is the same as Example 4, except for using the **ref** keyword in the method header and call. Any changes that take place in the method will affect the original variables in the calling program.

```
// PassingParams5.cs
// Passing an array to a method with the ref keyword.
// Compare the results to those of Example 4.
using System;
class PassingRefByRef
{
    static void Change(ref int[] arr)
    {
        // Both of the following changes will affect the original variables:
        arr[0]=888;
        arr = new int[5] {-3, -1, -2, -3, -4};
        Console.WriteLine("Inside the method, the first element is: {0}", arr[0]);
    }

    public static void Main()
    {
        int[] myArray = {1,4,5};
        Console.WriteLine("Inside Main, before calling the method, the first element is: {0}",
myArray [0]);
        Change(ref myArray);
        Console.WriteLine("Inside Main, after calling the method, the first element is: {0}",
myArray [0]);
    }
}
```

Output

```
Inside Main, before calling the method, the first element is: 1
Inside the method, the first element is: -3
Inside Main, after calling the method, the first element is: -3
```

Code Discussion

All of the changes that take place inside the method affect the original array in Main. In fact, the original array is reallocated using the **new** operator. Thus, after calling the Change method, any reference to myArray points to the five-element array, which is created in the Change method.

Example 6: Swapping Two Strings

Swapping strings is a good example of passing reference-type parameters by reference. In the example, two strings, str1 and str2, are initialized in Main and passed to the SwapStrings method as parameters modified by the **ref** keyword. The two strings are swapped inside the method and inside Main as well.

```
// PassingParams6.cs
using System;
class SwappinStrings
{
    static void SwapStrings(ref string s1, ref string s2)
    // The string parameter x is passed by reference.
    // Any changes on parameters will affect the original variables.
    {
        string temp = s1;
        s1 = s2;
        s2 = temp;
        Console.WriteLine("Inside the method: {0}, {1}", s1, s2);
    }
    public static void Main()
    {
        string str1 = "John";
        string str2 = "Smith";
        Console.WriteLine("Inside Main, before swapping: {0} {1}",
            str1, str2);
        SwapStrings(ref str1, ref str2);    // Passing strings by reference
        Console.WriteLine("Inside Main, after swapping: {0}, {1}",
            str1, str2);
    }
}
```

Output

```
Inside Main, before swapping: John Smith
Inside the method: Smith, John
Inside Main, after swapping: Smith, John
```

Code Discussion

In this example, the parameters need to be passed by reference to affect the variables in the calling program. If you remove the **ref** keyword from both the method header and the method call, no changes will take place in the calling program.

For more information on strings, see the section "string" on page 160.

See Also

Passing Arrays Using ref and out (pg. 254)

Main Method

The Main method is the entry point of your program, where the program control starts and ends. It is declared inside a class or struct. It must be static. It can either be **void** or return an **int**. The Main method is where you create objects and invoke other methods. The Main method can be written without parameters or with parameters. The latter form allows your program to read command-line arguments.

See the following topics for more information and examples on using the Main method:

- Return Values

- Command-Line Arguments

Return Values

The Main method can be of the type **void**:

```
static void Main()
{
}
```

It can also return an **int**:

```
static int Main()
{
    return 0;
}
```

Example

In this example, the program contains two classes, Factorial and MainClass. The Main method, which resides in the MainClass class, is used to read a number from the keyboard, invoke the Fac method from the Factorial class, and calculate and display the factorial of the input number.

```
// cs_main.cs
using System;
public class Factorial
{
    public static long Fac(long i)
    {
        return ((i <= 1) ? 1 : (i * Fac(i-1)));
    }
}
```

(continued)

(continued)

```
class MyClass
{
    public static void Main()
    {
        // Read a string from the keyboard:
        Console.Write("Enter an integer: ");

        string s = Console.ReadLine();

        // Convert the string to long:
        long num = Int64.Parse(s);

        Console.WriteLine("The Factorial of {0} is {1}.",
                            num, Factorial.Fac(num));
    }
}
```

Input

5

Sample Output

```
Enter an integer: 5
The Factorial of 5 is 120.
```

See Also

Command-Line Arguments (pg. 316), Main Method (pg. 315)

Command-Line Arguments

The Main method can use arguments, in which case, it takes one of the following forms:

```
static int Main(string[] args)
static void Main(string[] args)
```

The parameter of the Main method is a string array that represents the command-line arguments. Usually you check for the existence of the arguments by testing the Length property, for example:

```
if (args.Length == 0)
{
    Console.WriteLine("Please enter a numeric argument.");
    return 1;
}
```

You can also convert the string arguments to numeric types by using the Convert class or the Parse method. For example, the following statement converts the string to a long number by using the Parse method on the Int64 class:

```
long num = Int64.Parse(args[0]);
```

It is also possible to use the C# type `long`, which aliases `Int64`:

```
long num = long.Parse(args[0]);
```

You can also use the `Convert` class method `ToInt64` to do the same thing:

```
long num = Convert.ToInt64(s);
```

Example

In this example, the program takes one argument at run time, converts the argument to a long number, and calculates the factorial of the number. If no arguments are supplied, the program issues a message that explains the correct usage of the program.

```
// Factorial_main.cs
// arguments: 3
using System;
public class Factorial
{
    public static long Fac(long i)
    {
        return ((i <= 1) ? 1 : (i * Fac(i-1)));
    }
}

class MainClass
{
    public static int Main(string[] args)
    {
        // Test if input arguments were supplied:
        if (args.Length == 0)
        {
            Console.WriteLine("Please enter a numeric argument.");
            Console.WriteLine("Usage: Factorial <num>");
            return 1;
        }

        // Convert the input arguments to numbers:
        long num = long.Parse(args[0]);
        Console.WriteLine("The Factorial of {0} is {1}.",
                          num, Factorial.Fac(num));
        return 0;
    }
}
```

Output

```
The Factorial of 3 is 6.
```

The following are two sample runs of the program assuming that the program name is `Factorial.exe`.

Run #1:

Enter the following command line:

```
Factorial 10
```

You get the following result:

```
The Factorial of 10 is 3628800.
```

Run #2:

Enter the following command line:

```
Factorial
```

You get the following result:

```
Please enter a numeric argument.
Usage: Factorial <num>
```

See Also

Return Values (pg. 315), General Structure of a C# Program (pg. 2)

Conditional Methods Tutorial

This tutorial demonstrates conditional methods, which provide a powerful mechanism by which calls to methods can be included or omitted depending on whether a preprocessor symbol is defined.

Further Reading

- Command-Line Arguments

- Conditional

- #define

- /define (Preprocessor Definition)

- System.Diagnostics Namespace

Tutorial

Conditional methods allow developers to create methods whose calls can be placed in the code and then either included or omitted during compilation based on a preprocessing symbol.

Suppose that you want to enable some assertion code in the debug builds and disable it in the retail builds. In C++, there are two ways to have this functionality in your code:

- Using **#ifdef**, define both debug and release versions of a macro. The debug version calls the tracing code, and the release version does nothing. Because C# doesn't support macros, this method doesn't work.

- Have two implementations of the code being called—in the debug version have full functionality; in the retail version have empty stubs for the methods. Users then choose which one to include when linking the project. The problem with this approach is that the retail builds contain calls to empty methods, and the configuration is more complex.

C# conditional methods provide a simple solution to this problem that is similar to the first approach listed above. There are two basic mechanisms to do this:

- **#define** the preprocessing identifier in the source code directly. (See an example of this approach in "Conditional" on page 219.)

- Define the preprocessing identifier on the C# command line via the /define option (/d). This approach is used in the following example.

Conditional methods are used in the .NET Framework. The **System.Diagnostics** namespace contains a number of classes that support tracing and debugging in applications. Use the **System.Diagnostics.Trace** and **System.Diagnostics.Debug** classes to add sophisticated tracing and debugging to your application (functionality that can be compiled out of your retail builds through the use of conditional methods).

The example below shows how to implement a very simple tracing mechanism using conditional methods. **System.Diagnostics.Trace** provides much more sophisticated tracing mechanisms, but it uses the fundamental mechanism below to provide this functionality.

Example

This example consists of two source files: the first file is the library that provides a tracing mechanism, and the second file is the client program that uses this library.

File #1: Creating Conditional Methods

The code below shows a simple library that provides a tracing mechanism that displays trace messages to the system console. Clients can embed trace calls in the code and then be able to control whether the tracing gets called by defining symbols in their own compilation phase.

```
// CondMethod.cs
// compile with: /target:library /d:DEBUG
using System;
using System.Diagnostics;
namespace TraceFunctions
{
    public class Trace
    {
        [Conditional("DEBUG")]
        public static void Message(string traceMessage)
        {
            Console.WriteLine("[TRACE] - " + traceMessage);
        }
    }
}
```

Code Discussion

The following line:

```
[Conditional("DEBUG")]
```

marks the Message method as being conditional (via the **Conditional** attribute). The **Conditional** attribute takes one parameter—the preprocessing identifier that controls whether the method call is included when clients are compiled. If the preprocessing identifier is defined, the method is called; otherwise, the call is never inserted in the client's code.

Notice that there are a few restrictions on which methods can be marked as conditional:

- The **Conditional** attribute cannot be applied to interface methods.

- Conditional methods must have a void return type.

File #2: Using the Conditional Method

The following client program uses the Trace class defined in file #1 to do some simple tracing.

```
// TraceTest.cs
// compile with: /reference:CondMethod.dll
// arguments: A B C
using System;
using TraceFunctions;

public class TraceClient
{
    public static void Main(string[] args)
    {
        Trace.Message("Main Starting");

        if (args.Length == 0)
        {
            Console.WriteLine("No arguments have been passed");
        }
        else
        {
            for( int i=0; i < args.Length; i++)
            {
                Console.WriteLine("Arg[{0}] is [{1}]",i,args[i]);
            }
        }

        Trace.Message("Main Ending");
    }
}
```

Code Discussion

Conditional code is included in client code depending on whether the preprocessing identifier is defined when the client code gets compiled.

Compiling with client code with the /d:DEBUG flag means that the compiler inserts the call to the Trace method. If the symbol is not defined, the call is never made.

Sample Run

The command:

```
tracetest A B C
```

gives the following output:

```
[TRACE] - Main Starting
Arg[0] is [A]
Arg[1] is [B]
Arg[2] is [C]
[TRACE] - Main Ending
```

The command:

```
tracetest
```

gives the following output:

```
[TRACE] - Main Starting
No arguments have been passed
[TRACE] - Main Ending
```

Delegates Tutorial

This tutorial demonstrates the delegate types. It shows how to map delegates to static and instance methods, and how to combine them (multicast).

Further Reading

- delegate
- Events Tutorial

Tutorial

A delegate in C# is similar to a function pointer in C or C++. Using a delegate allows the programmer to encapsulate a reference to a method inside a delegate object. The delegate object can then be passed to code which can call the referenced method, without having to know at compile time which method will be invoked. Unlike function pointers in C or C++, delegates are object-oriented, type-safe, and secure.

A delegate declaration defines a type that encapsulates a method with a particular set of arguments and return type. For static methods, a delegate object encapsulates the method to be called. For instance methods, a delegate object encapsulates both an instance and a method on the instance. If you have a delegate object and an appropriate set of arguments, you can invoke the delegate with the arguments.

An interesting and useful property of a delegate is that it does not know or care about the class of the object that it references. Any object will do; all that matters is that the method's argument types and return type match the delegate's. This makes delegates perfectly suited for "anonymous" invocation.

This tutorial includes two examples:

- Example 1 shows how to declare, instantiate, and call a delegate.

- Example 2 shows how to combine two delegates.

In addition, it discusses the following topics:

- Delegates and Events

- Delegates vs. Interfaces

Example 1

The following example illustrates declaring, instantiating, and using a delegate. The BookDB class encapsulates a bookstore database that maintains a database of books. It exposes a method ProcessPaperbackBooks, which finds all paperback books in the database and calls a delegate for each one. The **delegate** type used is called ProcessBookDelegate. The Test class uses this class to print out the titles and average price of the paperback books.

The use of delegates promotes good separation of functionality between the bookstore database and the client code. The client code has no knowledge of how the books are stored or how the bookstore code finds paperback books. The bookstore code has no knowledge of what processing is done on the paperback books after it finds them.

```
// bookstore.cs
using System;

// A set of classes for handling a bookstore:
namespace Bookstore
{
    using System.Collections;

    // Describes a book in the book list:
    public struct Book
    {
        public string Title;        // Title of the book.
        public string Author;       // Author of the book.
        public decimal Price;       // Price of the book.
        public bool Paperback;      // Is it paperback?
```

```
        public Book(string title, string author, decimal price, bool paperBack)
        {
            Title = title;
            Author = author;
            Price = price;
            Paperback = paperBack;
        }
    }

    // Declare a delegate type for processing a book:
    public delegate void ProcessBookDelegate(Book book);

    // Maintains a book database.
    public class BookDB
    {
        // List of all books in the database:
        ArrayList list = new ArrayList();

        // Add a book to the database:
        public void AddBook(string title, string author, decimal price, bool paperBack)
        {
            list.Add(new Book(title, author, price, paperBack));
        }

        // Call a passed-in delegate on each paperback book to process it:
        public void ProcessPaperbackBooks(ProcessBookDelegate processBook)
        {
            foreach (Book b in list)
            {
                if (b.Paperback)
                // Calling the delegate:
                    processBook(b);
            }
        }
    }
}

// Using the Bookstore classes:
namespace BookTestClient
{
    using Bookstore;

    // Class to total and average prices of books:
    class PriceTotaller
    {
        int countBooks = 0;
        decimal priceBooks = 0.0m;
```

(continued)

(continued)

```
    internal void AddBookToTotal(Book book)
    {
       countBooks += 1;
       priceBooks += book.Price;
    }

    internal decimal AveragePrice()
    {
       return priceBooks / countBooks;
    }
}

// Class to test the book database:
class Test
{
    // Print the title of the book.
    static void PrintTitle(Book b)
    {
       Console.WriteLine("   {0}", b.Title);
    }

    // Execution starts here.
    static void Main()
    {
       BookDB bookDB = new BookDB();

       // Initialize the database with some books:
       AddBooks(bookDB);

       // Print all the titles of paperbacks:
       Console.WriteLine("Paperback Book Titles:");
       // Create a new delegate object associated with the static
       // method Test.PrintTitle:
       bookDB.ProcessPaperbackBooks(new ProcessBookDelegate(PrintTitle));

       // Get the average price of a paperback by using
       // a PriceTotaller object:
       PriceTotaller totaller = new PriceTotaller();
       // Create a new delegate object associated with the nonstatic
       // method AddBookToTotal on the object totaller:
       bookDB.ProcessPaperbackBooks(new ProcessBookDelegate(totaller.AddBookToTotal));
       Console.WriteLine("Average Paperback Book Price: ${0:#.##}",
          totaller.AveragePrice());
    }
```

```
    // Initialize the book database with some test books:
    static void AddBooks(BookDB bookDB)
    {
        bookDB.AddBook("The C Programming Language",
            "Brian W. Kernighan and Dennis M. Ritchie", 19.95m, true);
        bookDB.AddBook("The Unicode Standard 2.0",
            "The Unicode Consortium", 39.95m, true);
        bookDB.AddBook("The MS-DOS Encyclopedia",
            "Ray Duncan", 129.95m, false);
        bookDB.AddBook("Dogbert's Clues for the Clueless",
            "Scott Adams", 12.00m, true);
    }
  }
}
```

Output

```
Paperback Book Titles:
    The C Programming Language
    The Unicode Standard 2.0
    Dogbert's Clues for the Clueless
Average Paperback Book Price: $23.97
```

Code Discussion

- **Declaring a delegate** The following statement:

```
public delegate void ProcessBookDelegate(Book book);
```

  declares a new delegate type. Each delegate type describes the number and types of the arguments, and the type of the return value of methods that it can encapsulate. Whenever a new set of argument types or return value type is needed, a new delegate type must be declared.

- **Instantiating a delegate** Once a delegate type has been declared, a delegate object must be created and associated with a particular method. Like all other objects, a new delegate object is created with a **new** expression. When creating a delegate, however, the argument passed to the **new** expression is special—it is written like a method call, but without the arguments to the method.

  The following statement:

```
bookDB.ProcessPaperbackBooks(new ProcessBookDelegate(PrintTitle));
```

  creates a new delegate object associated with the static method `Test.PrintTitle`. The following statement:

```
bookDB.ProcessPaperbackBooks(new
    ProcessBookDelegate(totaller.AddBookToTotal));
```

  creates a new delegate object associated with the nonstatic method `AddBookToTotal` on the object `totaller`. In both cases, this new delegate object is immediately passed to the `ProcessPaperbackBooks` method.

  Note that once a delegate is created, the method it is associated with never changes—delegate objects are immutable.

- **Calling a delegate**   Once a delegate object is created, the delegate object is typically passed to other code that will call the delegate. A delegate object is called by using the name of the delegate object, followed by the parenthesized arguments to be passed to the delegate. An example of a delegate call is:

```
processBook(b);
```

Example 2

This example demonstrates composing delegates. A useful property of delegate objects is that they can be composed using the "**+**" operator. A composed delegate calls, in order, the two delegates it was composed from. Only delegates of the same type can be composed, and the delegate type must have a **void** return value. The "**-**" operator can be used to remove a component delegate from a composed delegate.

```csharp
// compose.cs
using System;

delegate void MyDelegate(string s);

class MyClass
{
    public static void Hello(string s)
    {
        Console.WriteLine("  Hello, {0}!", s);
    }

    public static void Goodbye(string s)
    {
        Console.WriteLine("  Goodbye, {0}!", s);
    }

    public static void Main()
    {
        MyDelegate a, b, c, d;

        // Create the delegate object a that references
        // the method Hello:
        a = new MyDelegate(Hello);
        // Create the delegate object b that references
        // the method Goodbye:
        b = new MyDelegate(Goodbye);
        // The two delegates, a and b, are composed to form c,
        // which calls both methods in order:
        c = a + b;
        // Remove a from the composed delegate, leaving d,
        // which calls only the method Goodbye:
        d = c - a;
```

```
        Console.WriteLine("Invoking delegate a:");
        a("A");
        Console.WriteLine("Invoking delegate b:");
        b("B");
        Console.WriteLine("Invoking delegate c:");
        c("C");
        Console.WriteLine("Invoking delegate d:");
        d("D");
    }
}
```

Output

```
Invoking delegate a:
  Hello, A!
Invoking delegate b:
  Goodbye, B!
Invoking delegate c:
  Hello, C!
  Goodbye, C!
Invoking delegate d:
  Goodbye, D!
```

Delegates and Events

Delegates are ideally suited for use as events—notifications from one component to "listeners" about changes in that component. For more information on the use of delegates for events, see "Events Tutorial" on page 328.

Delegates vs. Interfaces

Delegates and interfaces are similar in that they enable the separation of specification and implementation. Multiple independent authors can produce implementations that are compatible with an interface specification. Similarly, a delegate specifies the signature of a method, and authors can write methods that are compatible with the delegate specification. When should you use interfaces, and when should you use delegates?

Delegates are useful when:

- A single method is being called.

- A class may want to have multiple implementations of the method specification.

- It is desirable to allow using a static method to implement the specification.

- An event-like design pattern is desired (for more information, see "Events Tutorial" on page 328).

- The caller has no need to know or obtain the object that the method is defined on.

- The provider of the implementation wants to "hand out" the implementation of the specification to only a few select components.

- Easy composition is desired.

Interfaces are useful when:

- The specification defines a set of related methods that will be called.

- A class typically implements the specification only once.

- The caller of the interface wants to cast to or from the interface type to obtain other interfaces or classes.

Events

This section shows how to declare, invoke, and hook up to events in C#.

Further Reading

- event

- delegate

- Handling and Raising Events

- Delegates Tutorial

- Introduction to Event Handlers in Windows Forms

Tutorial

An *event* in C# is a way for a class to provide notifications to clients of that class when some interesting thing happens to an object. The most familiar use for events is in graphical user interfaces; typically, the classes that represent controls in the interface have events that are notified when the user does something to the control (for example, click a button).

Events, however, need not be used only for graphical interfaces. Events provide a generally useful way for objects to signal state changes that may be useful to clients of that object. Events are an important building block for creating classes that can be reused in a large number of different programs.

Events are declared using delegates. If you have not yet studied the Delegates Tutorial, you should do so before continuing. Recall that a delegate object encapsulates a method so that it can be called anonymously. An event is a way for a class to allow clients to give it delegates to methods that should be called when the event occurs. When the event occurs, the delegate(s) given to it by its clients are invoked.

In addition to the examples on declaring, invoking, and hooking up to events, this tutorial also introduces the following topics:

- Events and Inheritance

- Events in Interfaces

- .NET Framework Guidelines

Example 1

The following simple example shows a class, `ListWithChangedEvent`, which is similar to the standard `ArrayList` class, but also invokes a `Changed` event whenever the contents of the list change. Such a general-purpose class could be used in numerous ways in a large program.

For example, a word processor might maintain a list of the open documents. Whenever this list changes, many different objects in the word processor might need to be notified so that the user interface could be updated. By using events, the code that maintains the list of documents doesn't need to know who needs to be notified—once the list of documents is changed, the event is automatically invoked and every object that needs to be notified is correctly notified. By using events, the modularity of the program is increased.

```csharp
// events1.cs
using System;
namespace MyCollections
{
   using System.Collections;

   // A delegate type for hooking up change notifications.
   public delegate void ChangedEventHandler(object sender, EventArgs e);

   // A class that works just like ArrayList, but sends event
   // notifications whenever the list changes.
   public class ListWithChangedEvent: ArrayList
   {
      // An event that clients can use to be notified whenever the
      // elements of the list change.
      public event ChangedEventHandler Changed;

      // Invoke the Changed event; called whenever list changes
      protected virtual void OnChanged(EventArgs e)
      {
         if (Changed != null)
            Changed(this, e);
      }

      // Override some of the methods that can change the list;
      // invoke event after each
      public override int Add(object value)
      {
         int i = base.Add(value);
         OnChanged(EventArgs.Empty);
         return i;
      }
```

```csharp
        public override void Clear()
        {
            base.Clear();
            OnChanged(EventArgs.Empty);
        }

        public override object this[int index]
        {
            set
            {
                base[index] = value;
                OnChanged(EventArgs.Empty);
            }
        }
    }
}

namespace TestEvents
{
    using MyCollections;

    class EventListener
    {
        private ListWithChangedEvent List;

        public EventListener(ListWithChangedEvent list)
        {
            List = list;
            // Add "ListChanged" to the Changed event on "List".
            List.Changed += new ChangedEventHandler(ListChanged);
        }

        // This will be called whenever the list changes.
        private void ListChanged(object sender, EventArgs e)
        {
            Console.WriteLine("This is called when the event fires.");
        }

        public void Detach()
        {
            // Detach the event and delete the list
            List.Changed -= new ChangedEventHandler(ListChanged);
            List = null;
        }
    }
```

(continued)

(continued)

```
class Test
{
   // Test the ListWithChangedEvent class.
   public static void Main()
   {
   // Create a new list.
   ListWithChangedEvent list = new ListWithChangedEvent();

   // Create a class that listens to the list's change event.
   EventListener listener = new EventListener(list);

   // Add and remove items from the list.
   list.Add("item 1");
   list.Clear();
   listener.Detach();
   }
}
}
```

Output

```
This is called when the event fires.
This is called when the event fires.
```

Code Discussion

- **Declaring an event**   To declare an event inside a class, first a delegate type for the event must be declared, if none is already declared.

  ```
  public delegate void ChangedEventHandler(object sender, EventArgs e);
  ```

  The delegate type defines the set of arguments that are passed to the method that handles the event. Multiple events can share the same delegate type, so this step is only necessary if no suitable delegate type has already been declared.

  Next, the event itself is declared.

  ```
  public event ChangedEventHandler Changed;
  ```

  An event is declared like a field of delegate type, except that the keyword **event** precedes the event declaration, following the modifiers. Events usually are declared public, but any accessibility modifier is allowed.

- **Invoking an event**   Once a class has declared an event, it can treat that event just like a field of the indicated delegate type. The field will either be null, if no client has hooked up a delegate to the event, or else it refers to a delegate that should be called when the event is invoked. Thus, invoking an event is generally done by first checking for null and then calling the event.

  ```
  if (Changed != null)
  Changed(this, e);
  ```

  Invoking an event can only be done from within the class that declared the event.

- **Hooking up to an event**   From outside the class that declared it, an event looks like a field, but access to that field is very restricted. The only things that can be done are:

  - Compose a new delegate onto that field.

  - Remove a delegate from a (possibly composite) field.

  This is done with the **+=** and **-=** operators. To begin receiving event invocations, client code first creates a delegate of the event type that refers to the method that should be invoked from the event. Then it composes that delegate onto any other delegates that the event might be connected to using **+=**.

  ```
  // Add "ListChanged" to the Changed event on "List":
  List.Changed += new ChangedEventHandler(ListChanged);
  ```

  When the client code is done receiving event invocations, it removes its delegate from the event by using operator **-=**.

  ```
  // Detach the event and delete the list:
  List.Changed -= new ChangedEventHandler(ListChanged);
  ```

Events and Inheritance

When creating a general component that can be derived from, what seems to be a problem sometimes arises with events. Since events can only be invoked from within the class that declared them, derived classes cannot directly invoke events declared within the base class. Although this is sometimes what is desired, often it is appropriate to give the derived class the freedom to invoke the event. This is typically done by creating a protected invoking method for the event. By calling this invoking method, derived classes can invoke the event. For even more flexibility, the invoking method is often declared as virtual, which allows the derived class to override it. This allows the derived class to intercept the events that the base class is invoking, possibly doing its own processing of them.

In the preceding example, this has been done with the `OnChanged` method. A derived class could call or override this method if it needed to.

Events in Interfaces

One other difference between events and fields is that an event can be placed in an interface while a field cannot. When implementing the interface, the implementing class must supply a corresponding event in the class that implements the interface.

.NET Framework Guidelines

Although the C# language allows events to use any delegate type, the .NET Framework has some stricter guidelines on the delegate types that should be used for events. If you intend for your component to be used with the .NET Framework, you probably will want to follow these guidelines.

The .NET Framework guidelines indicate that the delegate type used for an event should take two parameters, an "object source" parameter indicating the source of the event, and an "e" parameter that encapsulates any additional information about the event. The type of the "e" parameter should derive from the **EventArgs** class. For events that do not use any additional information, the .NET Framework has already defined an appropriate delegate type: **EventHandler**.

Example 2

The following example is a modified version of Example 1 that follows the .NET Framework guidelines. The example uses the **EventHandler** delegate type.

```
// events2.cs
using System;
namespace MyCollections
{
   using System.Collections;

   // A class that works just like ArrayList, but sends event
   // notifications whenever the list changes:
   public class ListWithChangedEvent: ArrayList
   {
      // An event that clients can use to be notified whenever the
      // elements of the list change:
      public event EventHandler Changed;

      // Invoke the Changed event; called whenever list changes:
      protected virtual void OnChanged(EventArgs e)
      {
         if (Changed != null)
            Changed(this,e);
      }

      // Override some of the methods that can change the list;
      // invoke event after each:
      public override int Add(object value)
      {
         int i = base.Add(value);
         OnChanged(EventArgs.Empty);
         return i;
      }

      public override void Clear()
      {
         base.Clear();
         OnChanged(EventArgs.Empty);
      }
```

(continued)

(continued)

```csharp
        public override object this[int index]
        {
            set
            {
                base[index] = value;
                OnChanged(EventArgs.Empty);
            }
        }
    }
}

namespace TestEvents
{
    using MyCollections;

    class EventListener
    {
        private ListWithChangedEvent List;

        public EventListener(ListWithChangedEvent list)
        {
            List = list;
            // Add "ListChanged" to the Changed event on "List":
            List.Changed += new EventHandler(ListChanged);
        }

        // This will be called whenever the list changes:
        private void ListChanged(object sender, EventArgs e)
        {
            Console.WriteLine("This is called when the event fires.");
        }

        public void Detach()
        {
            // Detach the event and delete the list:
            List.Changed -= new EventHandler(ListChanged);
            List = null;
        }
    }

    class Test
    {
        // Test the ListWithChangedEvent class:
        public static void Main()
        {
        // Create a new list:
        ListWithChangedEvent list = new ListWithChangedEvent();
```

```
    // Create a class that listens to the list's change event:
    EventListener listener = new EventListener(list);

    // Add and remove items from the list:
    list.Add("item 1");
    list.Clear();
    listener.Detach();
    }
  }
}
```

Output
```
This is called when the event fires.
This is called when the event fires.
```

XML Documentation

In C# you can document the code you write using XML. C# is the only programming language in Visual Studio .NET with this feature. For details on creating an XML file with documentation comments, see the following sections.

For information about	See
Tags you can use to provide commonly used functionality in documentation	Tags for Documentation Comments
The ID strings that the compiler produces to identify the constructs in your code	Processing the XML File

Tags for Documentation Comments

The C# compiler will process documentation comments in your code to an XML file. Processing the XML file to create documentation is a detail that needs to be implemented at your site.

Tags are processed on code constructs such as types and type members.

Note Tags are not processed on namespaces.

The compiler will process any tag that is valid XML. The following tags provide commonly used functionality in user documentation:

<c>	<include>[1]	<paramref>[1]	<see>[1]
<code>	<list>	<permission>[1]	<seealso>[1]
<example>	<para>	<remarks>	<summary>
<exception>[1]	<param>[1]	<returns>	<value>

1. Compiler verifies syntax.

<c>

```
<c>text</c>
```

where:

text
    The text you would like to indicate as code.

Remarks

The <c> tag gives you a way to indicate that text within a description should be marked as code. Use <code> to indicate multiple lines as code.

Compile with /doc to process documentation comments to a file.

Example

```
// xml_c_tag.cs
// compile with: /doc:xml_c_tag.xml

/// text for class MyClass
public class MyClass
{
    /// <summary><c>MyMethod</c> is a method in the <c>MyClass</c> class.
    /// </summary>
    public static void MyMethod(int Int1)
    {
    }
    /// text for Main
    public static void Main ()
    {
    }
}
```

<code>

```
<code>content</code>
```

where:

content
    The text you want marked as code.

Remarks

The <code> tag gives you a way to indicate multiple lines as code. Use <c> to indicate that text within a description should be marked as code.

Compile with /doc to process documentation comments to a file.

Example

For an example of using <code>, see the section "<example>" on page 337.

<example>

```
<example>description</example>
```

where:

description
    A description of the code sample.

Remarks

The <example> tag lets you specify an example of how to use a method or other library member. Commonly, this would involve use of the <code> tag.

Compile with /doc to process documentation comments to a file.

Example

```
// xml_example_tag.cs
// compile with: /doc:xml_ctag.xml

/// text for class MyClass
public class MyClass
{
    /// <summary>
    /// The GetZero method.
    /// </summary>
    /// <example> This sample shows how to call the GetZero method.
    /// <code>
    ///    class MyClass
    ///    {
    ///        public static int Main()
    ///        {
    ///            return GetZero();
    ///        }
    ///    }
    /// </code>
    /// </example>
    public static int GetZero()
    {
        return 0;
    }
    /// text for Main
    public static void Main ()
    {
    }
}
```

<exception>

```
<exception cref="member">description</exception>
```

where:

cref = "*member*"
 A reference to an exception that is available from the current compilation environment. The compiler checks that the given exception exists and translates *member* to the canonical element name in the output XML. *member* must appear within double quotation marks (" ").

description
 A description.

Remarks

The <exception> tag lets you specify which exceptions a class can throw.

Compile with /doc to process documentation comments to a file.

Example

```
// xml_exception_tag.cs
// compile with: /doc:xml_exception_tag.xml
using System;

/// <exception cref="System.Exception">Thrown when... .</exception>
public class EClass : Exception
{
    // class definition ...
}

class TestClass
{
    public static void Main()
    {
        try
        {
        }
        catch(EClass)
        {
        }
    }
}
```

<include>

```
<include file='filename' path='tagpath[@name="id"]' />
```

where:

filename
> The name of the file containing the documentation. The file name can be qualified with a path. Enclose *filename* in single quotation marks (' ').

tagpath
> The path of the tags in *filename* that leads to the tag *name*. Enclose the path in single quotation marks (' ').

name
> The name specifier in the tag that precedes the comments; *name* will have an *id*.

id
> The id for the tag that precedes the comments. Enclose the id in double quotation marks (" ").

Remarks

The <include> tag lets you refer to comments in another file that describe the types and members in your source code. This is an alternative to placing documentation comments directly in your source code file.

The <include> tag uses the XML XPath syntax. Refer to XPath documentation for ways to customize your <include> use.

Example

This is a multifile example. The first file, which uses <include>, is listed below:

```
// xml_include_tag.cs
// compile with: /doc:xml_include_tag.xml
/// <include file='x.doc' path='MyDocs/MyMembers[@name="test"]/*' />
class Test
{
    public static void Main()
    {
    }
}

/// <include file='x.doc' path='MyDocs/MyMembers[@name="test2"]/*' />
class Test2
{
    public void Test()
    {
    }
}
```

The second file, x.doc, contains the documentation comments:

```
<MyDocs>

<MyMembers name="test">
<summary>
The summary for this type.
</summary>
</MyMembers>

<MyMembers name="test2">
<summary>
The summary for this other type.
</summary>
</MyMembers>

</MyDocs>
```

Program Output

```
<?xml version="1.0"?>
<doc>
    <assembly>
        <name>t2</name>
    </assembly>
    <members>
        <member name="T:Test">
            <summary>
The summary for this type.
</summary>
        </member>
        <member name="T:Test2">
            <summary>
The summary for this other type.
</summary>
        </member>
    </members>
</doc>
```

<list>

```
<list type="bullet" | "number" | "table">
   <listheader>
      <te<!---->rm>term</te<!---->rm>
      <des<!---->cription>description</des<!---->cription>
   </listheader>
   <item>
      <te<!---->rm>term</te<!---->rm>
      <des<!---->cription>description</des<!---->cription>
   </item>
</list>
```

where:

term

A term to define, which will be defined in *text*.

description

Either an item in a bullet or numbered list or the definition of a *term*.

Remarks

The <listheader> block is used to define the heading row of either a table or definition list. When defining a table, you only need to supply an entry for term in the heading.

Each item in the list is specified with an <item> block. When creating a definition list, you will need to specify both *term* and *text*. However, for a table, bulleted list, or numbered list, you only need to supply an entry for *text*.

A list or table can have as many <item> blocks as needed.

Compile with /doc to process documentation comments to a file.

Example

```
// xml_list_tag.cs
// compile with: /doc:xml_list_tag.xml

/// text for class MyClass
public class MyClass
{
   /// <remarks>Here is an example of a bulleted list:
   /// <list type="bullet">
   /// <item>
   /// <description>Item 1.</description>
   /// </item>
```

(continued)

(continued)

```
/// <item>
/// <description>Item 2.</description>
/// </item>
/// </list>
/// </remarks>
public static void Main ()
{
}
}
```

<para>

```
<para>content</para>
```

where:

content
    The text of the paragraph.

Remarks

The <para> tag is for use inside a tag, such as <remarks> or <returns>, and lets you add structure to the text.

Compile with /doc to process documentation comments to a file.

Example

For an example of using <para>, see the section "<summary>" on page 347.

<param>

```
<param na<!---->me='name'>description</param>
```

where:

name
    The name of a method parameter. Enclose the name in single quotation marks (' ').

description
    A description for the parameter.

Remarks

The <param> tag should be used in the comment for a method declaration to describe one of the parameters for the method.

Compile with /doc to process documentation comments to a file.

Example

```
// xml_param_tag.cs
// compile with: /doc:xml_param_tag.xml

/// text for class MyClass
public class MyClass
{
    /// <param name="Int1">Used to indicate status.</param>
    public static void MyMethod(int Int1)
    {
    }
    /// text for Main
    public static void Main ()
    {
    }
}
```

<paramref>

```
<paramref na<!---->me="name"/>
```

where:

name

    The name of the parameter to refer to. Enclose the name in double quotation marks (" ").

Remarks

The <paramref> tag gives you a way to indicate that a word is a parameter. The XML file can be processed to format this parameter in some distinct way.

Compile with /doc to process documentation comments to a file.

Example

```
// xml_paramref_tag.cs
// compile with: /doc:xml_paramref_tag.xml
/// text for class MyClass
public class MyClass
{
    /// <remarks>MyMethod is a method in the MyClass class.
    /// The <paramref name="Int1"/> parameter takes a number.
    /// </remarks>
    public static void MyMethod(int Int1)
    {
    }

    /// text for Main
    public static void Main ()
    {
    }
}
```

<permission>

`<permission cref="`*member*`">`*description*`</permission>`

where:

cref = "*member*"

A reference to a member or field that is available to be called from the current compilation environment. The compiler checks that the given code element exists and translates *member* to the canonical element name in the output XML. *member* must appear within double quotation marks (" ").

description

A description of the access to the member.

Remarks

The <permission> tag lets you document the access of a member. The **System.Security.PermissionSet** lets you specify access to a member.

Compile with /doc to process documentation comments to a file.

Example

```
// xml_permission_tag.cs
// compile with: /doc:xml_permission_tag.xml
using System;
class TestClass
{
    /// <permission cref="System.Security.PermissionSet">Everyone can access this
method.</permission>
    public static void Test()
    {
    }
    public static void Main()
    {
    }
}
```

<remarks>

```
<remarks>description</remarks>
```

where:

description
    A description of the member.

Remarks

The <remarks> tag is where you can specify overview information about a class or other type. <summary> is where you can describe the members of the type.

Compile with /doc to process documentation comments to a file.

Example

```
// xml_remarks_tag.cs
// compile with: /doc:xml_remarks_tag.xml
/// <remarks>
/// You may have some overview information about this class.
/// </remarks>
public class MyClass
{
    /// text for Main
    public static void Main ()
    {
    }
}
```

<returns>

```
<returns>description</returns>
```

where:

description
    A description of the return value.

Remarks

The <returns> tag should be used in the comment for a method declaration to describe the return value.

Compile with /doc to process documentation comments to a file.

Example

```
// xml_returns_tag.cs
// compile with: /doc:xml_returns_tag.xml

/// text for class MyClass
public class MyClass
{
    /// <returns>Returns zero.</returns>
    public static int GetZero()
    {
        return 0;
    }

    /// text for Main
    public static void Main ()
    {
    }
}
```

<see>

```
<see cref="member"/>
```

where:

cref = "*member*"
>   A reference to a member or field that is available to be called from the current compilation environment. The compiler checks that the given code element exists and passes *member* to the element name in the output XML. *member* must appear within double quotation marks (" ").

Remarks

The <see> tag lets you specify a link from within text. Use <seealso> to indicate text that you might want to appear in a See Also section.

Compile with /doc to process documentation comments to a file.

Example

For an example of using <see>, see the section "<summary>" on page 347.

<seealso>

```
<seealso cref="member"/>
```

where:

cref = "*member*"
   A reference to a member or field that is available to be called from the current compilation environment. The compiler checks that the given code element exists and passes *member* to the element name in the output XML. *member* must appear within double quotation marks (" ").

Remarks

The <seealso> tag lets you specify the text that you might want to appear in a See Also section. Use <see> to specify a link from within text.

Compile with /doc to process documentation comments to a file.

Example

For an example of using <seealso>, see the section "<summary>" on page 347.

<summary>

```
<summary>description</summary>
```

where:

description
   A summary of the object.

Remarks

The <summary> tag should be used to describe a member for a type. Use <remarks> to supply information about the type itself.

Compile with /doc to process documentation comments to a file.

Example

```
// xml_summary_tag.cs
// compile with: /doc:xml_summary_tag.xml

/// text for class MyClass
public class MyClass
{
    /// <summary>MyMethod is a method in the MyClass class.
    /// <para>Here's how you could make a second paragraph in a description. <see
cref="System.Console.WriteLine"/> for information about output statements.</para>
```

(continued)

(continued)

```
/// <seealso cref="MyClass.Main"/>
/// </summary>
public static void MyMethod(int Int1)
{
}

/// text for Main
public static void Main ()
{
}
}
```

<value>

```
<value>property-description</value>
```

where:

property-description
    A description for the property.

Remarks

The <value> tag lets you describe a property. Note that when you add a property via code wizard in the Visual Studio .NET development environment, it will add a <summary> tag for the new property. You should then manually add a <value> tag to describe the value that the property represents.

Compile with /doc to process documentation comments to a file.

Example

```
// xml_value_tag.cs
// compile with: /doc:xml_value_tag.xml
using System;
/// text for class Employee
public class Employee
{
    private string name;
    /// <value>Name accesses the value of the name data member</value>
    public string Name
    {
        get
        {
            return name;
        }
```

```
      set
      {
         name = value;
      }
   }
}

/// text for class MainClass
public class MainClass
{
   /// text for Main
   public static void Main()
   {
   }
}
```

Processing the XML File

The compiler generates an ID string for each construct in your code that is tagged to generate documentation. (For information on how to tag your code, see "Tags for Documentation Comments" on page 335.) The ID string uniquely identifies the construct. Programs that process the XML file can use the ID string to identify the corresponding .NET Framework metadata/reflection item that the documentation applies to.

The XML file is not a hierarchical representation of your code, it is a flat list with a generated ID for each element.

The compiler observes the following rules when it generates the ID strings:

- No whitespace is placed in the string.

- The first part of the ID string identifies the kind of member being identified, via a single character followed by a colon. The following member types are used:

Character	Description
N	namespace
T	type: class, interface, struct, enum, delegate
F	field
P	property (including indexers or other indexed properties)
M	method (including such special methods as constructors, operators, and so on)
E	event
!	error string; the rest of the string provides information about the error. The C# compiler generates error information for links that cannot be resolved.

- The second part of the string is the fully qualified name of the item, starting at the root of the namespace. The name of the item, its enclosing type(s), and namespace are separated by periods. If the name of the item itself has periods, they are replaced by the hash-sign ('#'). It is assumed that no item has an hash-sign directly in its name. For example, the fully qualified name of the String constructor would be "System.String.#ctor".

- For properties and methods, if there are arguments to the method, the argument list enclosed in parentheses follows. If there are no arguments, no parentheses are present. The arguments are separated by commas. The encoding of each argument follows directly how it is encoded in a .NET Framework signature:

  - Base types. Regular types (ELEMENT_TYPE_CLASS or ELEMENT_TYPE_VALUETYPE) are represented as the fully qualified name of the type.

  - Intrinsic types (for example, ELEMENT_TYPE_I4, ELEMENT_TYPE_OBJECT, ELEMENT_TYPE_STRING, ELEMENT_TYPE_TYPEDBYREF. and ELEMENT_TYPE_VOID) are represented as the fully qualified name of the corresponding full type. For example, System.Int32 or System.TypedReference.

  - ELEMENT_TYPE_PTR is represented as a '*' following the modified type.

  - ELEMENT_TYPE_BYREF is represented as a '@' following the modified type.

  - ELEMENT_TYPE_PINNED is represented as a '^' following the modified type. The C# compiler never generates this.

  - ELEMENT_TYPE_CMOD_REQ is represented as a '|' and the fully qualified name of the modifier class, following the modified type. The C# compiler never generates this.

  - ELEMENT_TYPE_CMOD_OPT is represented as a '!' and the fully qualified name of the modifier class, following the modified type.

  - ELEMENT_TYPE_SZARRAY is represented as "[ ]" following the element type of the array.

  - ELEMENT_TYPE_GENERICARRAY is represented as "[?]" following the element type of the array. The C# compiler never generates this.

  - ELEMENT_TYPE_ARRAY is represented as [*lowerbound*:*size*,*lowerbound*:*size*] where the number of commas is the rank - 1, and the lower bounds and size of each dimension, if known, are represented in decimal. If a lower bound or size is not specified, it is simply omitted. If the lower bound and size for a particular dimension are omitted, the ':' is omitted as well. For example, a 2-dimensional array with 1 as the lower bounds and unspecified sizes is [1:,1:].

  - ELEMENT_TYPE_FNPTR is represented as "=FUNC:*type*(*signature*)", where *type* is the return type, and *signature* is the arguments of the method. If there are no arguments, the parentheses are omitted. The C# compiler never generates this.

The following signature components are not represented because they are never used for differentiating overloaded methods:

- calling convention

- return type

- ELEMENT_TYPE_SENTINEL

- For conversion operators only (op_Implicit and op_Explicit), the return value of the method is encoded as a '~' followed by the return type, as encoded above.

Examples

The following examples show how the ID strings for a class and its members would be generated:

```
namespace N  // "N:N"
{
class X     // "T:N.X"
{
    X();   // "M:N.X.#ctor"
    static X(); // "M:N.X.#cctor"  a class constructor
    X(int);  // "M:N.X.#ctor(System.Int32)"
    ~X();  // "M:N.X.Finalize"   destructor's representation in metadata
    string q;  // "F:N.X.q"
    const double PI = 3.14;  // "F:N.X.PI"
    int f();  // "M:N.X.f"
    int bb(string s, ref int y, void * z); //
"M:N.X.bb(System.String,System.Int32@,=System.Void*)"
    int gg(short[] array1, int[,] array); // "M:N.X.gg(System.Int16[], System.Int32[0:,0:])"
    X operator+(X, X); // "M:N.X.op_Addition(N.X,N.X)"
    int prop {get; set;} // "P:N.X.prop"
    event MyDelegate d; // "E:N.X.d"
    int this[string s]; // "P:N.X.Item(System.String)"
    class Nested{} // "T:N.X.Nested"
    delegate void D(int i); // "T:N.X.D"
    explicit operator int(X x); // "M:N.X.op_Explicit(N.X)~System.Int32"
}
}
```

C# Compiler Options

The compiler produces executable (.exe) files, dynamic-link libraries (.dll), or code modules (.netmodule).

Every compiler option is available in two forms: *-option* and */option*. The documentation only shows the */option* form.

Building from the Command Line

The C# compiler can be invoked at the command line by typing the name of its executable file (csc.exe) on the command line. You may need to adjust your path if you want csc.exe to be invoked from any subdirectory on your computer.

This topic provides details on the following:

*   Running VCVARS32.BAT

*   Differences Between C# Compiler and C++ Compiler Output

*   Rules for Command-Line Syntax

*   Sample Command Lines

Running VCVARS32.BAT

vcvars32.bat sets the appropriate environment variables to enable command line builds.

To run VCVARS32.BAT

1. At the command prompt, change to the \bin subdirectory of your installation.

2. Run VCVARS32.bat by typing VCVARS32.

> **Caution**   VCVARS32.bat can vary from machine to machine. Do not replace a missing or damaged VCVARS32.bat file with a VCVARS32.bat from another machine. Rerun setup to replace the missing file.

For more information about vcvars32.bat, see the following Knowledge Base article:

*   Q248802 : Vcvars32.bat Generates Out of Environment Message

If the current version of Visual Studio is installed on a computer that also has a previous version of Visual Studio, you should not run vcvars32.bat from different versions in the same command window.

Differences Between C# Compiler and C++ Compiler Output

There are no object (.obj) files created as a result of invoking the C# compiler; output files are created directly. As a consequence of this, the C# compiler does not need a linker.

Rules for Command-Line Syntax

The C# compiler code uses the following rules when interpreting arguments given on the operating system command line:

- Arguments are delimited by white space, which is either a space or a tab.

- The caret character (^) is not recognized as an escape character or delimiter. The character is handled completely by the command-line parser in the operating system before being passed to the argv array in the program.

- A string surrounded by double quotation marks ("string") is interpreted as a single argument, regardless of white space contained within. A quoted string can be embedded in an argument.

- A double quotation mark preceded by a backslash (\") is interpreted as a literal double quotation mark character (").

- Backslashes are interpreted literally, unless they immediately precede a double quotation mark.

- If an even number of backslashes is followed by a double quotation mark, one backslash is placed in the argv array for every pair of backslashes, and the double quotation mark is interpreted as a string delimiter.

- If an odd number of backslashes is followed by a double quotation mark, one backslash is placed in the argv array for every pair of backslashes, and the double quotation mark is "escaped" by the remaining backslash, causing a literal double quotation mark (") to be placed in argv.

Sample Command Lines

- Compiles File.cs producing File.exe:

  ```
  csc File.cs
  ```

- Compiles File.cs producing File.dll:

  ```
  csc /target:library File.cs
  ```

- Compiles File.cs and creates My.exe:

  ```
  csc /out:My.exe File.cs
  ```

- Compiles all of the C# files in the current directory, with optimizations on and defines the DEBUG symbol. The output is File2.exe:

  ```
  csc /define:DEBUG /optimize /out:File2.exe *.cs
  ```

- Compiles all of the C# files in the current directory producing a debug version of File2.dll. No logo and no warnings are displayed:

```
csc /target:library /out:File2.dll /warn:0 /nologo /debug *.cs
```

- Compiles all of the C# files in the current directory to Something.xyz (a DLL):

```
csc /target:library /out:Something.xyz *.cs
```

See Also

C# Compiler Options Listed Alphabetically (pg. 357), C# Compiler Options Listed by Category (pg. 355)

C# Compiler Options Listed by Category

The following compiler options are sorted by category. For an alphabetical list, see "C# Compiler Options Listed Alphabetically" on page 357.

Optimization

Option	Purpose
/filealign	Specify the size of sections in the output file.
/optimize	Enable/disable optimizations.

Output Files

Option	Purpose
/doc	Process documentation comments to an XML file.
/out	Specify output file.
/target	Specify the format of the output file using one of four options: /target:exe /target:library /target:module /target:winexe

.NET Framework Assemblies

Option	Purpose
/addmodule	Specify one or more modules to be part of this assembly.
/lib	Specify the location of assemblies referenced via /reference.
/nostdlib	Do not import standard library (mscorlib.dll).
/reference	Import metadata from a file that contains an assembly.

Debugging/Error Checking

Option	Purpose
/bugreport	Create a file that contains information that makes it easy to report a bug.
/checked	Specify whether integer arithmetic that overflows the bounds of the data type will cause an exception at run time.
/debug	Emit debugging information.
/fullpaths	Specify the absolute path to the file in compiler output.
/nowarn	Suppress the compiler's ability to generate specified warnings.
/warn	Set warning level.
/warnaserror	Promote warnings to errors.

Preprocessor

Option	Purpose
/define	Define preprocessor symbols.

Resources

Option	Purpose
/linkresource	Create a link to a managed resource.
/resource	Embed a .NET Framework resource into the output file.
/win32icon	Insert an .ico file into the output file.
/win32res	Insert a Win32 resource into the output file.

Miscellaneous

Option	Purpose
@	Specify a response file.
/?	List compiler options to stdout.
/baseaddress	Specify the preferred base address at which to load a DLL.
/codepage	Specify the code page to use for all source code files in the compilation.
/help	List compiler options to stdout.
/incremental	Enable incremental compilation of source code files.
/main	Specify the location of the Main method.
/noconfig	Do not compile with the global or local versions of csc.rsp.
/nologo	Suppress compiler banner information.
/recurse	Search subdirectories for source files to compile.
/unsafe	Compile code that uses the unsafe keyword.
/utf8output	Display compiler output using UTF-8 encoding.

See Also

C# Compiler Options Listed Alphabetically (pg. 357), Building from the Command Line (pg. 353)

C# Compiler Options Listed Alphabetically

The following compiler options are sorted alphabetically. For a categorical list, see "C# Compiler Options Listed By Category" on page 355.

Option	Purpose
@	Specify a response file.
/?	List compiler options to stdout.
/addmodule	Specify one or more modules to be part of this assembly.
/baseaddress	Specify the preferred base address at which to load a DLL.
/bugreport	Create a file that contains information that makes it easy to report a bug.
/checked	Specify whether integer arithmetic that overflows the bounds of the data type will cause an exception at run time.

(continued)

(continued)

Option	Purpose
/codepage	Specify the code page to use for all source code files in the compilation.
/debug	Emit debugging information.
/define	Define preprocessor symbols.
/doc	Process documentation comments to an XML file.
/filealign	Specify the size of sections in the output file.
/fullpaths	Specify the absolute path to the file in compiler output.
/help	List compiler options to stdout.
/incremental	Enable incremental compilation of source code files.
/lib	Specify the location of assemblies referenced via /reference.
/linkresource	Create a link to a managed resource.
/main	Specify the location of the Main method.
/nologo	Suppress compiler banner information.
/nostdlib	Do not import standard library (mscorlib.dll).
/noconfig	Do not compile with the global or local versions of csc.rsp.
/nowarn	Suppress the compiler's ability to generate specified warnings.
/optimize	Enable/disable optimizations.
/out	Specify output file.
/recurse	Search subdirectories for source files to compile.
/reference	Import metadata from a file that contains an assembly.
/resource	Embed a .NET Framework resource into the output file.
/target	Specify the format of the output file using one of four options: /target:exe /target:library /target:module /target:winexe
/unsafe	Compile code that uses the unsafe keyword.
/utf8output	Display compiler output using UTF-8 encoding.
/warn	Set warning level.
/warnaserror	Promote warnings to errors.

Option	Purpose
/win32icon	Insert an .ico file into the output file.
/win32res	Insert a Win32 resource into the output file.

See Also
C# Compiler Options Listed by Category (pg. 355), Building from the Command Line (pg. 353)

@ (Specify Response File)

```
@response_file
```

where:

response_file
    A file that lists compiler options or source code files to compile.

Remarks
The @ option lets you specify a file that contains compiler options and source code files to compile. These compiler options and source code files will be processed by the compiler just as if they had been specified on the command line.

To specify more than one response file in a compilation, specify multiple response file options. For example:

```
@file1.rsp @file2.rsp
```

In a response file, multiple compiler options and source code files can appear on one line. A single compiler option specification must appear on one line (cannot span multiple lines). Response files can have comments that begin with the # symbol.

Specifying compiler options from within a response file is just like issuing those commands on the command line. See "Building from the Command Line" on page 353 for more information.

The compiler processes the command options as they are encountered. Therefore, command line arguments can override previously listed options in response files. Conversely, options in a response file will override options listed previously on the command line or in other response files.

C# provides the csc.rsp file, which is located in the vc7\bin directory. See "/noconfig" on page 372 for more information on csc.rsp.

To set this compiler option in the Visual Studio development environment
This compiler option is unavailable in Visual Studio.

To set this compiler option programmatically
This compiler option cannot be changed programmatically.

Example

The following are a few lines from a sample response file:

```
# build the first output file
/target:exe /out:MyExe.exe source1.cs source2.cs
```

/addmodule (Import Metadata)

```
/addmodule:file[;file2]
```

where:

file, file2
>   An output file that contains metadata. The file cannot contain an assembly manifest. To import more than one file, separate file names with either a comma or a semicolon.

Remarks

All modules added with /addmodule must be in the same directory as the output file at run time. That is, you can specify a module in any directory at compile time but the module must be in the application directory at run time. If the module is not in the application directory at run time, you will get a **System.TypeLoadException**.

file cannot contain an assembly. For example, if the output file was created with /target:module, its metadata can be imported with /addmodule.

If the output file was created with a /target option other than /target:module, its metadata cannot be imported with /addmodule but can be imported with /reference.

To set this compiler option in the Visual Studio development environment

This compiler option is unavailable in Visual Studio; a project cannot reference a module.

To set this compiler option programmatically

This compiler option cannot be changed programmatically.

Example

Compile source file input.cs and add metadata from metad1.netmodule and metad2.netmodule to produce out.exe:

```
csc /addmodule:metad1.netmodule;metad2.netmodule /out:out.exe input.cs
```

/baseaddress (Specify Base Address of DLL)

```
/baseaddress:address
```

where:

address
> The base address for the DLL. This address can be specified as a decimal, hexadecimal, or octal number.

Remarks

The /baseaddress option lets you specify the preferred base address at which to load a DLL. The default base address for a DLL is set by the .NET Framework common language runtime.

Be aware that the lower-order word in this address will be rounded. For example, if you specify 0x11110001, it will be rounded to 0x11110000.

To complete the signing process for a DLL, use -R of SN.EXE.

This option is ignored if the target is not a DLL.

To set this compiler option in the Visual Studio development environment

1. Open the project's **Property Pages** dialog box.

2. Click the **Configuration Properties** folder.

3. Click the **Advanced** property page.

4. Modify the **Base Address** property.

/bugreport (Report a Problem)

```
/bugreport:file
```

where:

file
> The name of the file that you want to contain your bug report.

Remarks

The /bugreport option will cause the following information to be placed in *file*:

- A copy of all source code files in the compilation.

- A listing of the compiler options used in the compilation.

- Version information about your compiler, runtime, and operating system.

- Compiler output, if any.

- A description of the problem, which you will be prompted for.

- A description of how you think the problem should be fixed, which you will be prompted for.

Because a copy of all source code files will be placed in *file*, you may want to reproduce the (suspected) code defect in the shortest possible program.

To set this compiler option in the Visual Studio development environment

This compiler option is unavailable in Visual Studio.

To set this compiler option programmatically

This compiler option cannot be changed programmatically.

Example

Compile `t2.cs` and put all bug reporting information in the file `problem.txt`:

```
csc /bugreport:problem.txt t2.cs
```

/checked (Check Integer Arithmetic)

```
/checked[+ | -]
```

Remarks

The /checked option specifies whether an integer arithmetic statement that is not in the scope of the checked or unchecked keywords and that results in a value outside the range of the data type shall cause a run-time exception.

An integer arithmetic statement that is in the scope of the **checked** or **unchecked** keywords is not subject to the effect of the /checked option.

If an integer arithmetic statement that is not in the scope of the **checked** or **unchecked** keywords results in a value outside the range of the data type, and /checked+ (/checked) is used in the compilation, then that statement will cause an exception at run time. If /checked- is used in the compilation, then that statement will not cause an exception at run time.

To set this compiler option in the Visual Studio development environment

1. Open the project's **Property Pages** dialog box.

2. Click the **Configuration Properties** folder.

3. Click the **Build** property page.

4. Modify the **Check for Arithmetic Overflow/Underflow** property.

Example

Compile `t2.cs` and specify that an integer arithmetic statement that is not in the scope of the **checked** or **unchecked** keywords and results in a value outside the range of the data type will cause an exception at run time.

```
csc t2.cs /checked
```

/codepage (Specify Code Page for Source Code Files)

```
/codepage:id
```

where:

id
> The id of the code page to use for all source code files in the compilation.

Remarks

If you compile one or more source code files that were not created to use the default code page on your computer, you can use the /codepage option to specify which code page should be used. /codepage applies to all source code files in your compilation.

If the source code files were created with the same codepage that is in effect on your computer or if the source code files were created with UNICODE or UTF-8, you need not use /codepage.

To set this compiler option in the Visual Studio development environment

This compiler option is unavailable in Visual Studio.

To set this compiler option programmatically

This compiler option cannot be changed programmatically.

/debug (Emit Debugging Information)

```
/debug[+ | -]
/debug:{full | pdbonly}
```

where:

+ | -

Specifying +, or just /debug, causes the compiler to generate debugging information and place it in a program database (.pdb file). Specifying -, which is in effect if you do not specify /debug, causes no debug information to be created.

full | pdbonly

Specifies the type of debugging information generated by the compiler. The full argument, which is in effect if you do not specify /debug:pdbonly, enables attaching a debugger to the running program. Specifying pdbonly allows source code debugging when the program is started in the debugger but will only display assembler when the running program is attached to the debugger.

Remarks

The /debug option causes the compiler to generate debugging information and place it in the output file(s). Use this option to create debug builds. If /debug, /debug+, or /debug:full is not specified, you will not be able to debug the output file of your program.

To set this compiler option in the Visual Studio development environment

1. Open the project's **Property Pages** dialog box.

2. Click the **Configuration Properties** folder.

3. Click the **Build** property page.

4. Modify the **Generate Debugging Information** property.

Example

Place debugging information in output file `app.exe`:

```
csc /debug /out:app.exe test.cs
```

/define (Preprocessor Definition)

```
/define:name[;name2]
```

where:

name, *name2*
> The name of one or more symbols that you want to define.

Remarks

The /define option defines *name* as a symbol in your program. It has the same effect as using a #define preprocessor directive in your source file. A symbol remains defined until an #undef directive in the source file removes the definition or the compiler reaches the end of the file.

You can use symbols created by this option with #if, #else, #elif, and #endif to compile source files conditionally.

/d is the short form of /define.

You can define multiple symbols with /define by using a semicolon or comma to separate symbol names. For example:

```
/define:DEBUG;TUESDAY
```

To set this compiler option in the Visual Studio development environment

1. Open the project's **Property Pages** dialog box.

2. Click the **Configuration Properties** folder.

3. Click the **Build** property page.

4. Modify the **Conditional Compilation Constants** property.

Example

```
// preprocessor_define.cs
// compile with: /define:xx
// or uncomment the next line
// #define xx
using System;
public class Test
{
    public static void Main()
    {
        #if (xx)
            Console.WriteLine("xx exists");
        #else
            Console.WriteLine("xx does not exist");
        #endif
    }
}
```

/doc (Process Documentation Comments)

```
/doc:file
```

where:

file

> The output file for XML, which is populated with the comments in the source code files of the compilation.

Remarks

The /doc option allows you to place documentation comments in an XML file.

For Visual Studio .NET, only the C# compiler provides this documentation comments feature.

In source code files, lines that begin with /// and that precede a user-defined type such as a class, delegate, or interface; member such as a field, event, property, or method; or a namespace declaration can be processed as comments and placed in a file.

The source code file that contains Main is output first into the XML.

To use the generated .xml file for use with the IntelliSense® feature, let the filename of the .xml file be the same as the assembly you want to support and then put the .xml file into the same directory as the assembly.

/doc will be ignored in a compilation that uses /incremental; use /incremental- to ensure that *file* is up to date.

Unless you compile with /target:module, *file* will contain <assembly></assembly> tags specifying the name of the file containing the assembly manifest for the output file of the compilation.

To set this compiler option in the Visual Studio development environment

1. Open the project's **Property Pages** dialog box.

2. Click the **Configuration Properties** folder.

3. Click the **Build** property page.

4. Modify the **XML Documentation File** property.

/filealign (Specify Section Alignment)

```
/filealign:number
```

where:

number
> A value that specifies the size of sections in the output file. Valid values are 512, 1024, 2048, 4096, 8192, and 16384. These values are in bytes.

Remarks

The /filealign option lets you specify the size of sections in your output file.

Each section will be aligned on a boundary that is a multiple of the /filealign value. There is no fixed default. If /filealign is not specified, the common language runtime picks a default at compile time.

By specifying the section size, you affect the size of the output file. Modifying section size may be useful for programs that will run on smaller devices.

Use DUMPBIN to see information about sections in your output file.

To set this compiler option in the Visual Studio development environment

1. Open the project's **Property Pages** dialog box

2. Click the **Configuration Properties** folder.

3. Click the **Advanced** property page.

4. Modify the **File Alignment** property.

/fullpaths (Specify Absolute Path in Compiler Output)

```
/fullpaths
```

Remarks

By default, errors and warnings that result from compilation specify the name of the file in which an error was found. The /fullpaths option causes the compiler to specify the full path to the file.

To set this compiler option in the Visual Studio development environment

This compiler option is unavailable in Visual Studio.

To set this compiler option programmatically

This compiler option cannot be changed programmatically.

/help, /? (Compiler Command-Line Help)

```
/help
/?
```

Remarks

This option sends a listing of compiler options, and a brief description of each option, to stdout. If this option is included in a compilation, no output file will be created and no compilation will take place.

To set this compiler option in the Visual Studio development environment

This compiler option is unavailable in Visual Studio.

To set this compiler option programmatically

This compiler option cannot be changed programmatically.

/incremental (Enable Incremental Compilation)

```
/incremental[+ | -]
```

Remarks

The /incremental compiler option enables the incremental compiler, which compiles only those methods that have changed since the last compilation. Information about the state of the previous compilation is stored in the following files, which are created by the compiler:

output_file_name.dbg
> When compiling with /debug, the status of debug information is stored in the program database (.pdb file).

output_file_name.extension.incr
> Information about the status of the compilation, other than debug information, is stored in a .incr file.

The first time you use /incremental, the .incr and .pdb files are updated and all subsequent compilations will be incremental. Changing the compiler options from the previous /incremental compilation will cause a full rebuild of the .incr and .pdb files.

If the compiler detects many changes since the last incremental build, it may perform a full build, as a full build would be at least as efficient as an incremental build. If the compiler cannot find the project's .pdb or .incr files, a full rebuild will occur.

In an incremental build, /doc is ignored. To ensure that your documentation file is up to date, build with /incremental-.

By default, /incremental- is in effect. Specifying /incremental is the same as specifying /incremental+.

Output files created with the /incremental option may be larger than those created with incremental compilation disabled. Because the output files can be larger, you should use /incremental- in the final build of your output file.

/incremental will speed compilation on projects with many, smaller files, and will have little or no speed improvement on projects with fewer, large files.

To set this compiler option in the Visual Studio development environment

1. Open the project's **Property Pages** dialog box.

2. Click the **Configuration Properties** folder.

3. Click the **Advanced** property page.

4. Modify the **Incremental build** property.

Example

Compile in.cs using the incremental compiler:

```
csc /incremental in.cs
```

/lib (Specify Assembly Reference Locations)

```
/lib:dir1[, dir2]
```

where:

dir1

> A directory for the compiler to look in if a referenced assembly is not found in the current working directory (the directory from which you are invoking the compiler) or in the common language runtime's system directory.

dir2

> One or more additional directories to search in for assembly references. Separate additional directory names with a comma.

Remarks

The /lib option specifies the location of assemblies referenced via the /reference option.

The compiler searches for assembly references that are not fully qualified in the following order:

1. Current working directory. This is the directory from which the compiler is invoked.

2. The common language runtime system directory.

3. Directories specified by /lib.

4. Directories specified by the LIB environment variable.

Use /reference to specify an assembly reference.

/lib is additive; specifying it more than once appends to any prior values.

An alternative to using /lib is to copy into the working directory any required assemblies; this will allow you to simply pass the assembly name to /reference. You can then delete the assemblies from the working directory. Since the path to the dependent assembly is not specified in the assembly manifest, the application can be started on the target computer and will find and use the assembly in the global assembly cache.

To set this compiler option in the Visual Studio development environment

1. Open the project's **Property Pages** dialog box.

2. Click the **Common Properties** folder.

3. Click the **References Path** property page.

4. Modify the contents of the list box.

Example

Compile t2.cs to create an .exe file. The compiler will look in the working directory and in the root directory of the C drive for assembly references.

```
csc /lib:c:\ /reference:t2.dll t2.cs
```

/linkresource (Link to .NET Framework Resource)

```
/linkresource: filename[, identifier]
```

where:

filename
> The .NET Framework resource file to which you want to link from the assembly.

identifier (optional)
> The logical name for the resource; the name used to load the resource. The default is the name of the file name.

Remarks

The /linkresource option creates a link to a .NET Framework resource in the output file; the resource file is not placed in the output file. /resource embeds a resource file in the output file.

Linked resources are public in the assembly when created with the C# compiler.

/linkresource requires one of the /target options other than /target:module.

If *filename* is a .NET Framework resource file created, for example, by Resgen.exe or in the development environment, it can be accessed with members in the **System.Resources** namespace. For all other resources, use the **GetManifestResource*** methods in the **System.Reflection.Assembly** class to access the resource at run time.

/linkres is the short form of /linkresource.

To set this compiler option in the Visual Studio development environment

This compiler option is unavailable in Visual Studio.

To set this compiler option programmatically

This compiler option cannot be changed programmatically.

Example

Compile `in.cs` and link to resource file `rf.resource`:

```
csc /linkresource:rf.resource in.cs
```

/main (Specify Location of Main Method)

```
/main:class
```

where:

class
    The type that contains the Main method.

Remarks

If your compilation includes more than one type with a Main method, you can specify which type contains the Main method that you want to use as the entry point into the program.

This option is for use when compiling an .exe file.

To set this compiler option in the Visual Studio development environment

1. Open the project's **Property Pages** dialog box.
2. Click the **Common Properties** folder.
3. Click the **General** property page.
4. Modify the **Startup Object** property.

Example

Compile `t2.cs` and `t3.cs`, specifying that the Main method will be found in `Test2`:

```
csc t2.cs t3.cs /main:Test2
```

/noconfig (Ignore csc.rsp)

```
/noconfig
```

Remarks

The /noconfig option tells the compiler not to compile with the global or local versions of csc.rsp.

By default, the C# compiler looks in the vc7\bin directory and in the directory from which the compiler was invoked for files called csc.rsp.

The csc.rsp file that is supplied in vc7\bin references the .NET Framework assemblies that would be included in a C# project created in the Visual Studio development environment. You can modify this global csc.rsp file to contain any other compiler options that you want to include in a compilation from the command line with csc.exe.

The compiler will then look for a csc.rsp file in the directory from which the compiler was invoked. The commands in the local csc.rsp file will be combined with the global csc.rsp file for the compilation. Since the global csc.rsp is processed first, any command that is also in the local csc.rsp file will override the setting of the same command in the global csc.rsp file.

Finally, the compiler will read the options passed to the csc command. Since these are processed last, any option on the command line will override a setting of the same option in either of the csc.rsp files.

If you do not want the compiler to look for and use the settings in the global and local csc.rsp files, specify /noconfig.

To set this compiler option in the Visual Studio development environment

This compiler option is unavailable in Visual Studio.

To set this compiler option programmatically

This compiler option cannot be changed programmatically.

/nologo (Suppress Banner Information)

```
/nologo
```

Remarks

The /nologo option suppresses display of the sign-on banner when the compiler starts up and display of informational messages during compiling.

This option is not available from within the development environment; it is only available when compiling from the command line.

To set this compiler option in the Visual Studio development environment

This compiler option is unavailable in Visual Studio.

To set this compiler option programmatically

This compiler option cannot be changed programmatically.

/nostdlib (Do Not Import Standard Library)

```
/nostdlib[+ | -]
```

Remarks

The /nostdlib option prevents the import of mscorlib.dll, which defines the entire System namespace. Use this option if you want to define or create your own System namespace and objects.

If you do not specify /nostdlib, mscorlib.dll will be imported into your program (same as specifying /nostdlib-). If you specify /nostdlib, it is the same as specifying /nostdlib+.

To set this compiler option in the Visual Studio development environment

This compiler option is unavailable in Visual Studio.

To set this compiler option programmatically

This compiler option cannot be changed programmatically.

/nowarn (Suppress Specified Warnings)

`/nowarn:number1[,number2[...]]`

where:

number1, *number2*
> A warning number that you want the compiler to suppress.

Remarks

The /nowarn option lets you suppress the compiler's ability to generate one or more warnings. Separate multiple warning numbers with a comma.

You only need to specify the numeric part of the warning identifier. For example, if you want to suppress CS0028, you could specify `/nowarn:28`.

To set this compiler option in the Visual Studio development environment

This compiler option is unavailable in Visual Studio.

To set this compiler option programmatically

This compiler option cannot be changed programmatically.

/optimize (Enable/Disable Optimizations)

`/optimize[+ | -]`

Remarks

The /optimize option enables or disables optimizations performed by the compiler to make your output file smaller, faster, and more efficient. /optimize also tells the common language runtime to optimize code at runtime.

By default, /optimize is in effect. Specifying /optimize is the same as specifying /optimize+.

All references (see "/reference" on page 377) in an assembly must have the same optimization settings.

To prevent an optimized output file, specify /optimize-.

/o is the short form of /optimize.

It is possible to combine the /optimize and /debug options.

To set this compiler option in the Visual Studio development environment

1. Open the project's **Property Pages** dialog box.

2. Click the **Configuration Properties** folder.

3. Click the **Build** property page.

4. Modify the **Optimize code** property.

Example

Compile t2.cs and enable compiler optimizations:

```
csc t2.cs /optimize
```

/out (Set Output File Name)

```
/out:filename
```

where:

filename
    The name of the output file created by the compiler.

Remarks

The /out option specifies the name of the output file. The compiler expects to find one or more source code files following the /out option.

If you do not specify the name of the output file:

- An .exe will take its name from the source code file that contains the Main method.

- A .dll or .netmodule will take its name from the first source code file.

On the command line, it is possible to specify multiple output files for your compilation. All source code files specified after an /out option will be compiled into the output file specified by that /out option. A source code file used to compile one output file cannot be used in the same compilation for the compilation of another output file.

Specify the full name and extension of the file you want to create.

To set this compiler option in the Visual Studio development environment

1. Open the project's **Property Pages** dialog box.

2. Click the **Common Properties** folder.

3. Click the **General** property page.

4. Modify the **Assembly Name** property.

Example

Compile `t2.cs` and create output file `t2.exe` and build `t3.cs` and create output file `t3.exe`:

```
csc t2.cs /out:t3.exe t3.cs
```

/recurse (Find Source Files in Subdirectories)

```
/recurse:[dir\]file
```

where:

dir (optional)

> The directory in which you want the search to begin. If this is not specified, the search begins in the project directory.

file

> The file(s) to search for. Wildcard characters are allowed.

Remarks

The /recurse option lets you compile source code files in all child directories of either the specified directory (*dir*) or of the project directory.

You can use wildcards in a file name to compile all matching files in the project directory without using /recurse.

To set this compiler option in the Visual Studio development environment

This compiler option is unavailable in Visual Studio.

To set this compiler option programmatically

This compiler option cannot be changed programmatically.

Example

Compiles all C# files in the current directory:

```
csc *.cs
```

Compiles all of the C# files in the dir1\dir2 directory and any directories below it and generates dir2.dll:

```
csc /target:library /out:dir2.dll /recurse: dir1\dir2\*.cs
```

/reference (Import Metadata)

```
/reference:file[;file2]
```

where:

file, file2
> One or more files that contains an assembly manifest. To import more than one file, separate file names with either a comma or a semicolon.

Remarks

The /reference option causes the compiler to make public type information in the specified files available to the project you are currently compiling.

The file(s) you import must contain a manifest; the output file must have been compiled with one of the /target options other than /target:module.

Use /addmodule to import metadata from an output file that does not contain an assembly manifest.

At run time, you should anticipate that only one .exe assembly can be loaded per process, even though, there may be times when more than one .exe might be loaded in the same process. Therefore, you are recommended to not pass an assembly built with /target:exe or /target:winexe to /reference if you are compiling with /target:winexe or /target:exe. This condition may be modified in future versions of the common language runtime.

If you reference an assembly (Assembly A), which itself references another assembly (Assembly B), you will need to reference Assembly B if:

* A type you use from Assembly A inherits from a type or implements an interface from Assembly B.

* If you invoke a field, property, event, or method that has a return type or parameter type from Assembly B.

Use /lib to specify the directory in which one or more of your assembly references is located. The /lib topic also discusses which directories the compiler searches for assemblies.

In order for the compiler to recognize a type in an assembly (not a module), it needs to be forced to resolve the type, which you can do, for example, by defining an instance of the type. There are other ways to resolve type names in an assembly for the compiler, for example, if you inherit from a type in an assembly, the type name will then become known to the compiler.

/r is the short form of /reference.

Example

Compile source file `input.cs` and import metadata from `metad1.dll` and `metad2.dll` to produce `out.exe`:

```
csc /reference:metad1.dll;metad2.dll /out:out.exe input.cs
```

/resource (Embed Resource File to Output)

```
/resource:filename[,identifier]
```

where:

filename
> The .NET Framework resource file you want to embed in the output file.

identifier (optional)
> The logical name for the resource; the name used to load the resource. The default is the name of the file name.

Remarks

Use /linkresource to link a resource to an assembly and not place the resource file in the output file.

Resources are public in the assembly when created with the C# compiler.

If *filename* is a .NET Framework resource file created, for example, by Resgen.exe or in the development environment, it can be accessed with members in the **System.Resources** namespace. For all other resources, use the **GetManifestResource*** methods in the **System.Reflection.Assembly** class to access the resource at run time.

/res is the short form of /resource.

To set this compiler option in the Visual Studio development environment

1.   Add a resource file to your project.

2.   Select the file you want to embed in Solution Explorer.

3.   Select **Build Action** for the file in the Properties window.

4.   Set **Build Action** to **Embedded Resource**.

Example

Compile in.cs and attach resource file rf.resource:

```
csc /resource:rf.resource in.cs
```

/target (Specify Output File Format)

The /target compiler option can be specified in one of four forms:

/target:exe
> Create an .exe file.

/target:library
> Create a code library.

/target:module
> Create a module.

/target:winexe
> Create a Windows® program.

Unless you specify /target:module, /target causes a .NET Framework assembly manifest to be placed in an output file. See "Global Attributes" on page 214 for information on how to specify assembly attributes.

The assembly manifest is placed in the first .exe output file in the compilation or in the first .dll, if there is no .exe output file. For example, in the following command line, the manifest will be placed in 1.exe:

```
csc /out:1.exe t1.cs /out:2.netmodule t2.cs
```

The compiler creates only one assembly manifest per compilation. Information about all files in a compilation is placed in the assembly manifest. All output files except those created with /target:module can contain an assembly manifest. When producing multiple output files at the command line, only one assembly manifest can be created and it must go into the first output file specified on the command line. If the first output file is an exe (/target:exe or /target:winexe) or code library (/target:library), then any other output files produced in the same compilation must be modules (/target:module).

If you create an assembly, you can indicate that all or part of your code is CLS compliant with the CLSCompliant attribute.

```
// target_clscompliant.cs
[assembly:System.CLSCompliant(true)]    // specify assembly compliance

[System.CLSCompliant(false)]    // specify compliance for an element
class TestClass
{
   public static void Main()
   {
   }
}
```

/target:exe (Create a Console Application)

```
/target:exe
```

Remarks

The /target:exe option causes the compiler to create an executable (EXE), console application. The /target:exe option is in effect by default. The executable file will be created with the .exe extension.

Use /target:winexe to create a Windows program executable.

Unless otherwise specified with the /out option, the output file name takes the name of the input file that contains the Main method.

When specified at the command line, all files up to the next /out, /target:winexe, or /target:library option are used to create the .exe file. The /target:exe option is in effect for all files since the previous /out or /target:library option.

One and only one Main method is required in the source code files that are compiled into an .exe file. The /main compiler option lets you specify which class contains the Main method, in cases where your code has more than one class with a Main method.

To set this compiler option in the Visual Studio development environment

1. Open the project's **Property Pages** dialog box.
2. Click the **Common Properties** folder.
3. Click the **General** property page.
4. Modify the **Output Type** property.

Example

Each of the following command lines will compile `in.cs`, creating `in.exe`:

```
csc /target:exe in.cs
csc in.cs
```

See Also

/target (Specify Output File Format) (pg. 379)

/target:library (Create a Code Library)

```
/target:library
```

Remarks

The /target:library option causes the compiler to create a dynamic-link library (DLL) rather than an executable file (EXE). The DLL will be created with the .dll extension.

Unless otherwise specified with the /out option, the output file name takes the name of the first input file.

When specified at the command line, all files up to the next /out, /target:winexe, or /target:exe option are used to create the .dll file.

When building a .dll file, a Main method is not required.

To set this compiler option in the Visual Studio development environment

1. Open the project's **Property Pages** dialog box
2. Click the **Common Properties** folder.
3. Click the **General** property page.
4. Modify the **Output Type** property.

Example

Compile `in.cs`, creating `in.dll`:

```
csc /target:library in.cs
```

See Also

/target (Specify Output File Format) (pg. 379)

/target:module (Create Module to Add to Assembly)

```
/target:module
```

Remarks

To not generate an assembly manifest, use the /target:module option. By default, the output file will have an extension of .netmodule.

A file that does not have an assembly cannot be loaded by the .NET Framework common language runtime. However, such a file can be incorporated into the assembly manifest of an assembly via /addmodule.

If more than one module is created in a single compilation, internal types in one module will be available to other modules in the compilation. When code in one module references **internal** types in another module, then both modules must be incorporated into an assembly manifest, via /addmodule.

To set this compiler option in the Visual Studio development environment

Creating a module is not supported in the Visual Studio development environment.

Example

Compile `in.cs`, creating `in.netmodule`:

```
csc /target:module in.cs
```

See Also

/target (Specify Output File Format) (pg. 379)

/target:winexe (Create a Windows Program)

```
/target:winexe
```

Remarks

The /target:winexe option causes the compiler to create an executable (EXE), Windows program. The executable file will be created with the .exe extension. A Windows program is one that provides a user interface from either the .NET Framework library or with the Win32® APIs.

Use /target:exe to create a console application.

Unless otherwise specified with the /out option, the output file name takes the name of the input file that contains the Main method.

When specified at the command line, all files until the next /out or /target option are used to create the Windows program.

One and only one Main method is required in the source code files that are compiled into an .exe file. The /main option lets you specify which class contains the Main method, in cases where your code has more than one class with a Main method.

To set this compiler option in the Visual Studio development environment

1. Open the project's **Property Pages** dialog box.

2. Click the **Common Properties** folder.

3. Click the **General** property page.

4. Modify the **Output Type** property.

Example

Compile `in.cs` into a Windows program:

```
csc /target:winexe in.cs
```

See Also

/target (Specify Output File Format) (pg. 379)

/unsafe (Enable Unsafe Mode)

```
/unsafe
```

Remarks

The /unsafe option allows code that uses the unsafe keyword to compile.

To set this compiler option in the Visual Studio development environment

1. Open the project's **Property Pages** dialog box.

2. Click the **Configuration Properties** folder.

3. Click the **Build** property page.

4. Modify the **Allow unsafe code blocks** property.

Example

Compile `in.cs` for unsafe mode:

```
csc /unsafe in.cs
```

/utf8output (Display Compiler Messages with UTF-8)

```
/utf8output
```

Remarks

The /utf8output option displays compiler output using UTF-8 encoding.

In some international configurations, compiler output cannot correctly be displayed in the console. In these configurations, use /utf8output and redirect compiler output to a file.

To set this compiler option in the Visual Studio development environment

This compiler option is unavailable in Visual Studio.

To set this compiler option programmatically

This compiler option cannot be changed programmatically.

/warn (Specify Warning Level)

```
/warn:option
```

where:

option

The minimum warning level you want displayed for the build. Valid values are 0–4:

Warning level	Meaning
0	Turns off emission of all warning messages.
1	Displays severe warning messages.
2	Displays level 1 warnings plus certain, less-severe warnings, such as warnings about hiding class members.
3	Displays level 2 warnings plus certain, less-severe warnings, such as warnings about expressions that always evaluate to true or false.
4	Displays all level 3 warnings plus informational warnings. This is the default warning level at the command line.

Remarks

The /warn option specifies the warning level for the compiler to display.

The Build Errors documentation describes the warnings, indicates each warning's level, and indicates potential problems (rather than actual coding errors) with statements that may not compile as you intend.

Use /warnaserror to treat all warnings as errors.

/w is the short form of /warn.

To set this compiler option in the Visual Studio development environment

1. Open the project's **Property Pages** dialog box.

2. Click the **Configuration Properties** folder.

3. Click the **Build** property page.

4. Modify the **Warning Level** property.

Example

Compile in.cs and have the compiler only display level 1 warnings:

```
csc /warn:1 in.cs
```

/warnaserror (Treat Warnings as Errors)

```
/warnaserror[± | -]
```

Remarks

The /warnaserror+ option treats all warnings as errors. Any messages that would ordinarily be reported as warnings are instead reported as errors, and the build process is halted (no output files are built).

By default, /warnaserror- is in effect, which causes warnings to not prevent the generation of an output file. /warnaserror, which is the same as /warnaserror+, causes warnings to be treated as errors.

Use /warn to specify the level of warnings that you want the compiler to display.

To set this compiler option in the Visual Studio development environment

1. Open the project's **Property Pages** dialog box.
2. Click the **Configuration Properties** folder.
3. Click the **Build** property page.
4. Modify the **Treat Warnings As Errors** property.

Example

Compile in.cs and have the compiler display no warnings:

```
csc /warnaserror in.cs
```

/win32icon (Import an .ico File)

```
/win32icon:filename
```

where:

filename
    The .ico file that you want to add to your output file.

Remarks

The /win32icon option inserts an .ico file in the output file, which gives the output file the desired appearance in the Windows Explorer. An .ico file can be created with the Resource Compiler. The Resource Compiler is invoked when you compile a Visual C++ program; an .ico file is created from the .rc file.

See "/linkresource" on page 370 (to reference) or "/resource" on page 378 (to attach) a .NET Framework resource file. See "/win32res" on page 386 to import a .res file.

To set this compiler option in the Visual Studio development environment

1. Open the project's **Property Pages** dialog box.

2. Click the **Common Properties** folder.

3. Click the **General** property page.

4. Modify the **Application Icon** property.

Example

Compile `in.cs` and attach an .ico file `rf.ico` to produce `in.exe`:

```
csc /win32icon:rf.ico in.cs
```

/win32res (Import a Win32 Resource File)

```
/win32res:filename
```

where:

filename
> The resource file that you want to add to your output file.

Remarks

The /win32res option inserts a Win32 resource in the output file. A Win32 resource file can be created with the Resource Compiler. The Resource Compiler is invoked when you compile a Visual C++ program; a .res file is created from the .rc file.

A Win32 resource can contain version or bitmap (icon) information that would help identify your application in the Windows Explorer. If you do not specify /win32res, the compiler will generate version information based on the assembly version.

See "/linkresource" on page 370 (to reference) or "/resource" on page 378 (to attach) a .NET Framework resource file.

To set this compiler option in the Visual Studio development environment

This compiler option is unavailable in Visual Studio.

To set this compiler option programmatically

This compiler option cannot be changed programmatically.

Example

Compile `in.cs` and attach a Win32 resource file `rf.res` to produce `in.exe`:

```
csc /win32res:rf.res in.cs
```

Index

Cordless Drill

A drill is a cutting tool for making round holes in wood, metal, rock, or other hard material. The simplest form of drilling machine is a small, hand-held electric motor with a chuck that grasps the drill. A **cordless drill** is a hand-held drill powered by a battery.*

At Microsoft Press, we use tools to illustrate our books for software developers and IT professionals. Tools are an elegant symbol of human inventiveness and a powerful metaphor for how people can extend their capabilities, precision, and reach. From basic calipers and pliers to digital micrometers and lasers, our stylized illustrations of tools give each book a visual identity and each book series a personality. With tools and knowledge, there are no limits to creativity and innovation. Our tag line says it all: *The tools you need to put technology to work.*

Hit the ground running *right now with Microsoft Visual C# .NET!*

U.S.A. **$39.99**
Canada $57.99
ISBN: 0-7356-1289-7

This step-by-step guide provides the solid foundation—and real-world examples—you need to begin building object-oriented applications with the versatile Microsoft® Visual C#™ .NET Web development language. Real-world programming scenarios and easy-to-follow, step-by-step exercises offer clear instruction to show you how to create stable, efficient business-level objects and system-level applications. You also get code samples on a companion CD-ROM to study and reuse in your own projects.

Microsoft®
microsoft.com/mspress

Get in-depth
architectural
information
about the hot new object-oriented language for Microsoft® .NET.

Take a detailed look at the internal architecture of the groundbreaking C# language with this in-depth book. It takes you inside this state-of-the-art, object-oriented programming language and its design parameters and construction to give you a complete understanding of how C# works—and why it works that way. Along the way, it reveals the full functionality of C# to enable you to write applications for Microsoft .NET. It also includes a searchable electronic copy of the book, sample code in C#, and a foreword by Scott Wiltamuth, coauthor of the C# Language Specification.

U.S.A. **$49.99**
Canada $72.99
ISBN: 0-7356-1288-9

mspress.microsoft.com

Get a **Free**
e-mail newsletter, updates,
special offers, links to related books,
and more when you

register on line!

Register your Microsoft Press® title on our Web site and you'll get a FREE subscription to our e-mail newsletter, *Microsoft Press Book Connections.* You'll find out about newly released and upcoming books and learning tools, online events, software downloads, special offers and coupons for Microsoft Press customers, and information about major Microsoft® product releases. You can also read useful additional information about all the titles we publish, such as detailed book descriptions, tables of contents and indexes, sample chapters, links to related books and book series, author biographies, and reviews by other customers.

Registration is easy. Just visit this Web page and fill in your information:

http://www.microsoft.com/mspress/register

Microsoft

- -

Proof of Purchase

Use this page as proof of purchase if participating in a promotion or rebate offer on this title. Proof of purchase must be used in conjunction with other proof(s) of payment such as your dated sales receipt—see offer details.

Microsoft® Visual C#™ .NET Language Reference
0-7356-1554-3

CUSTOMER NAME

Microsoft Press, PO Box 97017, Redmond, WA 98073-9830